The Soviet Era

The Soviet Era

Soviet Politics from Lenin to Yeltsin

Geoffrey Ponton

BLACKWELL
Oxford UK & Cambridge USA

The right of Geoffrey Ponton to be identified as author of this work has been asserted
in accordance with the Copyright, Designs and Patents Act 1988.

First published 1994

Blackwell Publishers
108 Cowley Road
Oxford OX4 1JF
UK

238 Main Street,
Cambridge, Massachusetts 02142
USA

British Library Cataloguing in Publication Data

A CIP catalogue record for this book is available from the British Library.

Library of Congress Cataloging-in-Publication Data

Ponton, Geoffrey.
    The Soviet era: From Lenin to Yeltsin/Geoffrey Ponton.
        p.   cm.
    Includes bibliographical references and index.
    ISBN 0-631-18775-8. – ISBN 0-631-18776-6 (pbk.)
    1. Soviet Union–History.   I. Title.
DK266.P615   1994
947 – dc20   93-14804
                                                       CIP

Typeset in 11 on 13 pt Plantin by Best-set Typesetter Ltd., Hong Kong
Printed in Great Britain by Page Brothers, Norwich

This book is printed on acid-free paper

To Mike and Pete

Contents

Preface

The rise, development and collapse of the Soviet Union has been one of the most dramatic spectacles of the twentieth century. This book aims to give a succinct overview of the political events of the period and the reasons for them, concentrating especially on the final years of *glasnost* and *perestroika* in which Mikhail Gorbachev struggled to reform the Soviet Communist system, but in the end failed to prevent its disintegration. Readers should note that economic statistics have been quoted for the political impact their announcement made at the time and should not be regarded as necessarily accurate. My thanks are due to Mary Dortch, Dr Eric Stenton and John Wallace.

Geoffrey Ponton
July 1993

Prologue:
A Revolution in the Soviet Union

Gorbachev's Achievements

Anyone contemplating staging a *coup d'état* in the Soviet Union in the early 1990s would have been wise to take into account the remarkable changes in politics and society effected by Mikhail Gorbachev. The central government had been much weakened and it was unlikely that the republics would ever again submit to control from Moscow. They had been developing horizontal contacts with each other, rather than vertical ones with the centre. With his policy of *glasnost* (openness) the elected soviets (councils) had become active at every level, often with Communists in a minority. There was a free press which, with the availability of fax machines, word-processors and photocopiers, could not easily be silenced. *Glasnost* had abolished fear. Once, Soviet citizens had been hesitant to state their opinions openly or to speak to foreigners. But in the new climate generated by Gorbachev's reforms they did so freely, and many did not hesitate to express themselves to foreign correspondents and soldiers even in the first hours of the coup of 19 August 1991.

Signs of the Impending Coup

Gorbachev centred power on himself, with the support of the Congress of People's Deputies (CPD) rather than that of the Communist Party of the Soviet Union (CPSU), but his avoidance of popular election (unlike Boris Yeltsin, President of the Russian Federation) eroded his claim to legitimacy. He had always lacked whole-hearted support in the Communist Party's Politburo, while conservatives remained a significant influence in the government and even among his advisers. The old system had been condemned, but as yet nothing had replaced it and people were suffering. In the autumn of 1990 Gorbachev had been forced by conservatives to abandon the radical '500-day' Shatalin economic plan and to appoint conservatives to many key posts. This was the beginning of a sustained conservative campaign to stop many of the political and economic changes – a campaign which culminated in the coup. Conservative provincial party bureaucrats continued to tell their local people that the reforms were not working. Soyuz, a strong hard-line faction in the Supreme Soviet and CPD consistently attacked Gorbachev's policies, especially the proposed Union Treaty, which they saw as breaking up the centralized Soviet state. They demanded his resignation. In addition, dramatic changes in foreign and defence policy, including arms reductions and the withdrawal from the East European states, provoked much discontent among the armed forces and conservatives generally. Weaknesses at home were not being compensated for in the traditional way by successes abroad.

The first public warning of an impending coup came from Eduard Shevardnadze during his resignation speech as Foreign Minister in December 1990. With hindsight it is possible to interpret various troop movements in the months preceding 19 August as preparations and practice for a coup. In particular, the army, MVD (Interior Ministry troops) and KGB forces had established control points in Moscow in connection with the banning of demonstrations there. Various alarmist statements had been made over preceding months, the most dramatic of which was published on 23 July by the nationalist newspaper *Sovetskaya Rossiya*. Entitled 'A Word to the People' and signed by prominent figures, including General Gromov, the Deputy Interior Minister, and General Valentin Varenikov, Commander of the Ground Forces, it called for the salvation of Russia (Crawshaw, 1992, pp. 181–3). On 17 June the Prime Minister, Valentin Pavlov, one of the coup perpetrators, had attempted to get powers from the Supreme Soviet which would have effectively put him and the Cabinet of Ministers, rather than Gorbachev, in control of the country. Pavlov was supported by the Defence Minister, Marshal Yazov, the head of the KGB, General Kryuchkov, and the Interior Minister, Boris Pugo, all later to become members of the coup's State Emergency Committee. Gorbachev firmly quashed this effort.

The Announcement of the Coup

The new Union Treaty was due to be signed from 20 August onwards, and the conservatives must have felt that they should strike before the signing, which they interpreted as the final breakup of the Soviet Union. A few days before, Alexander Yakovlev, a leading radical, had resigned from the Communist Party and predicted an imminent coup. Early on the morning of 19 August broadcast announcements said that the Deputy President, Gennadii Yanaev, was taking over the government because of Gorbachev's hitherto unannounced illness. But it was clear from those named as members of the State Emergency Committee, and by their 'Appeal to the Soviet People', that this was a take-over by conservatives connected to leading governmental and Party institutions and the military–industrial complex.[1] It also came to be suspected that Anatolii Lukyanov, the Chairman of the Supreme Soviet, was associated with the coup because he published a criticism of the Union Treaty very similar to that of the State Emergency Committee shortly after the coup started. One of the coup leaders, the Prime Minister, Valentin Pavlov, soon resigned on account of ill health.

National and Moscow television stations were taken over, and all but nine conservative newspapers banned. There were troop and naval movements in Russia and the Baltic republics. All communications with Gorbachev, on holiday in the Crimea, were cut. The 'Appeal' declared that Gorbachev's policies were a failure, the country had become ungovernable and was breaking up socially and politically. The elected legislatures were castigated as 'frivolous and clumsy parliamentarians who have set us against each other, and brought forth thousands of still-born laws' while the country's leaders were 'those who fawn on foreign patrons and seek advice and blessings across the sea'. They promised a new debate on the Union Treaty, a return to law and order, economic reform (including private enterprise, price cuts and allocation of more land for private plots) and the honouring of all international agreements (Crawshaw, 1992, pp. 185–6).

The main protest against the coup came from Yeltsin who, on the morning of the coup, read a message from the top of a tank outside the Russian parliament building (the 'White House') in which he said that 'the clouds of terror and dictatorship are gathering over the whole country. They must not be allowed to bring eternal night'. He called for the restoration of Gorbachev as the legitimate president of the country, a general strike, and declared sovereign control over the territory of the Russian Federation. Outside Moscow, the Leningrad and many other city soviets denounced the coup, as did the leader of one of the largest and most significant republics, Nazarbaev of Kazakhstan. But President Mutalibov of Azerbaijan welcomed it and others (such as Kravchuk of Ukraine) at first sat on the fence. Some autonomous republics also welcomed the coup.

Military control was tightened in Moscow but Yeltsin was not arrested and he was soon barricaded in the 'White House', gaining an increasing number of supporters both inside and out. When the 'White House' was not stormed on the night of Tuesday, 20 August, it began to seem that the coup was not succeeding. Although it appeared that the coup leaders had secured control of the main organs of power – the

Communist Party, the military and the KGB – it was also known that these organizations were not united in opposition to the policies of Gorbachev and his government. Many, especially middle- and lower-ranking personnel were thought to be supporters of the reformers. The army, composed of conscripts from many nationalities, was demoralized by recent events and not trained or willing to maintain law and order within the Soviet Union. Nor could the troops of the KGB be automatically relied on. The MVD were more united and disciplined but not numerous enough to subdue the whole country. Certainly, some army units soon expressed their support for Yeltsin's stand, including a unit of the elite airborne division.

Yeltsin was a highly popular, charismatic figure who had cultivated good relations with many in the army and had created his own Russian KGB. Moreover, he had legitimacy through being freely elected. In Leningrad too, where strong opposition was led by the mayor, Anatolii Sobchak, the army and navy were clearly not prepared to occupy and blockade the city. Resistance was building up in the Baltic republics, Ukraine and elsewhere. In fact, the radicals had done something to prepare resistance to a possible coup. Yeltsin had got the Russian presidential election brought forward, and the mayors of Moscow and Leningrad also ensured that they had electoral legitimacy. Yeltsin had appointed security officers who drew up plans to defend the 'White House'. Most important, Yeltsin got a Russian section of the KGB created with offices inside the Lubyanka, the KGB headquarters. During 18–19 July a conference of Russian KGB officers advocated the abolition of Communist Party control and the basing of KGB activities on legal authority. Thus during the coup there was a struggle for the support of the KGB between the coup leaders and the KGB Russian section.

Meanwhile, the army's Taman division which had, much to their surprise, been ordered to the centre of Moscow at the start of the coup, decided that they would not fire on civilians and would defend the 'White House' rather than storm it. The coup leaders then turned to the KGB's Alpha antiterrorist group and ordered it to take the building. They could have succeeded, but with Afghanistan veterans and armed police inside and a huge, virtually unarmed, crowd outside, serious bloodshed was inevitable. KGB communications officers loyal to Yeltsin were intercepting orders to the assault group, and the defence of the 'White House' was being adjusted accordingly, especially in the underground service tunnels. They also established that the coup was instigated by the top leaders only and did not have the active participation of the rank and file. In the end, KGB officers, too, refused to storm the building. Therefore it was, ironically, middle-ranking army and KGB officers who ensured the failure of the coup (BBC, 1991). Although the expected attack on the 'White House' on the night of 20 August did not occur, an army patrol moving away from it encountered barricades on the ring road and was ambushed. In the ensuing mêlée three people were killed. The coup was seen to crumble on 21 August when troops were given the order to leave Moscow and contact was re-established with Gorbachev, who speedily returned to the capital.[2]

Mistakes made by the Coup Leaders

The coup leaders failed to establish their authority – for example, an attempt to impose a curfew was ignored – and there was no public manifestation of support for them, in contrast to huge demonstrations against the coup in Moscow, Leningrad and elsewhere. The failure to arrest Yeltsin meant that opponents of the coup could rally around a popular and legitimately elected leader. It may be that Yeltsin's arrest was planned, but he escaped to the Russian parliament building before it could be accomplished. Some consider that Yeltsin's arrest would have triggered a popular uprising, which the coup leaders wished to avoid. They banned the radical press, radio and television but this did not prevent emergency issues being printed, and clandestine radio and television programmes being broadcast. Links with the West were not cut. The coup leaders failed to apply force effectively in the early hours, and the army and KGB were unwilling to fight when it became clear that there would be vigorous and bloody opposition from the people surrounding the 'White House'.

The overwhelming mistake was to assume that Gorbachev would sign the necessary state of emergency decree (as, indeed, he had often threatened to do). When he refused the coup leaders had to improvise. Invoking the constitution they made the Deputy President, Gennadii Yanaev, his successor, but their declaration of a state of emergency was legally very doubtful. It could have been declared by presidential decree and then would be required to be retrospectively approved by the soviets of the republics in which it was to be imposed or, failing that, by a two-thirds majority of the all-Union Supreme Soviet. But at least their concern with legal forms shows how far Soviet politics had developed towards constitutionality in the Gorbachev period.

Interpretations of the Coup

Some saw the failure of the coup as a demonstration that the people of the Soviet Union had at last become politically conscious and willing to defend their incipient democracy. They explained this by the fact that the population was now more sophisticated and better educated, was more aware of what went on in the rest of the world and had learnt a great deal from the experience of *glasnost* since 1985. For those who took this view, there could be no going back to the authoritarian past. Others argued that the coup was not the end, but merely a stage in the conflict between conservatives and radicals. The great majority of people in Moscow and elsewhere did not take part in the resistance, but went about their ordinary business, sometimes as concerned observers, sometimes apathetic, indifferent or cynical. While significant sections of the armed forces refused the coup leaders support (for example, the army and navy in the Leningrad region) others, such as the Black Sea naval command at Sevastopol, did support them.

For Galeotti (1991) the coup's failure reflected the polarization between two ideologies seeking to fill the vacuum left by the collapse of Communism. The first was a conservatism emphasizing discipline and order and the need to maintain the Soviet Union intact, linked to a nostalgic Russian nationalism and summed up in the slogan 'national salvation'. The alternative ideology saw developments in terms of decentralization based on greater grass-roots activism and an unwill- ingness on the part of the newly assertive decentralized authorities to finance services over which they had no control. But this decentraliza- tion could also be understood as disintegration, with both army and KGB facing great difficulty in maintaining their organizational struc- tures intact. There were divisions in the security forces over whether accountability was due to the old, albeit reinvigorated, centralized state or to the the new centres of power in the republics. Although there had been one or two tests of the security forces' effectiveness (for example, in the Baltic republics) there had been no test of the their unity of will – a unity which proved, in the event, to be absent. This, as Lenin had pointed out in another context, was a fatal weakness.

Another view is that the coup was an attempt to maintain *perestroika* (restructuring) but in the context of the old authoritarian system which was seen as essential to maintain order and stability. Davies (1991) pointed to Gorbachev's clear original intention to im- pose reform from above. He saw the hand of the KGB at work in that Gorbachev's rise was assisted by KGB chief and subsequent Party General Secretary, Yuri Andropov, himself a reformer. All leading Party and state organizations promoted *perestroika*, while Gorbachev kept the organization of the Party intact and retained the general secretaryship. Thus, he argued, Gorbachev had been able to place supporters of *perestroika* (but opponents of democratization) in all leading positions. There seemed to be a growing recognition in the Andropov circle (of whom Gorbachev was one) and the KGB that the Cold War policy was counter-productive, that the economy was de- monstrably inferior to those of the developed West, and that Soviet citizens no longer had belief in, or commitment to, the political system.

By mid-1991 reform appeared to have failed amid increasing chaos. The Cold War had been ended, but with what were seen by conservatives as losses for Soviet security and not for the western powers. A market economy was not replacing the old command economy and, above all, democratization was threatening to break up the Union. Moreover, in the spring of 1991 Gorbachev again began to show renewed sympathy with the radicals, reaching an agreement with Yeltsin and tending to sideline the conservatives. But, in staging a coup to save *perestroika*, Gorbachev's appointees would certainly have been forced to resort to authoritarian methods no longer tolerable in the contemporary Soviet Union.

Among emigrés and 'cold warriors' in the West it was believed that Gorbachev had always been a tool of the KGB, to be used and discarded as necessary, and that the Soviet Union's military strength exceeded that of the United States in spite of arms reduction treaties. The abandonment of Marxism-Leninism and the withdrawal from Eastern Europe were seen as merely tactical. For these interpreters the developments of *glasnost* and *perestroika* in the Soviet Union contributed to the strengthening, rather than weakening, of existing powerful interests. Where the vested interests appeared to have suffered a serious setback, as in the coup, it was argued that they were always strong enough to regroup and try again (Nazarov, 1991).

Brown (1991) felt that the dangers of a coup could have been mitigated if the radicals had given Gorbachev more support, and constructive – rather than negative – criticism. He regarded Gorbachev's support for conservatives in the period October 1990 to March 1991 as merely tactical, to avoid a coup during the winter. He had been presented with a virtual ultimatum by the government, the military–industrial complex and the KGB, which forced him into temporary retreat, while he himself remained a man of the centre. Still others, like Walker (1991) and Thompson (1991), blamed the coup on the failure of the West to give adequate backing to Gorbachev. Very few military concessions were made by the West in ending the Cold War compared to those by the Soviet Union. Gorbachev left the London summit of the Group of Seven (major industrial countries) in July 1991 without any significant commitment of western investment or technology to demonstrate that defence industries could be converted to civilian use and the public appeased by goods on sale in the shops.

The Coup's Aftermath

The failure of the coup provoked a crisis for all major institutions of the old regime. The members of the State Emergency Committee were arrested, but other leaders of the military, the KGB and the Communist Party were all implicated. The Party Politburo failed to condemn the coup and nearly all the Cabinet of Ministers supported it. Leading figures, such as the Foreign Minister Alexander Bessmertnykh and the acting editor of the Party newspaper, *Pravda*, had remained silent. Before the coup, although popular participation in politics had manifested itself in the Russian Federation by means of demonstrations, it was only in some of the other republics that 'people power' had directly influenced events. Now this phenomenon had effectively occurred on the streets of the capital itself, in conditions of physical bravery and moral courage. This indicated that, for many, a significant shift in political consciousness had taken place which would make any return to the authoritarianism of the past virtually impossible. It must be emphasized, however, that the immediate cause of the coup's failure was not 'people power' but disunity among the military and security forces.

The coup also changed the relationship between Gorbachev and Yeltsin. Undoubtedly, Yeltsin's position was greatly strengthened. Gorbachev was the symbol of legality and constitutional legitimacy, but Yeltsin emerged as the focus of resistance and the embodiment of elected authority. By 23 August, when the coup was over, the radicals, led by Yeltsin, were moving to consolidate their victory. Yeltsin issued a stream of decrees, many of them transferring control of key institutions from the central government to the Russian Federation. He suspended the activities of the Russian Communist Party and was soon followed by some other republics. Many officials were sacked, including the whole Soviet government, and radicals began to replace them. *Pravda* was suspended together with five other newspapers. The head of television and radio, as well as those of the two news agencies, Tass and Novosti, were sacked. Gorbachev's acting replacements for the head of the KGB and the defence and interior ministries were immediately replaced by radical nominees approved by Yeltsin.

At first, Gorbachev did not understand the extent of the political transformation which the failed coup had created. He told a news conference that the Communist Party still had an important role to play. But as a consequence of Yeltsin's initiatives, Gorbachev changed his position completely, the realities of the new situation having been at last brought home to him. He resigned from the Party secretaryship, suggested that the Central Committee dissolve itself, and issued a decree confiscating the Party's property and handing it over to local soviets for the time being. Another decree banned Party activity in the armed forces, the KGB and all other law enforcement agencies. On 29 August the Supreme Soviet suspended the activities of the Communist Party throughout the Soviet Union and directed the state prosecutor to investigate evidence of 'the participation of the Communist Party's leading organs in actions aimed at the violent overthrow of the constitutional system' (Roxburgh, 1991).

Western Reaction

Although there had been talk of a coup for some time the event, when it came, took western leaders by surprise. Their first reaction was to suspend aid to the Soviet Union. The question of how much financial and economic aid should be sent to the post-coup central government or to the separate republics – or to both – was a major point of discussion among the leading industrial nations. Pressure increased on the West to extend material and financial aid without insisting on a new political and economic order being fully in place. It was accompanied by fears of serious food shortages in the coming winter, and of economic chaos in the longer term, leading to prolonged social disorder. The West took varying attitudes to the many declarations of independence by the separate republics. There was a rush to recognize the independence of the Baltic republics, but no such hurry in the case of Georgia – considered to lack convincing democratic credentials – or Armenia, which had no powerful friends. There was concern over how far the new governmental authorities would adhere to the Soviet Union's international agreements, especially the arms reduction treaties, although rapid reassurance was given on that score. There were anxieties over the control of nuclear weapons and whether republics such as Russia would want to be represented at future arms reduction talks.

The Still-born Union of Sovereign States

Many other reforms, especially that of the economy, seemed far more feasible in the near future with the collapse of the conservative opposition. The main question to be dealt with was the setting up of a provisional covernment and reaching agreement on a revised treaty between the republics to replace the one intended to be signed from 20 August. Estonia and Latvia declared independence (as Lithuania had done long before). All the other republics were to soon do the same. Clearly, the fate of the new Union Treaty was crucial. The existing version already transferred many powers to the republics and weakened the centre. Now the role of the centre looked likely to be undermined completely. In a speech before the Supreme Soviet on 26 August Gorbachev offered full independence to those republics which did not wish to sign the treaty and proposed early elections for the presidency and a new parliament. But there was a feeling that events were overtaking Gorbachev, who was still talking in terms of retaining important economic powers at the centre. Meanwhile, the two most important republics, Russia and Ukraine, were agreeing to an economic and military alliance and calling on other republics to join them in a system of inter-republic relations with little or no role for the central government.

Gorbachev set about trying to establish a governmental structure to operate until the new Union Treaty had been signed and fresh elections held. In the interim, an Emergency Economic Committee was set up, but his attempts to persuade radicals to serve on a new Security Council failed. The most dramatic event was the meeting of the Congress of People's Deputies from 2 to 5 September, when Gorbachev, supported by leading radicals, cajoled and bullied the Congress into voting to abolish the existing constitutional arrangements (in effect, abolishing the Soviet Union) – including its own existence – and in their place to set up a 'Union of Sovereign States'. The new government institutions were: a *State Council*, replacing the Security Council, consisting of President Gorbachev and the leaders of the republics who agreed to sign the Union Treaty - its function would be to deal with foreign and domestic policy; and an *Inter-Republican Economic Council*, replacing the Emergency Economic Committee, to manage the economy and promote economic reforms until a new constitution was agreed. In place of the Congress of People's Deputies and Supreme Soviet was a *Council of Representatives*, consisting of twenty representatives from each republic. Republics could join a political union by signing the Union Treaty with full or associate membership, or could leave the Union altogether. All fifteen republics would be invited to join an economic union and to sign a collective security agreement aiming to maintain a single army and one 'military-strategic space'. It was very obvious that there had been a huge shift of power to the republics (Appendix D) (Pringle, 1991).

These arrangements were to remain in force until a new constitution was agreed and elections held. Much remained uncertain; for example, it was not clear whether the centre retained the power to negotiate with foreign powers on behalf of the republics, whether the 'Soviet Union' would retain its seat and veto on the United Nations Security Council, or whether the republics would have separate representation at the United Nations. It was also not certain how many of the old ministries would remain or how funds would be distributed. President Nazarbaev of Kazakhstan still argued that the republics would have to give up some powers voluntarily to the centre, particularly those involving economic policy.

Immediate Problems

Ironically, the collapse of the coup dramatically speeded up the very developments it was intended to halt. The breakup of the Union had been accelerated and the dominant role of the Communist Party ended, although many questions remained concerning the future of the Party's personnel (many of whom, as experienced officials, would be required to work in the administration of the new governmental structure) and the whereabouts and disposal of its very considerable assets. Although the Communist Party had apparently been destroyed, it was still in *de facto* control in Central Asia and attempting to reorganize under other names. The democratic parties were numerous, weak and argumentative; they were groups of intellectuals rather than mass parties. Yeltsin had as yet no organized basis for his power, no party to carry through difficult and unpopular reforms. As for Gorbachev, he would, in any circumstances, have difficulty in surviving, especially as he also now lacked any power base. The central presidency seemed to have no future except as a ceremonial institution, unless serious economic and political difficulties eventually drove the republics to seek a stronger co-ordinating structure.

The winter of 1991–2 was always going to be particularly difficult because of the poor harvest and falling production. Much depended on how far the West was willing and able to extend effective aid. Meanwhile, the republics were working to gain maximum advantage from the situation. The Baltic states were independent, while attempts were being made to establish authoritarian regimes in Central Asia and Georgia. There was complex political manoeuvring in republics such as Ukraine, with strong drives towards independence competing with pressures for close association with Russia. Overall, centrifugal forces seemed dominant, and it was difficult to see more than a very loose confederation emerging, with some economic and security links, institutionally much weaker than, for example, the European Community.

Gorbachev's Union Disintegrates

Gorbachev continued trying to get the republics to agree to a new treaty, albeit even more confederal than its draft predecessors. In interviews and speeches he argued (supported by President Nazarbaev of Kazakhstan) that economic and social reform would not succeed unless some form of union was preserved. But it was clear that the republics were increasingly reluctant to sign a new treaty. Instead, they were keen to assert their own independence and, above all, were suspicious of any initiative from the discredited centre. In particular, the Russian government, led by Yeltsin, moved with growing confidence to undermine Gorbachev's position. Yeltsin knew that the other republics would not do anything significant to support Gorbachev. He soon took control of crucial aspects of the central government: the official archives and the government communications system. Russian officials were transferred to head central government ministries and no top appointments were allowed without his approval. Meanwhile fewer and fewer representatives of the republics were turning up to meetings of central government institutions. The meeting of the Soviet parliament was postponed twice and, when it did meet, deputies from only seven of the twelve remaining republics attended.

Russia finally decided to do what it had long threatened: to push forward with economic reform without waiting for the agreement (apparently permanently stalled) of the other republics. Such was Russia's relative economic power that the other republics would be forced to fall into line. At the same time Russia announced the take-over of the state bank and other financial institutions formerly controlled by the centre. Russia also bailed out the state bank when the Supreme Soviet – lacking a quorum thanks to deliberate Russian absentees – was unable to sanction credits necessary to continue the financing of the central government. By the end of November Russia had been able to ensure the closure of eighty central ministries, simply by refusing to supply funds for their financing.

Yeltsin and others publicly demanded a confederal state (although privately preferring complete independence), but Gorbachev insisted on a single union to the end. He hoped that seven republics would agree and that others would sign later. In the event, on 25 November the seven refused even to initial the proposed treaty which would have created a 'Union of Sovereign States'. Although they had tentatively accepted the treaty they clearly lacked the political will to sign and would agree only to refer the text back to their parliaments for further consideration. The reality was that they could not agree on a text to be initialled and, in any case, the absence of Ukraine from the talks – Gorbachev said that a union without Ukraine was 'unthinkable' – rendered them virtually meaningless.

The Ukrainian Vote for Independence

On 30 November Gorbachev's remaining financial powers were transferred to Yeltsin. On the following day an even more significant event occurred: Ukraine voted for independence by a large majority. This was the event which triggered moves leading to the creation of the new Commonwealth of Independent States. Even the army was more and more recognizing Russia as the main power, and when the United States Secretary of State, James Baker, visited Russia in the middle of December the Soviet Defence Minister was among Yeltsin's advisers at the talks. It had become imperative to negotiate an inter-republic arrangement which, unlike Gorbachev's proposals, would be acceptable to the republics. Gorbachev continued to utter dire warnings about the consequences of a breakup of the Union – not least to the large numbers living outside their own republics. He offended Ukrainians' susceptibilities by the scornful way he dismissed their vote on independence as against common sense. He tried to persuade Yeltsin to sign the Union Treaty, believing that if Russia signed, others would follow. Yeltsin refused, responding to the Ukrainian vote more subtly, at first by saying that he could not envisage a union without the Ukraine, and then by rapidly recognizing an independent Ukraine and suggesting the establishment of a new structure of inter-governmental relations between the republics. He summed up the situation as he saw it in a speech to the Belarus parliament:

> Experience has shown that some want to maintain at least the spirit of a system which allows for people to be dominated. This is fraught with huge losses. These games cannot be played for ever. Everyone is afraid of the centre and its rebirth in old forms. (Steele, 1991a)

Gorbachev believed that Yeltsin used the Ukrainian vote and the crisis over the Union budget finally to destroy the Union. But before the Ukrainian President Kravchuk had even left for the meeting with Yeltsin in Belarus he too was talking of a 'Commonwealth'.

The Brest Meeting

The three Slavic republics – Russia, Ukraine and Belarus, comprising 70 per cent of the Soviet population – got together on 8 December near Brest[3] and issued the Minsk Declaration, which declared that the Soviet Union no longer existed. Instead there would be a Commonwealth[4] of Independent States which other republics would be able to join. They met Presidents Gorbachev and Nazarbaev immediately afterwards to put the situation to them. Nazarbaev was clearly angry that he, as head of a republic with nuclear weapons, had not been invited to the Brest talks. But as a close ally of Gorbachev's he may have been perceived as potentially disruptive. His absence, however, did make the agreement look like an exclusively Slavic initiative. Although Gorbachev continued to stress the necessity of the centre to the republics, his final efforts were of no avail. He tried to argue that the Ukrainian vote did not mean that Ukraine was against a new union but Kravchuk made it clear that it did mean just that. He also argued that the Slavic republics could not decide the fate of the Union by themselves. To this last point, the Minsk signatories said that the Union had in reality collapsed before the Brest meeting. Two days after the Minsk Declaration the Central Asian republics met in Alma-Ata and agreed to join the Commonwealth. By then they had little choice. Even Gorbachev's strongest supporter among the presidents of the republics, Nazarbaev of Kazakhstan, now faced realities and deserted him. Only Georgia (and the now fully independent Baltic republics) were left outside the Commonwealth and even Georgia, although in the throes of an armed struggle, indicated an interest in joining. The Central Asian republics insisted on being treated as co-founders with equal rights and they also wanted the economic agreement, made shortly before the Minsk Declaration, to be implemented. It implied a greater degree of common economic policy than that envisaged by the new Commonwealth. They also said that they wanted the 'social and economic realities' of Central Asia to be taken into account, which meant economic aid for them as the Commonwealth's poorest members.

At the end Gorbachev tried to maintain the forms of legality and constitutionality, and to express his concern for stability and security at home and abroad. A last gesture was to call a meeting of all the army commanders of the Soviet Union's military districts. In the Soviet armed forces the Communist Party had underpinned discipline and ideological loyalty but it was not now clear who was in charge of the military. His speech appears to have been a failure, making generalized appeals not to panic as they saw the Union in disarray, for the army not to get involved in politics and for reforms to continue. When Yeltsin met the military he stuck to basic issues, like salaries and housing; Yeltsin now held the purse strings. By 19 December Gorbachev was saying, 'The main work of my life is done' and that there was no place for him in the new Commonwealth. A further meeting of the eleven Commonwealth republics took place in Alma-Ata on the weekend of 21–2 December. It was at this meeting that the Soviet Union and its presidency were formally declared no longer to exist. They rejected the idea of a Commonwealth citizenship for people living outside their own republic since the Commonwealth was not a state. They agreed on the inviolability of their present borders and that Russia should occupy the Soviet seat at the United Nations, the other republics applying for membership separately. But there was still no clear agreement on economic reforms.

Desperately, Gorbachev was still calling for the Minsk Declaration to be put to the Soviet parliament, or even to a referendum, but it was too late. What remained of the central government was taken over by Russia and, a few minutes after Gorbachev made his resignation speech on 25 December, control of the former Soviet Union's nuclear weapons was transferred to Yeltsin as President of the Russian Federation. The red hammer and sickle flag of the Soviet Union was lowered from the Kremlin to be replaced by the flag of the Russian Federation. The Soviet parliament formally dissolved itself a day later.

Notes

1   The members of the State Emergency Committee were: Gennadii Yanaev, vice-president; Vladimir Kryuchkov, head of the KGB; Dmitrii Yazov, Defence Minister; Valentin Pavlov, Prime Minister; Alexander Tizyakov,

President of the Association of State Enterprises and Industrial, Construc-
tion, Transport and Communications Facilities; Oleg Baklanov, CPSU
Secretary responsible for the Defence Industry; Boris Pugo, Interior
Minister; and Vasilii Starodubtsev, Chairman of the Farmers' Union.
Thus some of the very highest officials of the government, Party and
military–industrial complex were involved.

2 For a first-hand account of Gorbachev's imprisonment see Jonathan
Steele, *Guardian*, 23 August 1991, pp. 1–3.

3 Although the Slavic representatives met at Brest, they issued their Declaration from Minsk to avoid comparison with the humiliating peace made
by the Bolsheviks with the Germans at Brest in 1918, in which large areas
of Belorussia and Ukraine were ceded.

4 The Russian word for commonwealth (*sodruzhestvo*) literally means
'friendship association'. It has no Communist overtones and thus is
very different from *soyuz*, or 'union', a word with strong Communist
connotations.

Part I

The Growth and Decay of the Soviet Union

1

The Bolshevik Revolution Triumphs

The Long-term Causes of the Revolution

The Russian empire was created through expansion and conquest over several centuries, spreading outwards from its centre rather than by establishing separate colonies overseas. By no means all the colonized people regarded themselves as conquered subjects. In areas such as Central Asia the Russians were looked to as protectors in an unstable and threatened region. In others the Russians might be played off against rivals, like the Germans. The ruling Romanov dynasty tried to secure the loyalty of local elites by granting them status and privileges in return for their maintaining stability in the lands they ruled over. This worked quite effectively in many parts. At the centre, the up-holding of a firm autocracy was seen as essential for keeping the disparate empire together. But its weakness was its multitude of nationalities embracing varied cultures, religions, languages and aspirations. The seeds of disintegration were ready to germinate should the centre ever weaken. The same inherent weakness was present in the Soviet Union.

The tsarist regime experienced increasing economic and social trouble for most of the nineteenth century, and much debate took place among the intelligentsia as to the sort of reforms that would be appropriate. Previous reforms had not succeeded in modernizing the empire or enabling it to keep up with the industrialization of the West. It had failed to absorb the new social classes of an industrializing society into the government. Much of the dispute over the future of Russia centred around this very industrializing process: whether it should be pursued vigorously or whether Russia should aim at being a reformed, peasant society. Echoes of this dispute could still be discerned during discussions on Russia's future which flourished in the *glasnost* atmosphere of the Gorbachev period.

The Revolutionary Mentality

In the latter part of the nineteenth century, and with the accession of a weak tsar, Nicholas II, many believed that the regime was losing its grip on power and that revolution rather than reform was necessary and ultimately inevitable. Things came to a head with the defeat of Russia by Japan in the war of 1904–5 and, from then on, the country was in a quasi-revolutionary situation. But it took a major war, the First World War, and the consequent chaos, to precipitate the revolution proper. At this time an apocalyptic revolutionary mentality was prevalent in Russia: a belief that the old order must end and everything be created afresh. This utopianism, in its Russian form, was utilitarian, judging everything in relation to the goal and rejecting aesthetic and individual values. In such a context the idea of revolution was attractive, giving a straightforward meaning to life, especially after a traumatic war.

After defeat in the Russo-Japanese War and increasing unrest, the Tsar reluctantly conceded a constitution and parliament: the Duma. Although these concessions were very limited in their effect, the authority of the regime was clearly being undermined. A form of party politics developed in which the main parties were the *Socialist Revolutionaries* (representing the peasants and capable of violence); the *Constitutional Democratic Party* (Cadets, who were liberal-democratic and revolutionary only as a last resort); the *Octobrists* (liberal-democratic, for constitutional monarchy, and antirevolutionary); the *Union of the Russian People* (extremely right wing, in favor of upholding the Orthodox Church, autocracy and Russian nationalism); and the *Russian Social Democratic Labour Party* (RSDRP) (Marxist forerunners of the CPSU, led by Lenin and founded in 1898). These parties expressed alternatives which were to be a standard of reference for many when reform could once again be openly debated in the 1980s.

If the tsarist regime was doomed, the question arose: Who would seize power and how they would do it? In 1881 terrorists had assassinated Tsar Alexander II (who was introducing moderate reforms) and the subsequent repression gave an impetus to Marxists. Marxist groups sprang up all over Russia. While the 'purity' of their Marxist beliefs may not have been perfect, their existence nevertheless proved vital in stimulating action throughout the empire when a revolution finally occurred. While the Socialist Revolutionaries stressed the development of Russia as a peasant community and advocated terrorism as the way to create a revolutionary situation, Marxists were convinced that the country was inevitably moving in a capitalist direction and saw the class struggle led by the industrialized working class, not the peasantry, as the basis of the revolution.

Lenin

Lenin, the most outstanding of the Marxist leaders, was converted to Marxism in 1889. He was convinced that Russia was already capitalist, and that its capitalist nature was epitomized in the large state-sponsored industrial factory production units. There had been attempts by the Jewish *Bund* (a confederation of left-wing organizations) to organize conspiratorial groups into a wider movement, but this resulted in greater danger and therefore more secrecy and conspiracy. In the *Bund* there was also an emphasis on *practical* objectives, such as seeking better wages and conditions of work. These objectives were believed to be more likely to lead to revolution. Lenin, however, was very much opposed to all this. His ideas on how to precipitate a revolution and consolidate power were more ideological and looked to worsening conditions and a heightening of class struggle as the way forward.

In *What is to be Done?*, written in 1902, Lenin argued that, left to itself, the proletariat would not develop a revolutionary self-consciousness, but would merely pursue economic aims. Therefore a core leadership party was needed to build up class consciousness from the outside. It was this vanguard party which was the revolutionary organization, and it was not a mass workers' party or a mass movement. Many felt that such an argument was a major departure from Marx's own idea that the Party would be the leading section of the working class. Lenin, however, saw himself as expanding Marx's not-very-well-developed ideas and as applying himself to the practical situation as he found it. At the subsequent Party Congress differences arose between two factions, which became known as the Bolsheviks (led by Lenin) and the Mensheviks. The Mensheviks believed in a strict adherence to Marxist theory with a clearly identified bourgeois revolution preceding the socialist one. For the Bolsheviks the proletariat could control and speed up the bourgeois revolution and create a situation of permanent revolution. They also disagreed on organization: a broad-based trade union organization for the Mensheviks and a centralized and disciplined Party-based organization for the Bolsheviks. The Mensheviks drew most of their support from non-Russians and the skilled working class, while the Bolsheviks found support largely among Russians and the unskilled working class.

The Bolsheviks decided to separate themselves from other revolutionaries on the questions of leadership, discipline and their attitude to the Duma. Lenin tried to build up a disciplined, elite organization. He did not propagandize or seek recruits among the workers because, for him, the immediate enemies were not capitalists or the supporters of the Tsar or the Duma, but the rival socialist parties which could undermine his support. His central ideas were, first, *democratic centralism*: initiative from the top, then full and free discussion followed by absolute obedience to decisions once taken; and second, *permanent revolution*: the continuous pressurizing and harassing of the bourgeoisie until their political regime collapsed and the Bolsheviks could take over. These same ideas, in a debased and corrupted form, were eventually to undermine the very political system that the Bolsheviks created.

The Revolutions of 1917

The outbreak of the First World War finally ended the tsarist regime. Huge defections of soldiers from the front and large-scale food riots in Petrograd (the capital, formerly called St Petersburg) in February 1917, which troops refused to suppress, created a massive crisis. The autocracy collapsed with the abdication of the Tsar. In a time of confusion, following the 'February Revolution', there were two potential governments: the Provisional Government led, from July, by Alexander Kerensky, and the Petrograd Soviet, which was much more radical and a constant challenge to the Provisional Government. Unofficial soviets (councils of workers and, later, soldiers) had come into existence in the years preceding the war. From February to October there was an uneasy dual authority. The RSDRP, still divided between Bolsheviks and Mensheviks, was usually in a minority, with the Socialist Revolutionaries the dominant party. There were disagreements in the RSDRP, including a row between Lenin on the one hand, and Kamenev and Zinoviev (leading members of the Bolsheviks) on the other. The latter believed the Bolsheviks could win enough support democratically without the need for a coup. But, for Lenin, violence was justified against the evils of compromise. The *real* majority was that of soldiers, sailors and workers. The orthodox Marxist development could occur somewhere else (like Germany) and the Russian revolution could be consolidated on it. The fundamental point was that the revolutionary moment had come and must be grasped, not quibbled over. The Bolsheviks emerged as the only group with confidence enough to create a viable government.

The consolidation of the Revolution, as of the Gorbachev reforms much later, depended very much on sustaining an efficient food supply to urban areas. Rural administration collapsed in 1917 owing to peasant direct action. They turned to traditional village institutions as rural society fragmented and each community concentrated on self-preservation. There was little sense of class consciousness or of wider social group interests among the peasants. There was also not much awareness or understanding of developments in Petrograd, but enough to realize that the Provisional Government would not grant their demands. The result was peasant direct action which interrupted the urban food supply. In turn, this quickened the radicalization of the urban population and, combined with the war weariness of the army, weakened the Provisional Government. Lenin emphasized the importance of the peasants in precipitating and consolidating the Revolution, but the significance of their role in events as they unfolded is still disputed.

The Mensheviks in 1917

The Mensheviks argued that Russia was not ready for a socialist revolution in 1917. Since it had not completed the stages of capitalist development, its industrial proletariat was too small and disorganized. Menshevik strategy in 1917 as prominent leaders of the Petrograd soviet, the trade unions and the three coalition governments of May to October, was to stabilize 'bourgeois' democracy, while organizing the working class for power and responsibility. Their weakness was to fail to respond to the rapidly changing mood on the streets, where power now lay. Before July 1917 there had been widespread support for the concept of dual power, meaning that the leaders of the Petrograd soviet would refrain from entering the 'bourgeois' Provisional Government. Fear of counter-revolution, and the widely recognized need for national unity during the war, enabled the Mensheviks in the trade unions to moderate the workers' demands, while the Ministry of Trade and Industry persuaded many employers to make concessions to the workers, such as the eight-hour day. This was seen as compatible with Menshevik aspirations to reconcile class conflict and stabilize democracy. These practical achievements persuaded the Mensheviks to abandon 'dual power' and enter the Provisional Government in May, contrary to the dictates of their ideology and the views of many of their leaders. The workers did not share their trust in the bourgeoisie and expected their entry into the government to bring more concessions from employers. As workers' strikes and demands for control of industry increased in May and June employers grew more militant, forcing the Mensheviks to abandon most of their labour legislation and impose a wages policy. The ideal of class cooperation was overtaken by the violent class conflicts of the summer, which were themselves in part the outcome of the workers' disappointment in – and bourgeois fears of – the Menshevik leaders in the government.

The Bolsheviks in 1917

The Mensheviks rejected the growing radicalism of the workers, seeing it as politically 'immature', the result of Bolshevik manipulation. But they failed to recognize that they themselves were steadily becoming the party of the radical urban intelligentsia divorced from the workers (Figes, 1990b, p. 466). Later, from September to November, there was a prospect that those in the Socialist Revolutionary Party, together with the Mensheviks and Bolsheviks, concerned by the drift towards civil war, would form a socialist coalition to halt the process of polarization. But the principle of coalition was discredited after the Kornilov affair (which involved a Provisional Government general who was thought to be attempting a military coup, and who was crushed largely by the efforts of the soviets rather than the Provisional Government itself).

Under the Provisional Government the influence of the soviets had grown. They controlled the army, communications and the streets. Lenin saw them as created by the proletariat and thus a more democratic form of government than liberal democratic bourgeois parliaments could ever be. The St Petersburg soviet, in particular, had an importance going beyond the 'politicized strike committees' which existed elsewhere. It was the prototype for its successor, the Petrograd soviet, which became the basis on which Lenin created the Soviet government. The early days were chaotic and a small group of socialist intellectuals predominated. The decision not to join the Provisional Government, for example had been made by a small self-appointed 'executive government'. In the end, the Bolsheviks, with a clearer sense of priorities and better led by Lenin, ruthlessly overwhelmed all opposition. The idea of opposition as a negative rather than a positive force in government then took root.

Because of their relatively spontaneous democratic origins, the soviets had a legitimacy which was lacking in all other 'alternative' institutions and was there to be revived when, decades later, the Communist order decayed. Although Lenin made much of the soviets as the only possible form of revolutionary government, he was not wholly committed to them because, at first, the Bolsheviks were in a minority on the Petrograd soviet. But it became more and more clear that real power increasingly lay with the Petrograd soviet and not with the Provisional Government. It was the popularity that the Bolsheviks gained by their key role in defeating Kornilov that finally enabled them to get a majority on the Petrograd soviet; Leon Trotsky became its chairman. The Bolsheviks could now take over the government. Whether Lenin sincerely believed that the soviets were to be the foundation of government, a policy he was forced to abandon in the crisis of the civil war, or whether he was never really interested in them and simply used them to make the Revolution, is still a matter of debate.

The Bolsheviks Seize Power

Lenin had returned to Russia in April (helped by the Germans who wished to undermine the Russian contribution to the war), advocating the telescoping of the bourgeois and proletarian revolutions. The Provisional Government was dithering, taking no firm action and supporting the war. The Bolsheviks believed in getting out of the war, a highly popular view and one which enhanced their support, leading many to believe that they deserved a chance. In November (October in the old calendar)[1] the Bolsheviks easily seized Petrograd by armed force and had their action legitimized by a Congress of Soviets: the 'October Revolution' had taken place. Elections were due for a constituent assembly to draw up a new constitution to replace the Provisional Government, and it was elected in November. The election turned out to be a defeat for the Bolsheviks who gained a quarter of the votes (but majorities in Petrograd and Moscow), while the Socialist Revolutionaries had an overall majority. The Bolsheviks refused to accept this result and forcibly broke up the Assembly. This ostensibly undemocratic act was justified by Lenin with the argument that the elections had been held too soon, before the workers had full power and become a strong political force. In addition, he said that the Bolsheviks had a majority among the industrial proletariat, which was the majority that really mattered. Significantly, there was little resistance to the Bolshevik take-over. At this time, although by no means totally single-minded, they were more resolute and better organized than the other parties, and had outstanding leaders in Lenin and Trotsky. But the Bolsheviks inherited the old problems: inadequate productive capacity, social and cultural inequalities, racial and religious prejudice, political rivalries and hostile foreign powers. Lenin might not have been so determined and resolute if he had not been so deeply influenced by his belief in an imminent general Western European insurrection – an insurrection which did not happen.

Lenin and the Party after the Revolution

In spite of Lenin's, strongly expressed belief in the soviets and their important role in the events of 1917, their influence was short-lived, since the Party–government bureaucracy was largely outside their control. The tendency was for Lenin to carry on into the post-revolutionary period the organization and strategy which had succeeded before 1917. Society as a whole was still largely sceptical or even hostile to the Bolsheviks but they were well equipped to deal with this. Lenin had kept them apart from other groups and, from 1918 to 1920, gradually eliminated the other parties from government until only Bolsheviks remained. In 1921, at the Tenth Party Congress the Resolution on Unity was passed, which outlawed internal Party disputes. The Congress also insisted that criticism by individuals must be communicated to the whole membership, thereby exposing and isolating critics. Consciously or not, the foundations of the monolithic Stalinist state were being laid, the state against which *glasnost* and *perestroika* were to be such a devastating reaction. Initiative was now solely in the hands of the Party leadership and bureaucracy, although unofficial divisions remained. The group called 'Left Communists' opposed centralization of power and the retention of features of the pre-revolutionary social and economic order. Forerunners of the opposition groups of the 1920s, they were not democrats in the western sense, but rather suspicious of all authority. In spite of denials, anarchist influences were also evident among the Bolsheviks at this time. Although Lenin moved to a standard Marxist position after the Revolution, many of his followers did not. They objected to the distribution of the landlords' estates to the peasants, although the need to placate the peasants was essential to the regime.

The main preoccupation of the new state was survival. It was faced with civil war, invasion, attempts to achieve independence by some of the nationalities and by economic and social collapse. Hence democracy and liberty were not sacrosanct if they were seen to threaten survival – while an effective centralized organization was deemed essential to ensure that survival. The creation of this centralized organization came from above, but such a development was by no means wholly opposed from below. Workers often saw democratic liberties as bourgeois manifestations of inequality: the intelligentsia and professional classes retaining their superiority. So, at first, the suppression of liberty was supported as much from below as from above. When the two movements joined together they contributed to the plebeian, rough, anonymous characteristics of Stalinism. A major priority was to decide what to do about the war with Germany. Lenin wanted to get out of the war as quickly as possible and was prepared to pay a heavy price to do so. The 'Left Communists' argued for a revolutionary war. They thought that if Germany no longer had to fight a war in the East, the defeat of the western allies was very likely. A victorious Germany would then turn to eliminating the Communist regime in Russia. Thus Communist Russia should pursue a pre-emptive revolutionary war against Germany. But the disintegrating Russian army was incapable of either defending the country or of carrying out a revolutionary war. Lenin's decision to get out of the war, although desperate and costly, was, from his point of view, the only realistic course.

The Civil War, 'War Communism' and the New Economic Policy

The Bolshevik monopoly was consolidated by the Red Army and by the secret police (the 'Cheka'). The latter had been established by Lenin to deal with an immediate crisis, but it soon established a power and authority of its own. Whether Lenin expected the Cheka to be a permanent institution is another matter for debate. Certainly, in the confused aftermath of the Revolution, the emergency was real. A major civil war raged in many parts, with the Whites, the counter-revolution-aries, being supported by troops from various foreign powers (including Britain and the United States). A number of nationalities were struggling to achieve independence and the regime controlled only one-seventh of Russian territory. In addition it had great difficulty in feeding the urban population. Peasant support was decisive; they feared the counter-revolutionary Whites who wanted to reverse many of the revolutionary changes and would take away the land the peasants had seized. But they soon discovered that the 'war Communism' of the Bolsheviks meant the forcible confiscation of their grain to feed the cities. As a result, the Bolsheviks were simultaneously faced with counter-revolutionaries, peasants' and workers' strikes, as well as a naval rebellion (ruthlessly crushed) at Kronstadt in favour of more democracy.

In these desperate economic conditions it was not possible to institute a thorough reform of the economic system. Supplying the basic need of food to the urban population was essential to the survival of the Bolshevik government. To meet the emergency a relaxation of authoritarian pressure was necessary. Lenin therefore agreed to the reintroduction of a limited market mechanism: the New Economic Policy (NEP). Appropriation of food from the peasants was abolished and replaced by a tax in kind. These concessions were not a weakening of Bolshevik control, however. Rather the Bolsheviks used them to consolidate their power and restore order. They kept control of banks, heavy industry, foreign trade and transport. Private traders and peas-ants had no, or diluted, voting power.

The NEP lasted throughout most of the 1920s and was a period in which the political machinations of Stalin and the economic evolution of the country were intimately connected. In view of the traumatic events and experiences of the Stalin period, and given the success of the NEP in improving the country's economic position, was the price paid for collectivization of agriculture by Stalin from the end of the 1920s either justified or even necessary? Lenin appears to have seen the NEP as a long-term policy and not one of his 'successive assaults'. An opponent of the ruthlessness of the collectivization of agriculture and a leading figure in the NEP was Bukharin. He had been an idealistic 'Left Communist' in 1918 and a great believer in the NEP. Later he was vilified by Stalin and his successors, but was rehabilitated by Gorbachev and is seen as a Bolshevik who, unlike most of the other leaders, placed essential human considerations above abstract principles. Eventually the Bolsheviks had to decide what to do in the longer term. The alternatives were to make further concessions to the peasants in return for higher productivity – but this meant tolerating capitalism; or reorganization of agriculture to restrict peasant consumption, that is, collectivization. The latter alternative was adopted.

Interpretations of the Revolution

The official Soviet view of the Revolution before *glasnost* followed Marxist orthodoxy in understanding it as an event explained by the contradictions of capitalism and the logic of history. The older western view was that the Bolshevik victory could be attributed to superior discipline in the Bolshevik Party before 1917. Thus the Revolution was considered to be either a popular movement or a *coup d'état*. More recent commentators have recognized that the Bolsheviks had their own internal disciplinary problems, but they were able to exploit a situation in which belief in the need for radical action was gaining more and more support in the community generally. The Revolution could not have succeeded without a collapse of confidence in the old order and the radicalization of public opinion. The lack of a big commercial and industrial middle class caused the intelligentsia to throw in their lot with the Marxists. The revolutionaries were further helped by the creation of embryonic state institutions in the soviets, district committees, and trade unions. The new institutions fought for control of the bureaucratic organization and the parties tried to gain advantage from the struggle. The Bolsheviks had gathered much sympathy by promising to end the war, and were best placed because of the radicalization of influential public opinion, even though they did not have nationwide support. The institutions had to break completely with the old state in order to survive; hence the attraction of the thoroughgoing Bolsheviks who were more opposed by the other parties than by the institutions. In fact, the institutions constituted an embryonic state without formal legitimacy. On this interpretation the Revolution can be understood as a widely-based movement which was given coherence and direction by a small group and Lenin's crucial leadership.

Glasnost provided much more access to Soviet archives than hitherto and thus enabled a fundamental rethinking of the Revolution and its significance. Richard Pipes (1990) has come in for criticism because of his consistently hostile view of the Revolution and of the role of Lenin and the Bolsheviks. He sees Russian Communism as having its roots in the tsarist state where the two main obstacles to ending the tsarist empire were the peasantry, ghettoized and without respect for law and property and lacking a wider vision, and the intelligentsia, who were without roots in society, being excluded from legislation and administration. Society was thus polarized. But others argue that the centre was weakening. Although the Tsar was supported by the military, the other pillar of support – the Orthodox Church – had been turned into a department of state, was enfeebled and a source of discontent. Many of Russia's revolutionaries were former seminarists. Without a strong Church the peasants were in no condition to cope with an urban crisis perpetrated by secular revolutionaries. This ongoing discussion points to the conclusion that the Revolution was partly a product of the history of Russia, and of the attitudes and thinking of the Russians, but also of many other forces (Hosking, 1991, pp. 3–4).

Revolutionaries and liberal democrats were profoundly divided by ideological differences over the meaning of revolution and democracy. It was Lenin's ability to establish a pragmatic but effective link between ideology and the existing reality in which they found themselves that enabled the Bolsheviks ultimately to prevail in the struggle for power. They took advantage of a social and political collapse precipitated by popular uprising and army desertions. Although they were not as effectively disciplined as has sometimes been thought their strength was the single-mindedness and ruthlessness of their leader, Lenin, together with awareness of, and response to, popular demands for reform and a withdrawal from the war. Lenin did not believe in forming majority coalitions, but rather in forcefully overwhelming opponents. However, having effectively seized the initiative, the Bolsheviks still had the problem of creating a new legitimacy and authority upon which to base their power, in the face of many hazardous crises. Their ultimate success was by no means assured. The real social changes occurred in the collectivization and industrialization of the Stalin era. Before that the main shift of social power was based on the struggle of some nationalities for independence. Few got it, but they did get recognized representation in the new Soviet state.

The Reassessment of Lenin

The Soviet regime always used Lenin as a symbol of political legitimacy. After 1924 it fostered the cult of Lenin, placing his embalmed body on display and making him the centre of propaganda with the slogan, 'Lenin lives!'. In 1970, the one hundredth anniversary of his birth, this almost went too far with overkill, and the official slogan 'Lenin is always with us' became the subject of humorous interpretation (Tumarkin, 1983, pp. 262–4). Gorbachev tried to reduce Lenin to more human proportions but also stressed those aspects of Lenin's character and writings which fitted his own policies and style in order to bolster his own legitimacy. Perhaps Gorbachev saw some similarity between the two of them in that both combined firm ideological commitment with a strong sense of the needs dictated by political realities.

The human failings of Lenin began to be discussed as part of the policy of *glasnost. Pravda* published a reassessment of Lenin, describing him as a great leader and thinker, yet 'by no means a saint'. Some writers suggested that the key to his character was a cold and cruel ruthlessness expressed in his uncompromising drive for power in 1917 and readiness to use mass terror during the subsequent years of civil war. His writings were also re-examined. The collected works run to more than 10 million words and could be used to support hard-line or reformist views on all the main issues of *perestroika*. The old school saw Lenin's works as a fixed body of doctrines. It especially favoured the early works, which drew black and white distinctions between capitalism and socialism, and stressed the leading role of the Bolshevik Party with its strict discipline. But it also drew heavily on the period around October 1917, when Lenin – in opposition to the Mensheviks, the Socialist Revolutionaries, and several old Bolsheviks (such as Kamenev and Zinoviev) – rejected parliamentarism in favour of strong authoritarianism. The period of the civil war, when Lenin oversaw the construction of the centralized, one-party state and the planned economy known as 'war Communism', was also an inspiration to the hard-liners.

Communist reformers, on the other hand, argued that Lenin's writings should be understood in their proper historical context, since Lenin was essentially pragmatic in his approach. Gorbachev talked about *perestroika* as a restoration of 'Leninist norms', a return to the pure model of Soviet socialism perverted by Stalin and Brezhnev. '*Perestroika* is the rebirth of Lenin's conception of socialism' was a slogan used to mark his 120th anniversary. Gorbachev drew his inspiration from his last writings, in which he spoke of the need to make 'a radical change in our entire view of socialism'. Lenin was preoccupied in that later period by three issues, each of them vital to *perestroika*.

First, he encouraged free trade, co-operative ventures and small-scale capitalist production to revive the Soviet economy, devastated by seven years of war and revolution. The NEP was a pragmatic step away from the dogmatic system of 'war Communism'. Like the economic reforms proposed in the Gorbachev period, it met with considerable opposition from Communist hard-liners who believed there was no room for the market under socialism. Thus Gorbachev's programme originally rested on the belief that Lenin's political system, purged of its Stalinist aspects, might become the means for the regeneration of socialism. But radicals were doubtful. The market socialism of NEP did not have the attraction of the free market and large-scale privatization for those who wanted to see better performance in the Soviet economy, and were prepared to pay the likely costs of unemployment and higher prices.

Second, Lenin supported the idea of a loose Soviet federation to allow for the nationalist aspirations of the non-Russian republics, inclusive of the right of secession from the Soviet Union on the basis of a referendum. The effect of this was somewhat reduced by his simultaneous insistence on a single Communist Party for the whole of the Soviet Union, and the fact that Stalin was in charge of nationalities policy. But it did perhaps suggest a more workable federation than the Russian-dominated Soviet empire eventually built up by Stalin, from which stemmed most of the country's ethnic problems during the *glasnost* and *perestroika* period. Lenin had assumed that nationalist sentiments would be weakened by the process of democratization. Yet *glasnost* and *perestroika* revealed long-suppressed problems with the non-Russians, and created an explosive situation rather than circumstances in which they could be remedied.

Third, Lenin sought to reform the Communist party-state, which he acknowledged had become over-bureaucratic and unrepresentative, by increasing the number of ordinary workers and peasants in the Central Committee, introducing greater openness into government, and promoting the role of the soviets *vis-à-vis* the Party. It is necessary to question how far such administrative measures were able to overcome the basic problem of the Soviet regime in 1921: that it had virtually lost its basis of popular support. But it is also necessary to acknowledge them as the first real attempt to reform the Soviet political system and, as such, a major inspiration for *perestroika*. In his 'Testament' to the Twelfth Party Congress, dictated from his wheelchair in 1923, Lenin demanded the removal of Stalin as General Secretary of the Party. Historians disagree on what would have happened if the Party leaders had not chosen to ignore Lenin's recommendation. Some believe it might have thwarted the rise of Stalinism, while others feel that the seeds of authoritarianism and oppression had already been sown during Lenin's lifetime and with his approval.

Lenin's proposed reforms of the party-state were flawed. For one thing, they kept the ban on factions within the Party which was passed in 1921 to silence the growing opposition to the dictatorial trends of the leadership in the lower Party ranks. A critique in *Moscow News* argued that Lenin had sought the ban to 'secure the Party's monolithic unity, because in this way alone could it retain its dictatorship'. Removing Stalin from the post of General Secretary was thus not enough to prevent the emergence of an autocrat at the head of the Party, since the ban on factions assured a monopoly of power for whoever controlled its bureaucracy. The tragedy of Lenin, concluded *Moscow News*, was his inability to see the faults in the system he had created (Figes, 1990a, p. 17). The rejection of parliamentary democracy and a multi-party system in favour of the dictatorship of the proletariat (that is the Party) had always been the main distinction between Leninism and other forms of Marxist socialism. Lenin firmly believed that the Party naturally voiced the interests of the working class. A situation like that of 1921, when it had lost support in the country, could be remedied by a rigorous reform of the Party to restore its credibility.

Gorbachev's reforms were originally based on a similar confidence in the one-party system. At the beginning of 1989 Alexander Yakovlev, a leading Gorbachev supporter, warned that 'we probably have no more than two to three years to prove that Leninist socialism can work'. But a growing number of Gorbachev's critics, including the Democratic Platform group in the Communist Party, held the view that that only genuine multi-party elections could sanction the right to rule. Yuri Afanasiev, a leading Democratic Platform member, who left the Party just before the Twenty-Eighth Congress, argued that the legacy of Leninism was a 'dead weight on the mind of the nation' because it negated the system of parliamentary democracy the Soviet people now wanted. Radicals said that the question was not about restructuring the Leninist system but how to abandon it (Figes, 1990a, p. 17).

Conclusion

The causes and development of the October Revolution still give rise to debate, much of it polemical. Nevertheless, such a debate was a crucial element of *glasnost* as people tried to establish an understanding of the basis of the Soviet regime, where it went wrong, and what was to be done about it. Lenin had to deal with immediate and threatening crises both in the country and in the Bolshevik Party. He believed in a particular form of democracy and in ruthlessness in pushing his policies through. The question is whether these two beliefs were ultimately compatible and which would have prevailed if Lenin had lived longer. It is simplistic to say that Leninism was the root of Stalinism. Many factors before and after the Revolution helped to shape outcomes and the Revolution itself should not be highlighted and isolated from other events. Certainly there were many differences between Lenin's principles and Stalin's. However, Lenin's practical decisions did not always adhere to these principles, and argument rages over how far he was forced by the crisis to move in an authoritarian direction, and how far such authoritarianism was inherent in his beliefs and principles. The debate on Lenin's real motives will continue, and is also inevitably coloured by the political preconceptions of the participants. Lenin did not have a crystal clear vision of the sort of society he was instrumental in creating, and much of the argument revolves around whether the decisions which he took and policies he advocated 'inevitably' led to dictatorship. Gorbachev at first saw Lenin as an essential reference if his radical reforms were to retain legitimacy. Subsequently, however, Lenin, too, became tainted as condemnation of the Soviet regime grew.

Notes

1   The October Revolution is so called because, at the time, Russia was still using the old-style Julian calendar.

2

Stalinism: the Regime Bloodily Consolidated

Stalin's Aims and Achievements

It was Stalin who rose to power after the death of Lenin in 1924, in spite of Lenin's express wish that he should not do so. He was not regarded as one of the most outstanding revolutionaries, although he did have an important part in developing more aggressive policies towards the nationalities than Lenin had envisaged. As Party Secretary during a time of confusion he effectively managed the situation by means of political manoeuvring, control of Party appointments and his organizing ability in the New Economic Policy. Eventually he established and consolidated the foundations of the Soviet state and Soviet power. It had singular characteristics, many of which were evident in the Soviet Union's policies and behaviour until the 1980s, when Gorbachev attempted his drastic reforms. He aimed to create a large, centralized, Russian-dominated, controlling bureaucracy. The Party leader was elevated to the position of guide and inspiration of the nation. There was only one official view, prescribed by Stalin, who more and more insisted on absolute outward conformity to it. He relied on various sources of information and played one interest off against another. Increasingly the power of the secret police over both Party and government grew, although the extent of this is disputed.

Stalin's position as supreme ruler was not firmly established during the 1920s. Various opposition groups manifested themselves. The *Left Opposition* was composed of well-known revolutionary figures, but with no basis in the working class. It was a struggle largely in the bureaucracy and was weakened by a reluctance to split the Party. Before 1926 it denounced bureaucratization and the consequent weakening of the working class. Then it became more militant, openly organizing meetings and demonstrations. The *United Opposition* consisted of a regrouping of the Left Opposition with Trotsky, Zinoviev and Kamenev among its supporters. It denounced the policy of socialism in one country and wanted rapid industrialization together with action against the kulaks (the more efficient and prosperous peasant farmers). In 1928 a large quantity of grain was forcibly requisitioned. As a result Bukharin, Rykov and Tomsky formed the *Right Opposition*, a more moderate grouping which wanted an end to the use of force, a better deal for the peasants (with voluntary collectivization), and a less headlong rush to industrialization. By clever manoeuvring in relation to these rivals and adjusting his own position on policies as the situation suggested, Stalin steadily consolidated his power.

The Drive to Transform Society

Faced with many regime-threatening problems Stalin believed that economic difficulties should be dealt with by breakthrough in a few key areas as rapidly as possible. Other necessary socialist developments would follow with dramatic results. Hence the decision to collectivize agriculture, coinciding with the First Five Year Plan of 1928. It involved great suffering for the peasantry, but the towns were fed and political control enforced in the countryside. The decision on industrialization with the emphasis on the development of heavy industry rather than consumer goods proved of great benefit in the Second World War. Stalin achieved the rapid industrialization he aimed for, with a claimed six-fold increase in industrial output between 1928 and 1955. All this involved political oppression and suffering on a massive scale, which most commentators have found difficult to explain and impossible to justify. There was a suppression of all opposition to Soviet policy or to Stalin personally. The bureaucracy was in a constant state of change and so could not develop its own political base. Critics were killed or exiled, the most significant and famous of these being Trotsky. The ruthless drive to destroy enemies and enforce obedience by terror and repression was epitomized by the show trials of the 1930s. Large numbers of old-style revolutionaries were executed or consigned to labour camps, which were an important source of cheap labour. The result was a weakening of the top leadership but considerable upward social mobility for the younger generation educated under the new regime.

Stalin had considerable support; no one was playing by liberal democratic rules and many believed that the establishment of the new regime needed ruthless measures. A new generation stood to gain much from the hitherto unachievable opportunities opened up to them. All the emphasis was on unity and no compromise, with ideology as a dynamic, transforming force. Overt opposition hardly existed except outside the Soviet Union where Trotsky constantly proclaimed that Stalin had perverted Lenin's work, particularly by mistaken economic policies and his doctrine of consolidating the Revolution in one country – the Soviet Union – instead of fostering world revolution as Lenin intended. The end result was a centralized, authoritarian regime based on the tsarist autocratic heritage together with the results of the crisis circumstances of the Revolution. These, and the prevailing of Stalin's ideas and personality, created the regime which was firmly established by the end of the 1930s. The longer-term development of Stalinism resulted in a stultifying, bureaucratic conservatism which Khrushchev unsuccessfully sought to break down in the 1950s and early 1960s. Gorbachev, in his turn, was trying free the country from this decaying legacy.

Characteristics of the Stalinist State

Some features of Stalin's state were established before Lenin's death but changes subsequently occurred, such as the abandonment of egalitarianism and the reintroduction of bureaucratic and military ranks. The withering away of the state (a doctrine developed by Engels) was modified by the policy of concentrating on the consolidation of socialism in one country. Consequently, the fact that there were powerful surviving capitalist states meant that the Soviet Union had enemies whose existence justified prolonging the life of the socialist state and delaying the attainment of full Communism. The theory developed as a rationale for this powerful state structure was that, paradoxically, the withering away of the state came from its strengthening, not its weakening (the strong socialist state will the more quickly defeat capitalist enemies and thus bring nearer the advent of full Communism and the disappearance of the state). From time to time there was a proclamation of artificial stages of socialist development towards full Communism. The promulgation of the 1936 Constitution marked one of these 'stages'. Khrushchev, Stalin's successor, argued that Stalin's faults were ones of personality and directed towards undermining the authority of the Party. Certainly the Party, severely weakened as it was by the purges, declined in influence under Stalin. He was inclined to rely more on the secret police and his own private office. Party congresses were rarely called. His fear of the Party was based on its legitimacy, continuity and the authority of leading members.

The Theory of Totalitarianism

Glasnost brought about an agonized reappraisal of the Stalinist period. The desire to discover and to explain 'how all this could have happened' was overwhelming. The need was to understand the immediate past in order to know how to go about changing its consequences, and also in order to be aware of when the task has been completed. In the West a totalitarian model was first developed by Friedrich and Brzezinski (1956) to try to explain, not just Stalinism, but the rise of the Nazis and Fascists. It was understood in terms of political, economic and ideological control. A totalitarian regime was said to have six major characteristics: a single ideology, a single mass party led by one man, the use of terror and secret police control, government monopoly of the mass media, the recourse to armed force and tight central control of the economy. Such a model was ultimately seen to be far toosimplistic. It superficially explained Soviet society as simply Stalinism in practice. In reality, research showed that there were various and contradictory movements in the period, together with much confusion.

Although nationalists such as Solzhenitsyn would disagree, some felt that totalitarian thinking was deeply rooted in Russian history, and based on popular support, and was developed and strengthened by Lenin, Stalin and their supporters. Alexander Osovtsov argues that in totalitarianism the many disregard the rights and dignity of the minority in a developing, progressive 'totalitarianization'. This means that totalitarianism is understood as a response to pressure from the masses; totalitarianism has majority support and even popular acclaim. At some time, however, the oppressed minority can become a majority and a popular movement becomes a state of universal oppression. Alexander Shkreba relates the vigour of totalitarianism to the form and structure of the industrial proletariat as it was created by the Revolution. For him the Soviet industrial proletariat was formed through the destruction of all extant human bonds. Leonid Volkov understands totalitarianism as the result of a misalliance between borrowed Western European ideas and the pre-modern reality of some societies. There was a clash between the desire for the material prizes of western civilization (hence the massive industrialization programmes) and a hatred of their cultural forms (hence repression of western political and cultural attitudes). This led to over-rationality in ideas and policy and to over-industrialism, but also to an irrational impulse that in self-defence fought against the 'alien culture of the market'. All these writers are looking for a model of a self-contained, all-embracing system, moulding state politics and private lives. But this assumption (rather than taking a multi-model approach) is simplistic, itself a residue of the totalitarian experience (Bauman, 1990, p. 1095).

Collectivization

Collectivization on a massive scale got under way in the late 1920s. It was clear by 1927 that the anticipated world revolution was not going to happen. On the contrary, there was a need to defend the country from foreign enemies. In agriculture the requirement to improve supplies for the industrial population was becoming desperate, and there was a growing fear of a kulak-based counter-revolution. Bukharin and others in the Right Opposition put forward the 'proceed slowly' argument. The problem with this policy was that by placing so much reliance on the kulaks, it might leave the country militarily unprepared for too long, and would not boost Party morale. Stalin represented the argument for moving forward rapidly, which implied smashing peasant resistance. Collectivization could not be voluntary if it was to be implemented in a short period of time. Centralization and tough leadership were needed and only the Party could provide it. In the Party this policy had wide support.

Perhaps the worst disaster to hit Soviet agriculture at this time was the Ukrainian famine of 1932–3, which the Soviet authorities tried to cover up for fifty years. With *glasnost* the Ukrainian Communist Party (UKP) finally declared the famine to have been a 'national tragedy' and blamed it on Stalin and his 'criminal' policies of forced collectivization. Although the disaster had begun to be mentioned, this was the first time that a full public exposé was ordered. The UKP conceded that there had been a cover-up during the years since the famine occurred, both in the Ukraine and nationally. As a result it had not been possible to analyse the circumstances nor to reach a 'moral and political assessment of a national tragedy'.

The UKP agreed with western historians that the famine was caused by enforced 'dekulakization': the dispossession and deporting of millions of kulaks (wealthier peasants thought to be opposed to the regime). As a result, the grain output fell, and the Stalin leadership raised the quotas of grain which farms were obliged to deliver to the state. When this failed, thousands were arrested for 'connivance in kulak sabotage' and farmers had seeds, fodder and food supplies taken away 'which proved fatal for the population'. Officially, the peasants were seen as the allies of the working class but the kulaks were singled out as the last bastion of capitalism. The result was the loss of a million of the best farmers, and confusion from creating large-scale nationalized units out of a vast number of small private plots. There was a massive movement of peasants to the cities, causing considerable social upheaval. It is estimated that some 17 million peasants moved in the period 1928–35. The urban population doubled amid much distress and disorder. A huge mobilization by the bureaucracy was needed to try to keep control of these great emigrations.

Industrialization

Füredi (1986, p. 97) describes how the First Five Year Plan (beginning in 1928), which aimed at industrial self-sufficiency, contained a sense of threat, crisis and a shortage of time. State planning was to be the only regulator of the economy. The bureaucracy now had considerable power to allocate resources in line with state policy, but was handicapped by lack of detailed information and expertise in managing different aspects of the economy. Thus industrialization was achieved by sweeping aside political and social obstacles, not by effective economic management. In place of the market, a chain of command now decided the allocation of resources. Labour was abundant and used inefficiently because of bad planning, but Soviet bureaucracy had more freedom to deploy resources than would have been the case under capitalist market forces. Social demand was ignored and there was central control of resources regardless of cost. Cuts in living standards released more resources for invest-ment which central planning could concentrate in priority areas such as defence. However, non-priority areas languished, and there was no overall momentum.

Stalin's New Elite

A great problem in the 1920s was that the necessary experts were non-Communists. Communists tended to be working class and ill-educated. Hence experts often had to accept the authority of an untrained Communist director. Stalin wanted a professional work-ing-class Communist administrative elite. Fitzpatrick (1979) describes how in 1929–30 there was a big working-class influx into new tech-nical colleges for crash courses in technology. This was an attractive alternative for many young people compared to the possibility of being involved in collectivization or being sent to a distant indus-trial site. The link between hitherto unheard-of opportunities for upward social mobility and the Soviet regime must have greatly helped to legitimize the system. Many in the Khrushchev and Brezhnev lead-ership groups were of this generation. In addition to these, many more were promoted from the shop floor without training to meet immediate needs. Half did not belong to the Party. There were two distinct contradictory pressures from 1933 onwards: one relying on the mobilization of subordinates to oblige the Communist man-agement to become efficient, the other defending the management against any control from below. But they both aimed at the perfecting and strengthening of the bureaucracy. The new people made the elimi-nation of the old elite more viable. They showed their competence in the war and post-war period. Only in the 1980s were they replaced by those of the post-war generation.

The Terror

By 1933 Stalin and his allies were still dissatisfied with progress and the great purge trials were connected with this. They indicted a whole group of industrialists who were alleged to have hindered technological advance. The Terror is generally thought of as the means used by Stalin to ensure personal power. For example, Robert Conquest (1990) sees the origins of the Terror in Stalin's desire for total power and his paranoid suspicions of anyone who might stand in his way. At the Seventeenth Party Congress in 1934 he received fewer votes than his rival, Leningrad Party Secretary Sergei Kirov, but then rigged the results. The subsequent murder of Kirov, whether Stalin was directly involved or not (and the Soviet biography of Stalin by Dmitrii Volkogonov (1991, pp. 207–8) does not solve the matter), provided the pretext for the show trials which crushed the Party, the military, national minorities, cultural elites, and others. Ingerflom (1990, p. 10) draws attention to a different interpretation which considers that, after 1934, the regime underwent a crisis of legitimacy, because it had abandoned exclusive reference to the working class and claimed to be directly representative of the 'nationalized masses'. Loyal Communists (and Stalinists) from the early days thus became an obstacle that had to be eliminated, in order to establish a new legitimacy.

In February–March 1937 grass-roots opposition to management gained the upper hand. But criticism by the masses went beyond this to attack the inherent functioning of the system. Social antagonisms were manifesting themselves within the Party. The central authorities decided to give management a free hand to restore the situation. In May, they launched their counter-offensive and the workers now found themselves castigated as the enemy. They immediately responded with a drastic purge of management lasting until December. However, continuing it would have meant permanent damage to the administrative and managerial machinery. Terrified management no longer dared carry out orders, because they feared being the victims of the unpopularity which their management methods provoked. The result was an alarming breakdown in work discipline. By 1938 things had to be slowed down, as well as better controlled and organized. Thus from 1939, any hope of controlling management from below was abandoned, although this did not help to solve the problem of inefficiency.

Reassessment of the Purges

In the *glasnost* years new evidence and more open discussion gave rise to two broad schools of thought. On the one hand there was a tendency, even in the Soviet Union, to couple Stalin with Hitler as one of the two 'monsters' of the century. Some academics in Austria and West Germany go further in arguing that the Stalinist system was actually responsible for the Nazis and the Second World War. On the other hand Getty (1985) sees the development of the Terror as piecemeal and haphazard rather than monolithic, while Lewin (1985) interprets the ruthlessness as a desperate determination to bring order to the chaos the Revolution had created. It was the Cheka who were best equipped for swift, effective action. The Party in the regions was disorganized and overburdened, while law and order in the countryside remained a problem well into the 1930s. The majority of the population lived in the countryside but only 0.3 per cent of Party members did so. The poor quality of these people, in education and experience, made it easy for anyone with a modicum of organizing ability to get on in the Party. From 1933 to 1936 there was a weeding out of inactive, unreliable or degenerate members, but this was less effective than similar weedings out in the 1920s. Local Party officials were by now too preoccupied or inefficient to do the job properly.

At the centre of all this was Stalin, whom Getty thinks of as less of a 'great man' than as an arbiter between groups. The elaborate and bizarre cult of personality which rapidly developed around him was possibly a device to conceal very real divisions in the leadership. The purges of 1937–8 were separate from, and not a culmination of, earlier purges. They were part of a central–regional conflict, a factional struggle in Moscow and a breakdown in the balance between radicals and moderates. Stalin supported the radicals and made a savage pre-emptive strike. In other words, the purge was not for personal reasons (ambition, paranoia, megalomania) but for political ones. Getty still considers Stalin's role may have been crucial. His policy of rapid modernization, which involved squeezing the peasantry in 1932–3, support for the Stakhanovite (militant pro-Soviet workers) challenge to managerial authority, and the doctrine of intensification of class struggle as the victory of socialism approached, all provided a rationale to justify the search for heresy and treason in 1937–8. Personal, political and structural factors all interacted. Lewin points out that the show trials made the myth of 'enemies of the people' look real, but they were based on confessions, not evidence. 'Enemies' was a term used to explain away all that went wrong with the regime, and also played on the psychological and cultural dispositions of a disorientated population.

By the time of the Eighteenth Party Congress in 1939 very many of the delegates to the previous 1936 'Victory' Congress had been eliminated. Stalin did mention the excesses of the purges but emphasized the creation of a new intelligentsia. These people were not to be regarded as bourgeois and so could be permitted to join the Party. From now on the Party would recruit not solely from the working class but from the 'best people'. The new leadership was better educated but, because previous leaders were thought to have been too settled and demanding, the new bureaucracy was denied secure tenure until well after Stalin's death.

Stalin's Victims

A central question in the *glasnost* debate was the number of Stalin's victims. There were three basic categories: those executed for political offences, most of whom died in the Terror of 1937–8; those who died in the labour camps or during mass deportations; and those peasants who died in the famines of the early 1930s (almost certainly the biggest number). There are considerable difficulties in computing an accurate figure. The relevant archives are not all declassified and may no longer exist. Among Soviet specialists and western demographers the current majority view seems to be that Conquest's figure (20 million) is too high. Fitzpatrick states that the younger generation of Soviet historians incline to far lower figures and think there is no basis for Conquest's claims. In a newspaper article by Milne, Anderson and Silver in the United States it was estimated that the most likely figure for all 'excess' deaths – whether from purges, famine or deportations – between 1926 and 1939 lay in a range with a median of 3.5 million, and a limit of 8 million. But this growing consensus seens to be challenged by some Soviet historians such as Roy Medvedev who, using the same data, have reached conclusions closer to that of Conquest (Milne, 1990). In 1992 the head of the Commission for Rehabilitation of Victims of Unjust Repression, Nikolai Grashchoven, quoted KGB archives when stating that from 1935 to 1945 about 18 million people had been victimized, of whom about 7 million had been shot. These figure clearly differ from KGB figures published earlier (Keep, 1990, p. 1058; Tolz, 1992, pp. 8–10). The controversy has political overtones. Supporters of the lower figures are sometimes accused of playing down the horrors of Stalinism. Others feel that by minimizing the quantitative gulf between Stalin and Hitler it becomes easier to reduce the qualitative uniqueness of the Nazi genocide and war.

The Second World ('Great Patriotic') War

There was a sensation in 1939 when Stalin concluded a pact with Hitler which undermined the opposition to Nazism. It seemed a deeply cynical move in view of the hitherto profound ideological differences and hostility between the two regimes. But it suited both sides, for the Germans in buying time to concentrate on the western front and, for Stalin, in taking the pressure off the unprepared Soviet Union. For a

long time the Soviet authorities denied the existence of a secret protocol, which, among other things, allowed the Soviet Union to invade
eastern Poland, attack Finland, and annex Moldavia and the Baltic
republics in 1940. The Soviet authorities refused to admit the existence
of the protocol, in spite of the publication of the alleged text in the West
and in the Baltic republics, plus considerable indirect evidence. In June
1989 the West German government finally made available a microfilm
of the original document. The admission of the existence of the protocol by the Soviet authorities was particularly important to the Baltic
republics in their demand for independence. They claimed that they
were forcibly incorporated into the Soviet Union against their will,
while the official Soviet view was that they had joined the Soviet Union
voluntarily.

A dispute has emerged among *glasnost* historians about the relations of Stalin with Hitler. Alexander Nekrich argues that Stalin's
efforts to reach agreement with Hitler extended as far back as 1934.
This contrasts with the view held by Volkogonov (1991, pp. 384–92)
that the West's wooing of Hitler forced Stalin into this 'necessary'
improvisation in 1939. Stalin was unwilling to believe, in spite of
considerable intelligence from the West, that Hitler was preparing an
imminent invasion of the Soviet Union. Thus the invasion by Nazi
Germany, when it came, at first caused shock and indecision.
Volkogonov became the subject of attack by conservatives when volume 1 of the Soviet official history of the Second World War (the ten-
volume *Great Patriotic War of the Soviet People*) for which he had overall
responsibility was rejected for publication because it was 'anti-Soviet'.
Volkogonov was attacked by *Sovetskaya Rossiya* (the paper of the
Russian Communist Party) for his portrayal of Stalin in the months
leading up to the invasion in June 1941. He argued that the Soviet
forces were ill-trained and under-equipped and that Stalin hopelessly
underestimated the strength of the German army. Further, having
bought time with the 1939 pact, Stalin persisted in thinking, even as
late as the end of 1940, that war – although inevitable – was still two
or three years away. After these attacks Volkogonov resigned from the
project because he said that he did not want to write a false history.
Most Soviet historians agree that the huge wartime losses were the
consequence of the purges and errors committed in the run-up to the
war. But many still argued that there was no alternative to the pact with
Hitler because, if the Germans had attacked earlier, there would have
been an even greater defeat of the Soviet army in the first few days.
Current thinking is that Hitler, too, would have preferred a war in 1943
rather than 1939 or 1941 (Bullock, 1991, p. 600).

After the initial shock, Stalin took on an inspirational role. The
whole country was mobilized and Stalin did not hesitate to appeal
to the heroes of Russia's past – and to Russian nationalism and the

Orthodox Church – in order to boost morale and patriotism. Administrative effectiveness was achieved by the co-ordination of civilian and military aspects of government in the State Defence Committee chaired by Stalin. Military planning was based in the Supreme Command led by Stalin. Civilian control of the military was maintained, but Stalin gave initiative and responsibility to military leaders. Although he was prepared to sack the incompetent, serious mistakes were nevertheless made. All in all, however, the war effort was an impressive achievement of the Soviet people although at great cost. There was some defection to the Germans, hence the harsh treatment of some western nationalities and prisoners of war during and after hostilities.

Foreign Policy

The main foreign policy argument under Stalin was that international tension justified strict internal controls. The experience of being invaded by foreign troops during the civil war and the continuing political and economic hostility from all major powers in the inter-war period, created a siege mentality. However, this did not stop united front campaigns in which the Soviet Union encouraged western Communist parties to try to join with other left-wing parties against fascism. The idea of the Soviet Union being encircled by hostile capitalist states persisted, even after the allied co-operation during the war. It provided the rationale for the creation of a buffer of satellite states and the continuing industrialization policy to the neglect of the consumer. The sense of still being threatened, even after the war, gave rise to the so-called 'Cold War' with western countries, and internal paranoia illustrated by the supposed Jewish doctors' plot to poison Soviet leaders which was being 'exposed' just before Stalin's death (but quickly dropped afterwards).

World Communism was dominated by Stalin and the Soviet Union. Satellite states in Eastern Europe and elsewhere were forced to toe the line, although one or two, such as Yugoslavia and, later, China, refused to co-operate. Other non-ruling Communist parties (like Great Britain's) had to take their lead from Moscow. The main enemy was perceived to be, not the right, but the non-Communist left. The post-Stalin leadership could not sustain this domination, in spite of drastic action on occasions (for example, the invasions of Hungary in 1956 and Czechoslovakia in 1968). After 1985 Gorbachev and his Foreign Minister, Shevardnadze, undertook a drastic reappraisal of these policies which they perceived as directly harming the Soviet Union.

Conclusion

A characteristic of *glasnost* was the opportunity to re-examine Soviet history and to escape from the official versions, such as Stalin's own *Short Course* (a history of the CPSU). In October 1988 the Central' Committee announced that Gorbachev would chair a committee to prepare a new outline history of the CPSU. This was not universally welcomed. Some people, such as Yuri Afanasyev, Rector of the State Historical Archive Institute, felt that official versions of history, whatever their slant, were no substitute in the period of *glasnost* for a variety of research, books and lectures from different standpoints. Authors were now trying to contrast the totalitarian intentions of the rulers with what was actually achieved. The result was a revised understanding of the Stalin period which showed a diversified society, giving rise to both initiative and resistance. The usual image of the state as the sole initiator of action was replaced by a view revealing a state reacting to events and to national realities. Contrary to superficial notions, events did not follow a plan predetermined by a political will from on high.

Local officials aroused popular hostility as much through their authoritarian methods as because they were officials in a demanding regime. Mass opposition compelled them to bypass directives from the centre and they could not claim success except by falsifying production figures. The widening gap between their reports and reality produced crises for which they became the scapegoats. A loss of authority by these local powers made it impossible to implement decisions and the state's inability to exercise control led it to adopt repression as the main instrument of government. The Terror was disorganized and repression was the outcome of weakness, not power. The local bureaucracy had two means of pre-empting repressive measures which might at any moment be also applied to itself. Either it could inflict exemplary punishments on scapegoats so zealously that its enthusiasm had to be checked to avoid production being totally disrupted; or it could redirect the campaign against workers who were considered most closely to represent popular dissatisfaction. The workers, in turn, used the image of enemies of the people to get rid of bosses with a reputation for unfairness. All in all, the results of current research, although far from being totally in agreement, do generally point to the conclusion of Getty that the Soviet government, however authoritarian, lacked the technical and technological sophistication to become literally totalitarian (Ingerflom, 1990, p. 10).

By the death of Stalin in 1953 the Soviet Union had achieved great things but also experienced terrible crimes and suffering. It had become stale and moribund with a need to find a way to renew its vigour. This was the aim of Khrushchev, Stalin's eventual successor, and the catalyst was his 'Secret Speech' to the Twentieth Party Congress when he denounced Stalin's crimes against the Party. But the campaign to denounce Stalin was not sustained and he was partially rehabilitated by Brezhnev. The bureaucracy was reluctant to reject the regime from which it had benefited. Among the population at large Stalin was often seen as something of a hero. He was the man who established the foundations of a better standard of living, who imposed discipline and who raised workers to important positions. Many benefited from Stalin's policies; he created opportunities as well as victims. The Terror increased social mobility for some and, in any case, fell more on those in control (who 'do as they like now'). The strong centralized power was understood by many people as a guarantee of workers' rights against the local administration. Internationally, Stalin was considered to have kept the other Communist states firmly under Soviet control, in contrast to his successors. Some of the young saw Stalin as an exciting and purposeful leader with clear goals and there was sympathy for his anti-Semitism.

This attitude was gradually undermined under Gorbachev. The relative freedom given to Soviet historians by *glasnost* and the opening up of the archives had a profound effect. Gorbachev himself said that a society which cannot face its own past cannot face the future. Revealing the truth about Stalinism had a strong psychological impact, not least over the matter of the rehabilitation of Stalin's victims. A society was formed called Memorial (its first president was Andrei Sakharov) to lead a public campaign for the rehabilitation of Stalin's victims, monetary compensation for survivors and dependants and for the setting up of local monuments. Thousands of people had been rehabilitated under Khrushchev but many others were not. In order to speed up the processing of the huge number of applications from relatives, the Central Committee proposed a general rehabilitation to be passed by the Supreme Soviet, and greater efficiency in paying compensation to survivors and relatives. Memorial saw all this as an attempt by the Party to regain control of the situation. Ales Adamovitch, a prominent writer in Belorussia, applauded the Central Committee's call on local soviets to help Stalin's victims, but in a reference to the feeling among Memorial supporters that the Party was usurping their ideas, he said, 'No local Soviet committee can replace the initiative of that one young man who collected tens of thousands of documents about people who were repressed.' He was talking of a young historian, Dmitrii Yurasov, who had shocked people two years before by revealing details of Stalin's purges (Tolz, 1987a).

Meanwhile organizations such as Democratic *Perestroika* and Socialist Initiative which (in officially sanctioned meetings) had called for the rehabilitation of those falsely imprisoned or put in psychiatric hospitals since Stalin's death, did not see a response to their demands until August 1990. Then Gorbachev followed a decree rehabilitating thousands of Stalin's victims – the first official admission that vast numbers of people had died in the forced collectivization of agriculture in the late 1920s and early 1930s – with another restoring Soviet citizenship to people exiled between 1966 and 1988, which mainly covered the Brezhnev period. Memorial organized a Gulag exhibition in 1988, consisting of photograps and letters. In 1989 they arranged for a ceremonial ring of candles around the Lubyanka (KGB headquarters). At the end of October 1990 they finally achieved their main commemorative goal when a monument – a large granite stone inscribed 'In memory of the millions of victims of the totalitarian regime' – was dedicated in front of the Lubyanka.

3

Stalin's Successors: Change and Stagnation

De-Stalinization

The death of Stalin initiated the first attempt at significant reform of the Soviet system. Many of the young, finding themselves in a conservative, boring society, looked back nostalgically to the earlier social revolution of Stalin's time, to its idealism and the exciting and challenging opportunities it gave. Intellectuals, or certain sections of them, felt devalued under the new post-Stalin regime. Their jobs were held at the whim of the state and there were too many of them for the jobs available. But the broader reality was that Stalin's successors had to reinvigorate a stagnant society. Years of oppression and lack of innovation had led to low morale and inertia. Large numbers of people were confined in labour camps, although revolts in the camps had begun even before Stalin's death. After his death pressure came from relatives for a review of sentences. Reform of the security services was set in hand to bring them more under Party control. One of the first acts of the new leadership was to arrest and execute the head of the secret police, Lavrentii Beria, the last Soviet leader to lose his life in this way. An investigation started into Stalin's treatment of the Party. There was also a restoration of formal and more reliable legal process in the courts.

Immediately after Stalin's death there was a period when no one person predominated in the leadership. This state of affairs was officially rationalized and justified as 'collective leadership' and a rejection of the excessively individualistic rule of Stalin. The principle (and to some extent the practice) of collective leadership was, from then on, always officially upheld. Until February 1955 the Soviet Union was ruled by Georgii Malenkov, who was Chairman of the Council of Ministers, Nikita Khrushchev, First Secretary of the CPSU, and Vyacheslav Molotov, the Foreign Minister. They began a series of policy reversals aimed at de-Stalinization. The Party and state bureaucracies were reorganized to remove supporters of Stalin. A policy known as the New Course aimed to reduce the number of bureaucrats, provide material incentives, devolve decision-making to lower levels, and increase the authority of major factory directors and trade union officials. It was especially intended to raise the general standard of living. This policy was central to the power struggle among the leadership. Malenkov supported a programme to develop light industry and supply more consumer goods. Khrushchev, at that time, wanted emphasis to remain on heavy industry. The first stage of the power struggle ended in 1955 when Malenkov had to resign his post of Chairman of the Council of Ministers.

Before long, Khrushchev ran into trouble himself, as a result of the speed and nature of his de-Stalinization programme. The establishment of regional economic councils aroused special opposition because they affected the rights of the republics and interests within the Party. In 1957 he was being opposed by a majority in the Praesidium (as the Politburo was then named). He dramatically and successfully appealed against the so-called 'anti-Party group' to the Party's Central Committee (with pro-Khrushchev delegates being flown in by the air force). The army also supported him because of his tackling of the problem of KGB power. Khrushchev's survival of this crisis removed rivals and consolidated his position.

The 'Secret Speech'

By the time of the Twentieth Party Congress in 1956 Khrushchev and other Party leaders realized that a dramatic change of direction was needed. They were, however, afraid that they would be implicated in Stalin's crimes. Hence the so-called 'Secret Speech' (secret because it was never published in the Soviet Union, but merely read out to meetings of Party members), dramatically delivered by Khrushchev at the end of the Congress. It concentrated on Stalin's crimes against the Party after 1934 and there was no mention of ordinary people. It also limited its criticism to Stalin and his immediate entourage. It was designed to minimize questions like 'How were such things allowed to happen?' and 'Where were you during the Terror?' The immediate results of the 'Secret Speech' included a distinct change of the political climate in the Soviet Union and the satellite countries. In the Soviet Union there was a large-scale release of political prisoners followed by a considerable social impact when they returned to their towns and villages to tell of their experiences. They spread knowledge of the camps and of the conditions in them, which led to demands for the rehabilitation of, and compensation for, the wrongly accused – a campaign which continues to this day.

The immediate result of Khrushchev's secretaryship was that Party control was re-established. Its responsibility now focused on control and co-ordination, and its political and ideological role was played down. There was more public discussion on a rational basis (although it was not always listened to). As Stalin was demoted in official esteem greater emphasis was given to Lenin as a symbol of legitimacy. For a time there was relative cultural and artistic freedom. It centred around the literary magazine *Novy Mir* and the growth of the poetry movement. Some hitherto disapproved-of authors and their works were published (for example, Solzhenitsyn's *One Day in the Life of Ivan Denisovitch*). Consumer and social welfare legislation was passed, providing a minimum wage and improving the provision of social needs such as housing and social welfare. One of the difficulties for the leadership which arose from all this was an increase in social disturbance in both the Soviet Union and in the satellite countries.

The Soviet Economy

Post-war reconstruction had largely been completed by the 1950s and the economy was undergoing a vigorous expansion. Soviet industry had a 10 per cent annual growth rate from 1953 to 1959 and 9 per cent from 1959 to 1964. Its production was already surpassing that of Europe in key sectors such as steel, power, cement and fuels. But there were also serious economic problems. Consumer expectations had been heightened, but the quantity and quality of consumer goods and housing remained low. Khrushchev's economic policies were far-reaching. Regional councils were established with authority to take economic decisions independently of higher state bodies. The key positions in these councils were held by pro-Khrushchev Party officials who were granted full decision-making authority over the regions. Laws were passed introducing the principle of local economic control, and many central ministries were dissolved as new local ministries assumed their powers. Reformed economic management methods were implemented to help the development of production for profit. Campaigns were held between 1954 and 1957 to 'struggle against bureaucratism' and improve management skills. Managers were allotted wider powers, including the right to sell, transfer or lease factories, determine the number of workers, and hire and fire workers.

In 1962 the so-called Liberman debates were held on the complete reorganization of the economy. *Pravda* published Liberman's proposals in an article entitled 'Plan, Profit and Reward'. It called for the upholding of profitability as the measure of economic performance. Profit and material incentives were to be considered the nucleus of the management programme in the large factories, which would then receive rewards based on profit. Experiments took place in factories in Moscow, Leningrad and Ukraine but these were carried out under artificial conditions which could not be reproduced in the rest of the economy. In the later years Khrushchev increasingly stressed the importance of consumer goods, promising at the Twenty-second Party Congress to overtake the United States by 1970. But at the same time he alienated important conservative elements in the military by cutting the size, and denigrating the importance, of the ground forces while elevating the standing of the strategic rocket forces.

Agriculture

Despite Khrushchev's own agricultural background, agriculture remained the most serious problem area in the economy. He had inherited from Stalin a backward sector, with low productivity, misuse of labour, poor incomes for workers on collective farms, low prices for crops and heavy taxes on the private plots. After 1957 many campaigns and reorganizations were carried out, but the end result was disastrous and the government was forced to import food. The attempted decentralization of agricultural planning was very unpopular and did not work. Khrushchev also wanted a gradual reduction of the agricultural private sector but at the same time to avoid lowering the income and morale of the peasants and serious disruption of the food supply. This, too, proved unsuccessful and pressure on the private plots was gradually relaxed. The formation of Territorial Production Associations in 1962 was an attempt to bring *kolkhoz* (collective farms) and *sovkhoz* (state farms) closer together and to separate agricultural and industrial administration in both Party and ministries. But it was also a means of tighter control and it undermined attempts at greater productivity. The location and practices of Soviet agriculture were fundamentally altered in the long run. More resources were obtained and huge investment continued from that time forward.

Khrushchev's great 'virgin lands scheme' aimed vastly to increase grain production by utilizing land in Kazakhstan, western Siberia and the north Caucasus. Other policies depended on its success, for example, transferring land in Ukraine and the Caucasus to animal fodder production (maize was desperately needed). But Khrushchev expected too much, too soon. He paid insufficient attention to scientific ideas. North American advice was ignored and maize was grown in unsuitable areas. There was not enough preparation and inadequate resources were made available to sustain the plan. The result was enormous waste and large-scale desertion by the poorly-provided-for workforce. Was the 'virgin lands scheme' a success? Eventually, yes, but Khrushchev was too optimistic and hurried, ignoring warnings. He still believed the old revolutionary adage that anything could be achieved by commitment and will power (which in reality often meant bullying), while great political pressures for success affected his judgement.

Khrushchev's Foreign Policy

At the time of Stalin's death the Soviet Union's place in the world had been greatly enhanced, but there was also a legacy of enormous problems. There were clashes with the United States in the Korean War, and over West German unification and rearmament. The main gain was that the Soviet Union had moved from being under serious threat from Nazism in the early 1940s to a recognized great power (soon to become one of the two superpowers) after the Second World War. With Khrushchev there was a burst of diplomatic activity, the main theme of which was the achievement of peaceful relations with the West (in contrast to the hostile Stalinist Cold War attitude), the confirmation of the Soviet Union's superpower status and the expansion of Soviet influence in the Third World. One of the aims of attacking Stalin in the 'Secret Speech' was to show the West that there was to be a basic shift in Soviet foreign policy, founded on three principles: peaceful coexistence, peaceful competition and acceptance of the peaceful transition to socialism by the capitalist world. He abandoned the doctrine of an inevitable conflict between capitalism and socialism; instead they could exist side by side in co-operation and peace.

These changes were viewed with initial suspicion both in the West and throughout the Communist world. The Chinese, in particular, saw Khrushchev's anti-Stalinism as a step towards revisionism and collaboration with the capitalist West. It began the serious Sino–Soviet split which lasted until Gorbachev's time. In Eastern Europe the attack on Stalin undermined the legitimacy of the shaky regimes there and encouraged manifestations of popular resistance. There were disturbances in Poland, East Germany and Hungary, the last being suppressed by invasion in 1956. By the late 1950s Khrushchev had become more assertive. The success of the Soviet Union in getting the first man into space increased his self-confidence. He expressed his belief at the Twenty-first Party Congress in 1959 that the West was weakening and therefore a stepped-up campaign of global expansion and assertion of power was justified. Such a notion was destroyed when his bluff was finally called in the Cuban missile crisis of 1962 (Adelman and Palmieri, 1989, pp. 268–71). In 1963 he moved again towards a policy of *détente*, the most notable achievement of which was the Nuclear Test Ban Treaty of 1963.

Khrushchev's foreign policy certainly moved away from Stalin's hostility to the rest of the world and presented the Soviet Union in a more favourable light. Advances in the Soviet Union's influence in the Third World were made, and the Cold War experienced a definite thaw. But he was prone to high-risk foreign policy adventures and manifested boorish behaviour together with an erratic style. There was also a certain pragmatism; if major goals were unattainable, lesser ones would be pursued. Underneath all this, the limitations of Soviet power were evident.

Khrushchev's Fall

Khrushchev failed to decentralize Soviet agriculture effectively. The reforms were too hasty and pressurized. Bottlenecks and distortions occurred in the economy. Political and administrative reforms were not enough and were even counter-productive. Production fell after 1958 for lack of the real need investment. The investment eventually came through, but not soon enough to save Khrushchev. Problems increased in the period 1962–4. The output of the 'virgin lands' fell heavily. Prices for meat, butter and milk products were insufficient to secure voluntary production. Officials confiscated produce and seed, attacked the private sector, as well as engaging in fraud. All this was the result of excessive pressure ('campaignism'). Targets in the urban industrial sector were better met, so illustrating the industrial–agricultural gap. There was passive resistance by officials, and workers' riots in 1959, 1960 and 1962.

Khrushchev's response was more campaigning and confrontation. By 1964 he had offended nearly all the powerful elements in the Party, and alienated the secret police by achieving a sharp reduction in their power (including the closure of most labour camps in 1956). Some military sectors resented his attacks on their importance, size and budgets. The military were upset by their public humiliation at the hands of the United States in the Cuban missile crisis. The central government bureaucracy hated the frenetic government reorganizations and especially the 1957 regional and local reforms, which required much of it to leave Moscow to work in provincial capitals. The 1962 division of the Party into agricultural and economic wings was a great threat to the power of the Party bureaucracy. Many found Khrushchev to be a crude, simplistic ideologue. His strongest period as leader was in 1955–62. Although he was no Stalin and could not rely on terror, he could, on the whole, adhere to his policies. The difference was that he had to take into account a wider variety of interests than hitherto. He was eventually removed in 1964 by the device he had used to consolidate his power: the calling of a meeting of the Party Central Committee. He was brought back from holiday to learn of his removal. Gorbachev, too, was on holiday when his removal was attempted in the failed coup of 1991.

Khrushchev's Secretaryship in Perspective

In the end Khrushchev's belief in ideological principles, exhortation and bullying to achieve results – albeit without the Terror – was not a sufficient break with the past to cope with a new industrialized society where careful research and pragmatic experiment were more likely to achieve success. Above all, he alienated the CPSU bureaucracy, those who had put him in power in the first place, by a highly unpopular reorganization and by drastically reducing its members' job security. One of the priorities of Brezhnev when he replaced Khrushchev was the so-called policy of 'stability of cadres'; this was a guarantee of stability and consolidation for the Party bureaucrats after the uncertainties and eccentricities of the Khrushchev period. Under Gorbachev, Khrushchev was slowly rehabilitated, his achievement in ending the Stalinist bloodshed and making life more bearable for the Soviet people being recognized. More important, he came to be seen as a precursor of Gorbachev, and as someone who had attempted to breathe new life into the Soviet system. Like Gorbachev, he was thwarted by the powerful, conservative vested interests of Party, KGB and military– industrial complex. When his turn came, Gorbachev showed more intelligence, sophistication and pragmatism. But he was ruling a country which had changed dramatically in sociological and demographic terms since the Khrushchev period.

Brezhnev

The eighteen years of Brezhnev's rule were a good deal less eventful than Khrushchev's nine. Although there were difficult problems to deal with, the period was characterized by consistency and relative dullness. This was deliberate because Brezhnev realized from Khrushchev's experience that powerful interests should be placated. Hence a new genuinely collective and consensual policy-making process was established. Powerful politicians had a real degree of autonomy and a steady and regular enhancing of their budgets. There was a great increase in the use of technical experts in science, industry and the making of policy. Many of Khrushchev's schemes were called 'harebrained' and undone in 1965 – a popular move. The two-fold division of the Party was abolished and the agricultural reforms abandoned in favour of a strengthened Ministry of Agriculture. The remaining local ministries were dissolved and the industrial system was largely recentralized with some modifications.

A marked change came over incentives policy with a greater emphasis on material benefits immediately rather than the promise of future rewards. Instead of the objective of transforming society emphasis was placed on economic achievement, especially with regard to consumer goods. There was more reliance on expertise and less on the effect of a charismatic leader. While Khrushchev had emphasized the need for the Soviet Union to catch up with the West, Brezhnev proclaimed the superiority of the Soviet Union and the deficiencies of capitalism. Overall, emphasis was placed on moderate rather than radical expectations. Critics such as the Chinese said that Brezhnev had substituted material prosperity for the goal of Communism.

The Economy

There were major successes in the economic policy area during the Brezhnev period, but they were achieved alongside severe problems. The Soviet standard of living doubled and foreign trade tripled. But the high growth rates achieved in the Khrushchev era could not be sustained and, towards the end annual growth slowed to 3–5 per cent. The command economy which hitherto had been considered to work well, in spite of difficulties, was now inefficient and wasteful, with slow technical progress, poor information flows and unbalanced plans. The decline in the growth rate coincided with rising consumer expectations and continuing problems with the quantity and quality of consumer goods. The emphasis on heavy industry seemed more and more outdated as the western economies moved towards high technology, service-based societies. The Soviet economy lagged far behind the West in electronic, computer-based technology, and needed to import much of this from the West (unless the West forbade this for security reasons). Agriculture remained a serious problem in spite of high investment. To sustain the expectations of an improved standard of living required greater imports of grain and consumer goods, mainly from the West. Agricultural productivity remained low, far lower than western levels. The desire to increase rural wages but hold prices constant meant ever-growing food subsidies which, by the end of the Brezhnev period, had reached the staggering figure of over 20 billion roubles.

Foreign Policy

Brezhnev and his fellow leaders attempted to move away from the failures of Khrushchev and to create a positive long-term framework for Soviet–American relations (*détente*). In this they were only partially successful. They did achieve military parity with the West in the 1970s, signed the Strategic Arms Limitation Treaties (SALT I and SALT II), improved trade and economic integration with the West, and made major political gains through the Helsinki Accords (on co-operation and civil rights) in 1975 – without actually implementing them in the sense expected by the West. But none of this could hide the fundamental clash of interests and perceptions between the two superpowers. By the late 1970s and early 1980s these had brought the period of *détente* to an end. The emergence of a new Cold War demonstrated the major failure of Brezhnev's foreign policies. The far greater political and military resources of the United States, its western allies and China were mobilized against the Soviet Union. It was essential for Brezhnev's successors to extricate the country from this position.

From December 1979 the country had been involved in a war in Afghanistan. The intention was to defeat opposition to the pro-Soviet regime and to strengthen the Soviet frontier. The war lasted for eight years, involving half a million men, of whom nearly 10 per cent (according to official figures) became casualties. Although United States casualties in Vietnam had been three times as great, the war assumed great importance and engendered considerable discontent in the Soviet Union. Public opinion turned against the war and the legitimacy and authority of the Soviet system, already weakening, was further undermined. It was also very damaging to the Soviet Union's political standing in the West and the Third World. The withdrawal which followed Gorbachev's accession was an acknowledgement of defeat, and the Communist government of Afghanistan, which was supposed to be threatened, survived for some years.

Administrative Reform

Brezhnev never appealed to the masses over the heads of the elite or threatened the elite with the spectre of mass discontent as Khrushchev had been known to do. He aimed at administrative efficiency but with accommodation and consensus towards officials, replacing punishment with attention to their wishes. Soviet officials wanted political status, job security and stable expectations. In return they had to be more responsive to the public. Like Khrushchev (and Gorbachev), Brezhnev wanted to maintain the leading role of the Party, which he saw as emphasizing culture and welfare as well as economics, as protecting national as opposed to local interests and as initiating new programmes and new values to counter bureaucratic conservatism. The Prime Minister, Alexei Kosygin, had a different emphasis, placing more weight on consumer goods rather than the development of agriculture, on the general public rather than elites and wanting more decentralization than Brezhnev. At the same time, however, repression of dissenters was intensified after the relative relaxation under Khrushchev. Overall, a more empirical and open-ended approach was adopted although there was no change in authority relationships. From December 1977 onwards there was a reversion to the encouragement of reforms and economic experiments. Brezhnev hoped that all this would increase his authority and keep his critics off-balance. He took steps to consolidate his formal power, being made a Marshal of the Soviet Union in 1976 and Chairman of the Praesidium of the Supreme Soviet (head of state) in 1977. He removed opponents from the Politburo and installed supporters such as Konstantin Chernenko and Vladimir Tikhonov. In 1980 Kosygin died and the pro-Brezhnev Tikhonov became Chairman of the Council of Ministers in his place.

Dissent

Many leading poets, novelists and historians stayed in the country after the Revolution. Their influence remained until the 1970s, in spite of persecution, as in Stalin's 'anti-cosmopolitan' campaign of the 1940s and 1950s. Soviet dissent rested largely on the survival, against all odds, of this Russian intelligentsia. *Intelligentsia* is a Russian phenomenon. Developing in the second quarter of the nineteenth century, it was a movement of educated, morally sensitive Russians opposed to an obscurantist Church and oppressive state.

> They believed in personal and political liberty, in the removal of irrational social inequalities and in truth, which they identified to some degree with scientific progress. They held a view of enlightenment which they associated with Western liberalism and democracy.
>
> The intelligentsia, for the most part, consisted of members of the professions. The best known were the writers – all the great names (even Dostoyevsky in his younger days) were in various degrees and fashions engaged in the fight for freedom. It was the descendants of these people who were largely responsible for making the February Revolution of 1917. Some of its members who believed in extreme measures took part in the suppression of this revolution and the establishment of Soviet communism in Russia, and later elsewhere. In due course the intelligentsia was by degrees systematically destroyed, but it did not wholly perish.
> (Berlin, 1990, p. 149)

Kargarlitsky (Tolz, 1991) has drawn attention to the differences between these 'old dissidents', descended from the pre-revolutionary intelligentsia, and those whose parents were often active Bolsheviks and who themselves initially accepted the Soviet system as the best existing one. The 'pre-revolutionary' group saw the Bolsheviks as an alien force in Russian history but too strong to be opposed. They concentrated on their scholarly or scientific careers, which were often international in scope. They would sometimes oppose the authorities on particular matters but not in a general rejection of the official ideology. Those who originally supported the system had their eyes opened by the Twentieth Party Congress when Khrushchev made his 'Secret Speech' concerning Stalin's crimes against the Party. They reacted very strongly because, for them, Soviet power was not an alien force but something they and their parents had created and supported. For that reason, therefore, their demands for change were indignant and strong. Andrei Sakharov, who died at the end of 1989, and Alexander Solzhenitsyn are examples of those who grew up enthusiastic for the Soviet regime only to be bitterly disillusioned.

After the relatively limited relaxation of the Khrushchev period there was a tightening up, with significant criticism of Stalin now forbidden. Symbolic of the change in atmosphere were the trials of the writers Andrei Sinyavsky and Yuli Daniel in 1966 and Yuri Galanskov and Alexander Ginsburg in 1968. These evoked much protest at home and abroad but were clearly intended to signify that the Brezhnev regime would not tolerate dissent at the levels it had reached under Khrushchev. Sinyavsky and Daniel were arrested in September 1965, less than a year after Khrushchev was deposed. The charges were that they had published their work abroad under pseudonyms, and that they were disseminating anti-Soviet propaganda, a violation of Article 70 of the Criminal Code. But the trial was widely seen as an attack on all uncensored writing and a warning to all their colleagues. The Galanskov and Ginsburg affair was the subject of a famous appeal by Andrei Sakharov to the Party Central Committee. It proved to be the action that began his long persecution.

The late 1960s also saw a burgeoning of a lively dissenting campaign, the so-called Democratic Movement. The trials of important literary figures such as Sinyavsky and Daniel and the proclamation of 1968 as Universal Human Rights Year were the spur to a movement which aimed at furthering human rights and the rule of law. The movement also wanted to get rehabilitation and compensation for Stalin's victims or their dependants, and the fostering of a more rational application of the country's scientific expertise. The unifying factor was advocating (and practising) an adherence to the law and the liberalization of its interpretation (which was a contrast to the violent activity of nineteenth-century Russian dissidents). The movement concentrated on political and legal freedoms. Little was said about the economic and social rights of workers.

The movement failed because it violated important requirements of the political culture. That, together with the emphasis on communicating with public opinion abroad, in the hope of getting foreign governments to put pressure on the Soviet authorities, made it difficult to sustain alliances. It failed to activate the foreign governments effectively, overestimating its influence and the effect of its efforts both on third parties and on the Soviet authorities, and was open to charges of disloyalty. The authorities gradually tightened up their control by infiltrating, dividing its members and suppressing their activities. Dissent did not die out but remained relatively weak until Gorbachev's time.

A sustained achievement of the Democratic Movement was *samizdat*, the publication of unauthorized material by unofficial means. Its best-known publication was *The Chronicle of Current Events*: liberal, reformist, gradualist and sceptical of 'revolution'. In its economic outlook the publication was less clear, but adopted a more or less liberal-socialist line. It was clearly hostile to Slavophile, chauvinist and fascist groups, although defending the right of free speech. A striking feature of the *Chronicle* was its lack of editorializing. For the most part it tried to present straight news unavailable in the official media. Its correspondents were very widespread throughout the Soviet Union, and often in responsible jobs. There were a number of imitations of the *Chronicle*, notably in Ukraine, Lithuania and among the Jewish community.

In 1978 a mining engineer and local trade union organizer, Vladimir Klebanov, founded the Free Trade Union Association of Soviet Working People after long and unproductive efforts to get a response from the authorities. Its members aimed to correct abuses in what they considered a basically good system and their original criticisms were based on their workplace experience: overbearing management, incompetence, dishonesty and corruption. But it also involved claims for the right to strike, to emigrate and to show solidarity with workers in the West. The association was ruthlessly crushed and its leaders sent to prison or to psychiatric hospitals. Considerable dissenting activity was also generated by religious groups and nationalists. While some dissenting groups had an increasingly difficult time (including the churches) the Jews and the Germans fared differently. Internal protests by these groups, together with international pressure, resulted in their large-scale emigration. But, from 1980 to 1982, as *détente* crumbled, this, too, was severely curtailed.

Alexander Solzhenitsyn and Andrei Sakharov

Alexander Solzhenitsyn achieved prominence when Khrushchev sanctioned the publication of his novel of life in the Gulag. He single-mindedly fought the system, smuggling his writings abroad in the belief that the West, through its broadcasts, could reach the Soviet public and encourage the growth of a critical public opinion. He fought the Soviet regime with a spiritual intensity drawn from what he perceived as the Slavic soul. On being deported to the West he became disillusioned and disappointed with the West's acquiescence in the Brezhnev regime. He saw the West as being untrue to its own principles, because it was a culture where man was losing God. Western influence was, for him, alien to the Slavic world.

The other great dissident of this period, Andrei Sakharov, like Solzhenitsyn, had as a young man been a supporter of the Soviet regime. He was immersed in outstanding scientific work concerned with nuclear weapons. Doubts about the use to which these weapons might be put developed throughout the 1950s, and he came to realize the priority of ethical and political questions over the technical, military and economic. His life as a dissident began in Khrushchev's time and extended throughout the Brezhnev period, sustained by his wife, Elena Bonner. It embraced many causes but ended his scientific career. In contrast to Solzhenitsyn, Sakharov had the clear intellect of a rational humanist. He supported the highest values of western thought.

Later Developments against Dissidents

After a period of stabilization by the Soviet authorities, a time of relative repression started in 1972. Solzhenitsyn was deported to the West, while Sakharov was eventually exiled to Gorky. It was directed at the reactionary right as well as at liberals, and the Russian National Movement was crushed. The holding of the Olympic Games in Moscow in 1980 was an opportunity for a further crackdown. Organizations were shut down (including Christian groups, and those monitoring the abuse of psychiatry and the implementation of the Helsinki Accords). The reasons for this tough policy included the decline of Brezhnev's influence and a drive by KGB chief Yuri Andropov (later to succeed Brezhnev as General Secretary) against dissidents and corruption. Differences among dissidents again emerged, with Roy Medvedev, a historian, criticizing Sakharov for being too pro-western and Solzhenitsyn for being too nostalgic about the Russian past. Medvedev remained socialist in his views and was never imprisoned, exiled or deported in spite of some outspoken comments. Under Gorbachev he resisted the fundamental reform of the Communist Party's position in the political system.

The advent of Gorbachev as General Secretary soon gave rise to hopeful signs. The dissident movement provided the idealistic roots of the growth of civic awareness under *glasnost*, above all in its fight for freedom of speech regardless of a person's political views. Sakharov's exile in Gorky was revoked by Gorbachev personally in 1986, the poet Yevgenii Yevtushenko published a plea for freedom from censorship and more honest writing, while many dissidents were released. A dramatic development was the replacement of the old conservative leadership by a new radical one at both the Union of Writers and the Union of Cinema Workers.

The Brezhnev Regime Disintegrates

By the early 1980s Brezhnev's health was declining rapidly. Years of 'stability' had taken its toll on the country. Stagnation was deteriorating into disintegration. The *blat* (an elaborate system of reciprocal favours) which had kept the economy more or less going over the years had degenerated into plain corruption. The command structure had begun to decay, with orders being ignored. In some sectors of the economy and areas of the country 'feudal barons' appeared, building wealthy private empires based on exploitation and expropriation of state property, crime and (sometimes physical) intimidation of workers and other citizens. There was a series of corruption scandals, which came close to Brezhnev's own family, and much jockeying for position among the rivals for the succession (Remnick, 1992, pp. 45–50). His ultimate successor, Andropov, had himself transferred from head of the KGB to the Party secretariat (from which the new Party Secretary was likely to be chosen) some months before Brezhnev's death.

4

The Surge of Reform

Societal Changes in the Soviet Union

The death of Brezhnev in November 1982 generated considerable anticipation of fundamental reforms that had been long delayed. Soviet society had altered significantly since Stalin's time and reform seemed not only desirable but urgent. Aspects of this 'quiet revolution' included the fact that, by the 1960s, over half the Soviet population was urbanized, while in the 1970s there was a great increase in the number of white collar and highly qualified workers. The younger generation was more individualistic than its predecessors and more aware and appreciative of the West, both of its values and its material rewards. Moreover, it was increasingly obvious that the Soviet Union was not catching up with the standard of living in the West, nor could it keep up with technological advances or continue to sustain the arms race. In the later Brezhnev years, liberal Soviet sociologists, many of whom were working in Siberian research institutes, wrote about changes in Soviet society. Studying the results of the first Soviet opinion polls in sixty years, they found a decline in Soviet-style patriotism, in respect for socialist and Leninist values, and in allegiance to Party and state. They pointed to increases in juvenile delinquency, evasions of military service and other 'immoral' activities as a sign of a crisis in values. A decline in the attractiveness of public service careers and a shift to 'individualistic' lucrative private occupations, combined with respondents' expressed desire to get rich, seemed to herald a fundamental transformation in attitudes and social organization (Getty, 1990, pp. 16, 18).

Andropov

Yuri Andropov was very quickly chosen by the Politburo as General Secretary of the CPSU to succeed Brezhnev. Chernenko had been thought of as the natural successor to Brezhnev, but Andropov was probably seen as having superior qualities; others were too old, too narrow in their interests or (like Gorbachev) too young. He was ten years older than Khrushchev or Brezhnev had been on their accession and his health was poor. Therefore he knew that he probably had little time in which to make an impact. He was faced with the same increasingly worrying economic situation as Brezhnev. By 1982 high levels of corruption and inefficiency as well as low labour morale were seriously limiting growth. He started by launching an anti-corruption campaign and demanding major changes in the Party and government, relying on a number of men who were to become prominent later, notably Gorbachev and Ryzhkov. He also tried to tighten up work discipline, his most headline-catching move being to send police into shops to ask why shoppers were not at work.

An important area was agriculture, significant because it was an ongoing problem in the Soviet Union and agricultural initiatives were popular with the public. Politically, regional secretaries were responsible for agriculture and Andropov needed their support. But the rate of increase in agricultural expenditure had decreased since 1979. Inevitably, his priority was domestic rather than foreign and defence policy. However, he attempted to improve relations with the United States. Despite this, 1983 was one of the worst years of the new Cold War. The problem also affected relations with Western and Eastern Europe. The failure to prevent the deployment of American missiles in Western Europe led to East Germany, Czechoslovakia and others joining some western countries in expressing anxiety over the placing of missiles on their soil, and over the economic effects of heightened tension. There was strong public support in Eastern Europe for better relations with the West and for arms negotiations. They often spoke of a 'European community of interest' regardless of ideology. Thus disarray among the Eastern Europeans was evident by the beginning of 1984 and pointed to the increasing unreality of trying to keep them subservient. Overall, foreign policy and defence problems mounted during Andropov's short period in office and he left many unresolved issues for his successors. His health steadily deteriorated during the summer of 1983 and after September he was never again seen in public. He had little more than fourteen months in power and was ill most of the time. He died in February 1984.

Chernenko

On Andropov's death Konstantin Chernenko, a Brezhnev protégé, at last succeeded, to the surprise of many in the West, where it was thought his opportunity had passed with the succession of Andropov.

His elevation did not mean a return to Brezhnevian conservatism. There were now too many influential younger men in the Politburo. Nevertheless there was a serious dispute on Chernenko's succession. Unlike on the accession of Andropov there was a delay before his appointment was announced. Despite having been Brezhnev's confidant and chief of staff for over thirty years, he lacked the experience, youth or intelligence to cope with the demanding situation now facing the Soviet Union. But the old guard knew he would not challenge their power or launch many new initiatives. Gorbachev was another matter; he was Chernenko's number two man, leading the Politburo in his absences and taking full advantage of his position. Like Brezhnev, Chernenko was a firm believer in *détente* abroad. He was not a friend of the military and was more concerned with domestic unrest than foreign danger, although he managed to improve relations with the United States and Western Europe. But his period of office was so short that all policies and activities reflected its transitional nature. There were signs of division in the Politburo and of a continuous succession struggle. His health deteriorated suddenly and he died in March 1985 after only thirteen months in office.

Gorbachev

With the appointment of Mikhail Gorbachev as Party Secretary, a highly intelligent, well-educated man from a new post-war generation, the moment for change had at last arrived. There was no delay in electing him as Party Secretary. It is thought that he was supported by the KGB (Rahr, 1987b). Under Brezhnev the nation-wide Party bureaucracy had grown in influence. Gorbachev aimed to restore the authority of the centre and of the General Secretary. A remarkable feature of his early months was the biggest turnover of Party personnel since the 1930s, all the way down the hierarchy. But this was not a complete turnover. Many of the old elite remained for some time (for example, in the KGB, in Ukraine and in the military–industrial ministries) and some of the new appointees were quite old. Local officials were now frequently rotated to Moscow for a spell before taking up secretary posts. In this way they could be vetted and briefed. The introduction of contested elections and the limitation of holding office for two five-year terms only was intended to help avoid regional secretaries virtually appointing their own successors and creating local patronage networks. The overall influence of the Party in Moscow declined after its leader, Victor Grishin, was removed. In all this Gorbachev had the great advantage of being appointed a year before the Twenty-seventh Party Congress was due to be held, so giving him time to install numbers of his supporters before the Congress met.

From Dissent to Opposition: Glasnost *Takes Effect*

Soon there were hopeful signs that alternative opinions would be given expression. A landmark was the agreement reached at the Vienna Conference on Security and Co-operation in Europe in 1989 which, at that time, had thirty-five states as members. The Soviet Union made important concessions and Gorbachev, commenting on the agreement, said, 'We demand no privileges, no exemption from rules which are mandatory for all' (*Keesing's*, 1989, p. 36413).

The Soviet Union got agreement to hold a human rights conference in Moscow in 1991. Some saw this as premature or a sell-out, but the approval was conditional on the Soviet Union keeping to its undertakings. This put pressure on Gorbachev to keep up the momentum on human rights. Nothing similar was linked to the original Helsinki Accords in 1975, and the Brezhnev regime made little effort to observe them. Among other things, the conditions for the 1991 conference included the release of all political prisoners and prisoners of conscience, exit visas for 'refusniks' (Jews wanting to emigrate) and changes in the criminal code to abolish or amend political and religious articles, effective guarantees of free speech, freedom to emigrate, and judicial independence in addition to no going back on changes already made.

The Soviet Union claimed that all prisoners convicted of political and religious crimes had been released, but western sources still had doubts about a small number of cases. Emigration from the Soviet Union increased dramatically (but not for those deemed to hold state secrets). Thousands of ethnic Germans, Greeks and Jews emigrated and the first Soviet Jewish Cultural Centre opened in Moscow. Jamming of western radio broadcasts ended. Amnesty International was invited to visit the Soviet Union. A new criminal code was put into preparation which was intended to reduce prison sentences and limit the use of, or even abolish, the death penalty. The ancient sentence of internal exile was to be abolished. Changes in the 1977 Constitution were envisaged which would have enshrined extended rights and freedoms of the individual. But the penal code was still to retain an article against 'socially dangerous acts, damaging to the economic and political system of the Soviet Union'. All this had to be reconsidered afresh in each republic after the Soviet Union's demise.

The Rehabilitation of Solzhenitsyn

A number of exiled Soviet dissidents had their citizenship rights restored, the most notable being Alexander Solzhenitsyn. In July 1989 the Writers' Union voted to readmit him and asked the Supreme Soviet to restore his citizenship. It also voted for the publication of Solzhenitsyn's *Gulag Archipelago*. In September 1990 (a month after receiving back his citizenship) Solzhenitsyn published a manifesto in the newspaper, *Komsomolskaya Pravda* entitled 'Rebuilding Russia' (English version, Solzhenitsyn, 1991). He called for a pan-Slav state to replace the Soviet Union. It would be a Russian union made up of Russia, Belorussia, Ukraine and the northern part of Kazakhstan (largely inhabited by Russians). The other republics would be given full independence and he was against internationalist expansionism. The article began by stating that time had finally run out for Communism. But, 'its concrete edifice has not yet crumbled. May we not be crushed beneath its rubble instead of gaining liberty' (p. 9). He went on to complain that,

> The Iron Curtain of yesterday gave our country superb protection against all the positive features of the West: against the West's civil liberties, its respect for the individual, its freedom of personal activity, its high level of general welfare, its spontaneous charitable movements. But the Curtain did not reach all the way to the bottom, permitting the continuous seepage of liquid manure – the self-indulgent and squalid 'mass popular culture', the utterly vulgar fashions, and the by-products of immoderate publicity – all of which our deprived young people have greedily absorbed. (p. 40)

He attacked western electoral politics and television campaigning, and called for a return to 'the democracy of small areas' with special emphasis on rural councils: 'It decidedly does not depend on Moscow, Petrograd, Kiev, and Minsk whether our country will flourish economically; that depends on the provinces' (p. 37).

While the national president would be elected by popular suffrage, the local councils based on the pre-revolutionary model (*zemstvos*) would elect regional councils, which would, in turn, elect the national legislature. One chamber of 'an experienced and highly educated minority' would have to 'create an impediment to the unchecked spread of democracy' (p. 85).

He wanted to abolish the much disliked *propiska*, the residency permit which severely restricted people's ability to move to the town in which they wished to live. On economic freedom he asserted the fundamental principle that 'there can be no independent citizen without private property' (p. 33).

While some saw Solzhenitsyn simply as a reactionary, others thought of him as raising the vital question of whether Russian nationalism could be democratized. Gorbachev answered him in the Supreme Soviet:

> He is without doubt a great man. As for Solzhenitsyn the politician, his views are alien to me. I feel myself a democrat, more inclined to radical

views . . . As a Russian I resolutely disagree with Solzhenitsyn's position as regards other nationalities. It is not respectful, to put it mildly. (Rettie, 1990d)

In general, Solzhenitsyn's article was received lukewarmly by both conservatives and radicals. His views (for example, the rejection of empire and criticism of the Orthodox Church) did not please the extreme right, while many felt that he was out of touch with the prevailing situation in the Soviet Union and had unrealistic political views.

Abuses of Psychiatry

At the East–West Conference on Humam Rights in January 1989 Fyodor Burlatsky, head of the Soviet Committee on Humanitarian Co-operation and Human Rights, said that he had failed to get clear answers from the Soviet government on the cases of people allegedly sent to psychiatric hospitals for political reasons. Nevertheless, the conference recognized that much progress had been made. Permission had been obtained for foreign psychiatrists to visit Soviet hospitals and examine patients. This visit took place when a team of United States psychiatrists arrived in March 1989. Their initial reaction was cautious and their final report was crucial in deciding whether Soviet psychiatrists were to be readmitted to the World Psychiatric Association from which they were expelled in 1983, and also to a United States confirmation of its provisional agreement to attend the Moscow Human Rights Conference in 1991.[1] The co-operation which the American psychiatrists got was patchy. There appears to have been a struggle between the Foreign Ministry, which wanted an open, informative approach, and the Mimistry of Health, which had things to hide.

An Independent Soviet Association of Psychiatrists was against the readmission of the Soviet Union to the world body. It alleged that, although progress had been made, the mechanism remained in place by which a person could be detained for psychiatric treatment because of his or her political views. Fyodor Burlatsky, a distinguished journalist, said that an appeals system was needed as well as the abolition of such diagnoses as 'social delusions' and 'sluggish schizophrenia'.[2] Yuri Reshetov, head of the Foreign Ministry's humanitarian affairs department, said that decrees passed in 1988 protected the rights of mental patients and gave them a right of appeal. However, an article in *Kommunist* written by two lawyers severely criticized these decrees, ridiculing them as nothing but 'declarations and promises which are at times unclear'. The World Psychiatric Association provisionally re-admitted the Soviet Union to the association at the end of March 1989.

Political Demonstrations

In 1988 new rules on public demonstrations had been introduced which many thought were unduly restrictive. Gorbachev defended the rules in a meeting with intellectuals in January 1989. He said that only 7 per cent of recent requests had been refused and he pointed to the violence in Azerbaijan and Armenia as a justification for the rules. Nevertheless, the feeling persisted that the government was anxious to control demonstrations within narrow parameters. Evidence was produced that local soviets in some parts of the country were introducing tight conditions in an attempt to play down the impact of meetings. There were regional contrasts. A political meeting of 10,000 people in Lithuania would be tolerated while in Moscow, Leningrad or other republics it might not be. The Democratic Union, a group to promote *glasnost* and *perestroika*, was often given rough treatment. In March a Democratic Union rally in Mayakovsky Square was dispersed by the police but, noticeably, passers-by joined in to support the protesters. Only a few years before dissident protests were met at best with indifference from passing citizens, at worst with outright hostility. Now there was a groundswell of support for outspoken criticism even when it went beyond the limits of permitted *glasnost*. This was partly because people felt less afraid and partly because the flood of revelations in recent years had shaken people's faith in the rightness of the system itself.

In February 1990 the Central Committee issued a strong warning that some planned nation-wide demonstrations could lead to chaos and 'civil confrontation'. Whether this was a genuine fear of things getting out of hand or merely a ploy by Gorbachev to strengthen his campaign to get elected as executive president was not clear. A dramatic demonstration took place at the 1990 traditional May Day parade. Gorbachev and the assembled Politburo were hissed and booed by 10,000 demonstrators ranging from the monarchists to Stalinists and leftist radicals. The parade was organized, for the first time, by the official trade unions, and they allowed citizens to join in on condition that their banners 'did not run counter to the constitution or call for violence'. They were unprepared for the demonstration that followed. Shortly after this, a group of deputies in the Supreme Soviet brought in a bill giving harsh sentences to people who 'insult the President in public or slander him'. The bill was substantially amended in the Supreme Soviet. It was made clear that criticisms of the President's policies were not an offence, and that insults were punishable only if expressed 'in an indecent way'.

The Uzbekistan Investigation

Some felt that another affair was also linked with an attempt to turn people against the reformers. Two deputies, the prosecutors Telman Gdlyan and Nikolai Ivanov, were expelled from the Party. For six years they had been investigating corruption in Uzbekistan. They were officially supported, so long as their accusations involved only local officials, but they lost their posts in 1989 when they accused the Politburo member and leading conservative, Yegor Ligachev, of involvement. They themselves were alleged to have used undue pressure on witnesses, detained suspects' relatives and to have allowed bribe takers to go free in exchange for information. The pair had widespread popular support. Although many believed they may have exceeded their powers, it was pointed out that many people had fabricated cases against dissidents over the last thirty years, held them without trial, and not been removed from their jobs, let alone been expelled from the Party. In the event, the Supreme Soviet rejected a call for criminal proceedings against the two investigators and suggested instead that the discredited former local Party leaders be investigated. But deputies agreed to a dismissal of the two from their investigative posts and demanded the dismissal of officials who had failed to curb the investigators' alleged excesses.

Disappointment for the Opposition

In spite of constraints and controversies, great changes occurred. The problem was that the improvements did not rest on firm legal foundations. The Stalinist system of internal passports and strictly controlled rights of residence was still nominally in force. There was still an element of censorship. Members of the government were at first rarely criticized openly in the press. It caused a sensation when the Minister of Land Reclamation and Water Resources, Nikolai Vasilyev, was lampooned in the satirical magazine *Krokodil*. Newly elected leaders, too, showed sensitivity to criticism. An increasing number of former dissidents became disillusioned with Gorbachev. The feeling was that his words had been taken too much at their face value. Elena Bonner (the widow of Andrei Sakharov) wrote,

> Gorbachev proclaimed the need for *perestroika*, for reconstruction, but no one asked what he was going to build. Gorbachev's words – 'demo-

cratic and humane socialism' – were taken from the past. There was no more substantive content in them than there was in the slogans 'social-ism – the first phase of communism' and 'developed Socialism'. (Bonner, 1990)

The death of Sakharov in December 1989 had added to the feeling of disintegration among radicals. He was joint leader of the Inter-regional Group of Deputies in tactical alliance with Yeltsin, the nearest thing in the Supreme Soviet to an opposition party. The Inter-regional Group had been formed because radicals failed to secure adequate parliamentary representation in the March 1989 elections to the Con-gress of People's Deputies and the Supreme Soviet, although Soviet opinion polls showed that the group potentially had a large amount of popular support. Thus the group's existence seemed to be crucial to *perestroika* and the democratization of the Soviet Union. But many wondered how long this odd alliance of intellectuals and populists could stay together.

For the future, it seemed that opposition would most likely have to be expressed in a developing party system. Dissidents – in the sense of people who oppose the existing regime – would be those of the 'right' (for example, Pamyat, monarchists) and 'left' (old-style Stalinists, an-archists) whose role would be marginal to mainstream politics. If democracy took hold, the great issues of human rights and social reform which were upheld by dissidents in the post-Stalin period would in future become party issues, openly discussed and campaigned for. However, the economic, nationalist and political crises facing the Soviet Union meant that the rights of opposition could not be taken for granted.

Perestroika

Gorbachev had identified the key elements of his strategy; returning real power to the soviets, and stripping the managerial–industrial elite of many of its functions, while creating competing centres of power in factories and co-operatives. He was also determined to separate the Party from economic management. But could he demonstrate to a sceptical public that social and economic life would indeed change significantly? Discipline and order involved an attack on the problems of alcoholism, crime, corruption and privilege. Although the privileges of Party officials were denounced there was still ambiguity on the matter, with Ligachev (regarded as second in command to Gorbachev) defending them. There was disagreement over whether poor produc-tivity was the result of human failings (caution, laziness and corrup-tion) or technical difficulties (poor investment and planning).

Gorbachev stressed the latter until the Twenty-seventh Party Congress and then went over to stressing incentives (quoting Lenin and citing the NEP). He stopped short of advocating the market mechanism but more and more emphasized the need for reform.

In the first instance, Gorbachev's *perestroika* aimed to revitalize the economy and restore social discipline in a pragmatic way. Problems here included the fact that restructuring the economy interfered with growth, and technological innovation interfered with consumer welfare. Gorbachev was going for growth and primarily relying on restored discipline and order to sustain productivity. There was a flourishing 'second' (private) economy in the Soviet Union, illegal and contrary to socialist principles. The problem was that the 'first' economy relied on it. The first steps to doing something about this was to legalize co-operatives and family businesses, although they were seriously hampered by regulations and high taxes (as well as gravely compromised by protection rackets).

Major obstacles remained and were worsening. The biggest problem was conservatism and inertia in the Party and managerial–industrial bureaucracy. Managers had a direct interest in opposing decentralization and a shift to cost-accounting because their power was threatened. In many industrial towns in central Russia, Ukraine and Siberia there was an industrial mono-culture, a single huge factory which ran the place like a company town and controlled everyone from the local party secretary to the municipal authorities. Then there was the difficulty of switching from a centrally run economy to a mixture of market and plan. What seemed right on paper might be politically very hard to implement. Russian and Soviet history provided few examples of successful entrepreneurial or political culture. There had been a struggle with the planners and four draft's of the Twelfth Five Year Plan were rejected. In the end a compromise was reached. Gorbachev tried to build consensus by emphasizing both change *and* stability. He had also been trying to split the opposition by rewarding some and punishing others. But it was clear that divergent views were to be found at the top, and Ligachev was understood to be the most prominent of the more cautious members. Only in October 1988 was he removed from the influential post in charge of ideology, to that for agriculture.

Glasnost *and Democracy*

Gorbachev proclaimed that economic and social reform could not work without more *glasnost*, that is, openness and democracy. But what he meant by democracy is a matter of some debate. Certainly it did not originally mean the institutional set-up of a multiplicity of parties competing for office: the CPSU was to retain its unique and leading role. Answering questions on Soviet television in February 1989 he denounced the idea of a multi-party system as 'politically and theoretically unsound', and stressed in strong terms the need for the Party to retain its leading role. In the 1989 election campaign the conservative Ligachev also came out for a 'free dialogue and open comparison between different viewpoints' as long as the one-party system was maintained. He made it clear that pluralism was only acceptable if it 'serves the unification of society in the name of renewing and consolidating socialism'.

Some commentators, particularly on the political right and among the emigré community (see, for example, Paul, 1990) argued that the creation of a democratic civil society in the Soviet Union was impossible unless the 'totalitarianism' based on Marxist and Leninist ideology was completely destroyed. Such a society, they argued, was incompatible with the development of civil society, because the very purpose of its existence was to destroy such a society. They saw the necessity of civil war or a total collapse of the economy, with all the chaos and suffering that implied, if the Soviet Union was to escape from totalitarianism. But by 1989 the situation had indeed been reached where there was an upsurge of grass-roots activity, with the burgeoning of 'informal' (that is, not officially approved) groups. They were independent of him and hence Gorbachev had been equivocal about such a development. Most of these groups may have had no ostensible political aims, but some definitely did. They highlighted the tension between centralized 'mobilizational' policies and participatory local initiatives.

Achievements

In spite of the many and increasing difficulties which faced Gorbachev and the Soviet Union, it is important to note the significant changes which did take place in his early years. From 1985 to 1986 there had been a great breakthrough in public debate and criticism. Almost all the old taboos went. Emigrés were invited back and former dissidents such as Andrei Sakharov became prominent political figures. The election campaign of March 1989 illustrated the political changes by having a multiplicity of candidates, and crowded, highly participatory election meetings. The Congress of People's Deputies and Supreme Soviet proved no rubber stamps. The more open mass media gave full coverage to independent-minded deputies. A beginning was made in the creation of what was officially called a 'law-based state'. The draft penal code aimed to liberalize the system, minimize the category of 'political' crime, and to soften the regime in prison camps. Citizens would be able to challenge bureaucratic injustice and delay, and seek redress in the courts. There were greater opportunities to go abroad and to emigrate. In many republics Popular Fronts were formed, changes were made in the law to safeguard local languages and moves towards full economic sovereignty were accepted and approved in Moscow. Experiments began in new forms of property and economic management. Farms were being put under a lease contract system, so that peasants would be able to do almost anything with the land (deciding what to grow, where to sell products and how much to charge) except sell it for profit. Co-operatives were set up in the service sector, and even, hesitatingly, in manufacturing. People could buy their homes but not sell them; they could pass them on to their families or return them to the state. Profit and loss accounting was encouraged instead of fulfilling a rigid plan. Major cuts and reductions in conventional and nuclear weapons were achieved. Soviet troops were withdrawn from Afghanistan. At the same time the military's professionalism was recognized by encouraging military personnel to join in the public debates (Steele, 1989b).

Conclusion

In many respects the Soviet Union was not like an Eastern European Communist country. It had experienced a longer period of Communism than they had and some generations had been socialized effectively into support for Marxism-Leninism. The impact of the civil war and Stalinist repression had left no room for dissent or for alternative ideas to have wide currency. In Eastern Europe elements of a private economy had survived to provide the foundations of an alternative system. In the Soviet Union there was virtually nothing and people were not accustomed to looking to themselves for political and economic alternatives, or to taking risks. In these circumstances the tradition of relying on a strong leader to deal with a crisis remained strong. Gorbachev wanted reform and quick results, but he had to build bridges by emphasizing stability. Hence his message at first was a bit ambivalent but this may have been the only realistic approach. He was clearly carrying on where Andropov left off but had more definite policies. It was still too early to say whether he would succeed, but the elite now generally agreed that reform was necessary; they had acquired a more realistic and practical attitude than hitherto. The amount of reform needed and at what cost was still very controversial but the Twenty-seventh Party Congress of February 1986 endorsed his goals.

Gorbachev started changes the course of which must to some extent have been uncertain. Equally uncertain (even if his personal hold on office seemed to be secure) was whether Gorbachev could continue the pace of reform or whether vested interests or public discontent would force him to slow down, or even reverse, his direction. It can perhaps more effectively be argued, in reply to arguments from the left, that the problem was not that the central authorities remained authoritarian and dominant, but that they had become too weak and no longer had the administrative authority able to implement reform. Nationalism and criminality were threatening to undermine the state entirely, leaving only chaos and strife. Local soviets, with more potential power, seemed to be hoarding resources and building their own economic networks, often connected to local interests of dubious legality and to the bureaucracy. Certainly, political consciousness and activity from below was increasing dramatically – but so was disillusionment and cynicism.

Keane (1990, pp. 340–52) suggested that Gorbachev should not be understood as a charismatic leader, but rather as one of a type whose function was to contribute to the *dismantling* of a despotic political system by means of state-led liberalization from above. He cited Suarez in Spain, Kádár in Hungary, Karamanlis in Greece, and Jaruzelski in Poland as examples of the type. But the 'politics of retreat' is delicate and dangerous. The leaders of such a 'retreat' have a major problem of legitimacy as they face enemies resisting their reforms and the ingratitude of radical rivals. They inevitably cause uncertainty and confusion, while being unable to offer immediate benefits to their supporters. In the end they are overwhelmed by the political forces which they unleash and are victims of their own success. This analysis of Gorbachev's position proved most prophetic.

Notes

1 The Human Rights Conference was held but became overshadowed by the crisis overtaking the Soviet Union in 1991.

2 The Serbsky Institute of Psychiatry in Moscow developed a very broad definition of schizophrenia. Under one type known as 'sluggish schizophrenia' a patient retained abilities to function socially but developed paranoid symptoms, which led to the overvaluation of his or her own importance and exhibiting grandiose ideas of reforming the world. Schizophrenia was considered to remove the patient's entire responsibility for his or her actions and was continuous and irreversible. There was no notion of diminished or partial responsibility in Soviet law, so that the diagnosis put great power in the psychiatrists' hands. Since the disease was considered 'sluggish' a person behaving normally could, because of a past record of the illness, be diagnosed as still harbouring it.

Part II

From Party Power to Presidential Government

5

Soviet Government Transformed

The Organization of Soviet Government

Before the Gorbachev reforms the authority of the Soviet government was vested in the Council of Ministers. But, with more than a hundred members, it was too large to exercise real authority and generally met about four times a year to hear reports on the progress of the Five Year Plan. Its effective authority resided in the Praesidium of the Council of Ministers, a much smaller executive body. The chairman was often referred to as the Soviet Prime Minister, although he was head of government administration rather than political head of government in the British sense; that role was taken by the Party General Secretary. However, the chairman of the Praesidium of the Council of Ministers was always a member of the Communist Party Politburo. Government administration was undertaken by a large number of ministries and state committees. The difference between the two was not always clear-cut but, broadly speaking, ministries related to a single branch of government while state committee responsibilities normally cut across ministerial boundaries. The state committees best known in the West were the KGB (Committee for State Security) and Gosplan (Committee for State Planning). Ministers were nearly always professional administrators and they were not normally shifted from ministry to ministry but they could be replaced, promoted or demoted for proven ability (or lack of it) and for political reasons. A major role was given to scientific staff. Ministries and state committees were supposed to take a Party-national view but often lapsed into departmentalism and had disputes among themselves (Appendix A) (Smith, 1988, pp. 98–101).

Over the years there were many changes in the organization of Soviet government, but it was clear that the nature of the reforms envisaged under *perestroika* would entail fundamental reorganization. In June 1989 a big ministerial shake-up was announced. Ryzhkov, the Soviet Prime Minister, said that twenty of fifty-two ministries in the industrial, transport and farming sectors would be abolished. The remaining ministries would operate on the basis of minimum interference in production methods. 'We are talking about a completely new type of ministry, qualitatively different from what existed before', Ryzhkov explained (Evans, 1989).

Law and Order

Apart from the regular police force (known as the militia) and the KGB troops, law and order was in the hands of the troops of the Ministry of the Interior (MVD). These were the ones usually sent to deal with major outbreaks of trouble in places such as, in the last years, the Caucasus and Central Asia. Western analysts sometimes numbered these troops at around 300,000. However, most of them were uniformed but unarmed employees who carried out tasks done in the West by the police, security firms, the prison service and so on. The remainder were the 36,000 men of the so-called Osnaz 'special designation' forces. They were armed and equipped like regular Soviet troops, but many sources suggest that they were the least wanted of each year's military service draft. Troubles in the southern republics in the Gorbachev period compelled the government to use regular soldiers in addition to the MVD troops. The Soviet army was very reluctant to undertake this task, because it did not see its role as going into action against Soviet citizens, and did not relish the considerable unpopularity it engendered. Reservists were indeed sometimes mobilized, but there were instances where they refused to go to deal with trouble in other parts of the Soviet Union. In January 1991 it was reported that paratroopers from Vitebsk refused to go the Vilnius in Lithuania to deal with disturbances there when they discovered that they were to be under KGB control.

The KGB

The KGB was the direct successor of the 'Cheka', the security agency set up by Lenin soon after the Revolution. It acquired a fearsome reputation inside and outside the Soviet Union, being responsible for internal security as well as foreign operations. This meant that it was influenced by political changes in the Soviet Union and by the vagaries of Communist Party politics. It had never been quite the super-efficient and effective intelligence organization which some in the West believed. Now that more information has become available it is clear that it was seriously affected by the decline in standards and morale in the Communist Party during the last years of Brezhnev's rule, when it was more under the Party's control than ever before. As Gorbachev struggled to keep control and felt it necessary to placate conservative interests, the KGB acquired new powers, to enter business premises and confiscate documents, as well as over environmental matters. Yanaev, Gorbachev's Deputy President, held posts in organizations believed in the West to be linked to the KGB and was a member of the Presidential Security Council, as was General Vladimir Kryuchkov, the head of the KGB. Kryuchkov severely criticized the reforms and accused the West of trying to undermine the Soviet Union. Both were involved in the attempted coup.

As the Gorbachev reforms took effect democratic and nationalist groups fiercely attacked the KGB, while it tried to defend and restore its public image. It announced plans to hold regular press conferences and meetings and debates at institutes and factories. In the developing situation of the second half of the 1980s, the KGB saw itself as perhaps having a more significant role internally, less that of looking for individual critics of the system and more one of dealing with ethnic unrest. Along with other nominees for ministerial posts, the head of the KGB now had to be questioned and scrutinized by the Supreme Soviet. Later, the Supreme Soviet set up a Defence and State Security Committee which included the KGB among its responsibilities. Kryuchkov welcomed this, but some deputies complained that there were too many on the committee directly involved in security matters. Not everyone was convinced by these apparent changes. At a conference of Democratic Platform in June 1990 a leading KGB officer, Major-General Oleg Kalugin, told the audience 'the organization is unreformable and ought to be disbanded'. He went on to say that there were different currents of thought within the KGB. Some officers had difficulty coming to terms with the new situation and criticism of Gorbachev was on the increase (Steele, 1990c). For these public comments, Kalugin was sacked, stripped of his honours and was to be prosecuted. However, in August 1990 he won a by-election for the Congress of People's Deputies in the Krasnodar district and thus acquired parliamentary immunity.

The New Soviet Parliament

Before Gorbachev Soviet elections were based on non-western criteria and were taken very seriously - by the Party, at least. They were regarded as great demonstrations of united and virtually unanimous support for the regime and a great deal of effort went into preparing for them. A list of nominees was drawn up discreetly, by private consultation. The main responsibility was that of the Party officials who were expected to know which candidates would be acceptable. Nominations were made by officially approved organizations, such as trade unions or

Komsomol (the Party youth organization), and it can be assumed that some discussion that may have involved active disagreement took place at this stage. The final decision on the candidate was unanimous. Protest against, or rejection of, the candidate was possible but rare. Rejection implied criticism of local Party officials and attempts would always be made to smooth things over and make the candidate acceptable. Steps to introduce contested elections for soviet, Party and factory managerial posts were not originally envisaged as involving challenges to the Party or official Party policy. They were seen as contests between individuals based on individual competence or performance. They had the intention of making deputies and officials less secure and complacent in their roles, and more responsive to the people they ostensibly served. But the end of the Party's official 'leading role' and the rise of political groups with every intention of becoming political parties, meant that such elections were likely to develop into party political contests. This development had not gone very far by the time the Soviet Union collapsed.

A sign of things to come occurred even before the old Supreme Soviet had ceased to exist. In October 1988 two issues – the right of Interior Ministry troops to enter private homes without a warrant, and the right to control demonstrations without reference to the local authorities – came before the Supreme Soviet. After a debate in which strong criticism of the decrees came from some delegates, thirteen deputies voted against and four abstained on the measure to control public demonstrations. On the right of Ministry of the Interior police to enter homes without warrants, thirty-one of the 1,500 deputies voted against. This was the first significant opposition ever displayed in the old Supreme Soviet.

On 29 November 1988 the existing Supreme Soviet met to approve the law which would, in effect, end its existence. A new body called the Congress of People's Deputies (CPD) was to be created, with 2,250 members. Two-thirds were elected under the old system of 750 chosen in territorial constituencies of the nationalities and 750 from constituencies with an approximately equal number of voters. Another 750 were not elected directly by the ordinary citizens but were chosen by various established bodies such as the CPSU, Komsomol, the trade unions, the Academy of Sciences, and churches. Government ministers were not eligible for nomination to the CPD. Such a body was unwieldy as a functioning parliament. It was intended normally to meet only once a year and from its number chose a Supreme Soviet of 542 members, 271 each for the Soviet of the Union and the Soviet of the Nationalities. This was the real parliament and was to have spring and autumn sessions of three to four months each.

The new electoral law laid down how candidates could get on to the ballot. They had to be nominated at meetings of not less than 500 people called by the local authority. More than half of those attending the meeting had to accept the candidates. The names then went forward to a constituency election meeting, made up of people chosen from work collectives or local residents. Their task was to reduce the number of candidates to a small viable number. Again, more than half the people at the meeting had to accept the candidates before their names would get on to the ballot. Once chosen, candidates could campaign politically in the sense of presenting their personal pro-grammes. They did not have to be Party members. If more than two people ran, and no one got more than 50 per cent of the votes cast, the top two people took part in a run-off not more than two months later. (This often happened.) If only one candidate was nominated, he or she had to get over 50 per cent of the votes cast to be declared elected. Voters could cross out the name of the candidate. It was therefore possible for a candidate to be defeated even if he or she was the only candidate standing.

A public opinion survey by the Soviet Association of Social Sci-ences early in the life of the new Supreme Soviet demonstrated a wide demand for contested elections and a multi-party system. On the eve of the poll the association asked the public whether they favoured plural-ism. Forty-six per cent said yes, and only 10 per cent said no. The rest either declined to answer or said it would make no difference. The nomination process varied, with evidence of old-style manipulation in some places, and genuine involvement by the people in others. The Politburo of the CPSU nominated exactly one hundred candidates for its one hundred seats, which disappointed those who wanted contested elections. Outside the Party the choice of nominations was wider, with priests and members of co-operatives sometimes being selected. Can-didates put forward their own political programmes and debated with each other, a new experience for Soviet citizens. There could be drama, as in the meetings at the Academy of Sciences, which favoured con-servatives, and at first failed to nominate Andrei Sakharov and other reformers. They only did so after stormy protests.

The First Contested Elections

In the March 1989 elections for the CPD about a quarter of the 1,500 territorial constituency seats had only one candidate. More than 80 per cent of the candidates were CPSU members (a higher percentage than under the old system) and a fifth were women. The old quota system under which the Party nominated acquiescent non-Party candidates for the Supreme Soviet had given way to a contest in which activists and independents had a real chance to run. But without the quota local Party managers ensured that loyal Party nominees stood for election in disproportionate numbers. A number of prominent Party officials and military commanders were defeated, including five members of the Central Committee. In Leningrad six Party leaders lost, including Yuri Soloviev, Party Secretary of the Leningrad region and candidate member of the Politburo. He was defeated, although the only candidate, as voters crossed his name off the ballot paper. A number of prominent radicals were elected, including Andrei Sakharov and Roy Medvedev, and nationalists won about two-thirds of the seats in the Baltic republics, Committed radicals were thought to be in a minority of about three to four hundred in the CPD. Gorbachev asked the media not to dramatize the situation and blamed Party officials for losing contact with ordinary people.

In the republic and local elections of March 1990 the result in the major cities was victory for radical electoral groups. In Moscow, Democratic Russia won fifty-five of the capital's sixty-five seats in the Russian Federation's CPD. In the city soviet they won 56 per cent of the seats. In Leningrad, Democratic Elections 90 took 54 per cent of the places on the city soviet and 80 per cent of the city's CPD seats. In Kiev, capital of Ukraine, the nationalist movement, Rukh, won a majority on the city soviet and fifteen of the city's twenty-two Supreme Soviet seats. As the first opportunity for citizens to make a choice since the Revolution, the elections at all levels had aroused great interest and even passion. But disillusionment soon set in with the slow progress of *perestroika*, and subsequent by-elections had smaller turn-outs. Nevertheless many political parties were now registered and future elections could be expected to play a genuine role in deciding who exercised power.

Boris Yeltsin

A notable feature of the election was the role of Boris Yeltsin. Yeltsin was born in 1931 in Sverdlovsk. In a typical Soviet career he followed study at a polytechnical institute with various construction engineering jobs, rising to be head of a state house-building firm in 1965. Three years later he became a full-time Party official. At the age of 45 he was head of the Sverdlovsk Party organization, and soon won a popular reputation. In 1985, a month after Gorbachev came to power he was transferred to Moscow and was rapidly promoted to become Moscow Party chief and a candidate member of the Politburo. He made a great impact in Moscow, travelling on buses and stopping some perks for the elite. His popularity among the citizens contrasted with the hostility of the Party bureaucracy. He was disgraced in 1987 for publicly attacking leading politicians and the slow pace of reform. Removed from the Politburo, he remained a member of the Central Committee and

Deputy Minister of Housing Construction. Once a close ally of Gorbachev, he was now openly criticizing the results of Gorbachev's period of office and advocating policies which Gorbachev denounced as irresponsible.

He used the election campaign to try to stage a political come-back, standing for the Moscow seat in the Soviet of Nationalities which meant that all the Moscow electorate would have an opportunity to vote for him. Attempts were made to hinder his election campaign by denying him publicity, packing his meetings with hostile audiences and even by publishing the Central Committee minutes of 21 October 1987, when he was disgraced. Nevertheless, huge crowds attended his meetings and posters saying that he would 'free Moscow from the mafia of bureaucrats' were evident throughout Moscow. In the end, the election result was a great landslide victory for Yeltsin, who got 90 per cent of the vote in many wards. An estimated 80 per cent of the electorate voted. But when the results of the election to the Supreme Soviet were announced it was evident that many prominent radicals had been excluded, including Yeltsin. Later, a deputy from the Russian Federation resigned to make way for him to sit in the Soviet of Nationalities.

The Supreme Soviet in Action

The powers of the CPD and the Supreme Soviet were not entirely clear. It depended to a large extent on how, over time, they would develop their role and how assertive they would be, together with how far the bureaucracy could control their activities. The Party soon decided not to limit the course of discussion in the new parliament and from the start it was clear that the CPD would not be a rubber stamp. Challenges to the official line came straight away. Gorbachev was elected head of state with executive powers by a secret ballot, 2,123 votes in favour and 87 against, although some people had expressed a preference for a nation-wide election and for the election to be at least symbolically contested. The CPD soon showed that it would not accept nominations to government posts without examination. Gorbachev's nomination to the deputy presidency, Anatolii Lukyanov, and Nikolai Ryzhkov the nominated Prime Minister, were closely questioned. Committees rejected five of the people Gorbachev nominated to be senior ministers in his new Council of Ministers. The CPD also set up a large panel under Gorbachev's chairmanship to draft a new constitution in place of that of 1977. Its members included Yeltsin, who was already advocating a loose confederation of independent states. There was talk of the radicals drawing up an alternative, minority, programme but suggestions that this meant the formation of an opposition group were firmly denied. Rather, they would concentrate their activities on the committees and commissions of the CPD and Supreme Soviet. Some compromises were arrived at. The CPD was granted more power than originally expected. It was to have the right to review and amend any laws passed by the Supreme Soviet. Half of the seats on parliamentary committees were reserved for deputies who had not been elected to the Supreme Soviet.

On 31 May 1989 Yeltsin made an important speech to the Supreme Soviet in which he drew attention to the potential power of the president and to the continuing influence of the CPSU. He called for an annual vote of confidence in the president and told the deputies:

> Against the background of the general economic crisis and sharpening ethnic tensions, his growing power could lead to the temptation to solve our complex problems by force. Without even noticing it, we may again find ourselves captive of a new dictatorship. (Steele, 1989c)

He emphasized that power must be transferred from the Party to the elected soviets. The Supreme Soviet should pass a law on the Party to define its role. He complained that the existing CPD was a hostage to decisions taken by a meeting of the Party's Central Committee which took place three days before its inaugural session. Most of the decisions had already been made by the Central Committee and left for the CPD to rubber-stamp. He stated that 'the democratization of the Party is lagging behind the democratization of society'. The speech was coolly received by the predominantly conservative or pro-Gorbachev deputies. It was clear that the CPSU leaders were not prepared to surrender the Party's powers. The leading Party ideologist, Vadim Medvedev, made a speech to Moscow Communists in June in which he said,

> Opposing the Congress to the Party or the Supreme Soviet to the Central Committee leaves a demagogic aftertaste. Talk of bringing in legislation to subordinate public organizations, in particular the Party, to the Soviets is not only baseless. It represents the worst form of anti-democratism and statism. It shows total lack of understanding of realities. The Party works within the framework of the constitution, and has its own goals and methods . . .
>
> In the present complicated social situation, pressing for a multi-party system willy-nilly weakens the Communist Party's role, leads to the weakening of *perestroika*, and forces the country into a condition of unpredicability, from which it will be hard to emerge. (Steele, 1989d)

In spite of this speech, political developments soon made clear that it was not possible to hold to such a line. Groups formed in the Supreme Soviet on the radical side which, in turn, forced the conservatives into the open, so ending the artificial unity in Soviet politics. Nevertheless, as the crisis in the Soviet Union deepened, the Supreme Soviet became less outspoken and more inclined to support Gorbachev's proposals for a presidential government with very extensive powers.

The Gorbachev Presidency

Under the 1977 Constitution Gorbachev was head of state, officially known as the Chairman of the Praesidium of the Supreme Soviet. But his real power came from his being General Secretary of the CPSU. Although he put forward the idea at the February 1990 Central Committee meeting, it still came as a surprise when a proposal for an executive presidency was placed before the Supreme Soviet. Although the president was to be elected for a five-year term on the basis of 'general, equal and direct elections' the first election, as an exception, was to be by the CPD and for a four-year term to run concurrently with the term of the existing CPD. No one could serve more than two successive terms. The purpose of the change, apart from the need for quick, firm action in an emergency situation, was to transfer real power from the Party Secretary to the head of state. Gorbachev emphasized that an end was being put to the Party's 'direct interference in the solution of specific state and economic issues' (Millinship, 1990a). Instead, such decisions would be taken by the soviets. Unlike the Party, these were directly responsible to the electorate. The relationship between the president and the soviets was not made clear.

The radical group opposed the changes on the grounds that it was more important to establish an effective parliament with powers over the government budget and key ministries. Ironically, the radicals had originally supported the idea of a strong presidency to deal with the conservatives. They now saw it as a reversion to the Russian tradition of a powerful ruler. There were stormy debates, although the proposals were eventually passed by large majorities. However, Gorbachev's unopposed election as president was by only 1,329 votes (59.1 per cent) out of 2,250 deputies. Those voting against numbered 495, those abstaining or absent 426. Because of the need for a 51 per cent majority, abstentions are, in effect, votes against. This compares with the vote of 2,123 to 87 which he received ten months before when he was elected Chairman of the Supreme Soviet.

The president nominated the chairman and members of the *Council of Ministers* for acceptance by the Supreme Soviet, headed the *Defence Council*, and conducted international negotiations. He signed legislation into effect and exercised 'overall leadership' of the preparation of matters for the Supreme Soviet, submitting regular reports on the state of the country, and on important matters of domestic and foreign policy. He also appointed a *Presidential Council* to take over many of the Politburo's functions. It was not subordinate to the CPD or Supreme Soviet but had to 'work out measures to implement the cardinal planks of the home and foreign policy of the Soviet Union and to ensure the country's security' (Steele, 1990a). Its composition (which included non-politicians) suggested that Gorbachev wanted to involve a variety of different constituencies and force them to toe the line – or to resign. In addition to the Presidential Council, there was established a *Presidential Council of the Federation*, representing the nationalities. Its first major task was to be the renegotiation of the 1922 treaty governing relations between the nationalities. This would inevitably be a delicate and difficult task. There was still a *Praesidium of the Supreme Soviet*, but smaller than hitherto, consisting of twenty people plus the chairpersons of various committees. It had power to declare war or martial law in any pary of the country in time of trouble.

The new executive presidency caused concern among the non-Russian republics, who were already worried about a bill defining the central government's right to impose a state of emergency. The bill would have allowed the central authorities to suspend their Supreme Soviets, override decisions of their governments and take over their administrations during situations of widespread violence. After much protest, the republics were more or less appeased by amendments which required the president to warn republics of his intention to impose martial law in the event of an emergency, and to get their agreement. Failure to do so would require him to secure the approval of two-thirds of the all-Union Supreme Soviet. The president's power to declare a state of emergency and the rights of the Supreme Soviet and the republics in such an eventuality were crucial in interpreting the legality and constitutionality of the actions of the coup leaders in August 1991.

Another important concession concerned the newly established *Constitutional Review Committee*. The purpose of this committee was to check the validity of all legislation and decrees. Under the original draft the president would have appointed its members, a violation of separation of powers which upset many deputies. Now the job was to be given to the chairperson of the Supreme Soviet. The new committee was less than a Supreme Court of the United States, but it was the first move towards creating an independent system of judicial review of legislation. Its fifteen members (composed of lawyers and politicians) were to serve for ten years. The committee exerted itself in February 1991 over Gorbachev's decree establishing joint military–police patrols in major cities. In response to a referral by the Russian Federation, it found 'substantial flaws' in the decree and the regulations to implement it. It also nullified other decrees but it was not clear what, if any, action was likely to be taken as a result of these decisions (Appendix B).

The Conservatives Assert their Power

As the economic crisis deepened and discontent grew, Gorbachev began to seek extended powers. In the autumn of 1990 he got the Supreme Soviet to grant him special powers for eighteen months to deal with the economy, the budget, property relationships and the 'strengthening of law and order'. By November something approaching panic broke out, with calls in and out of the Supreme Soviet for action to improve food supplies and prevent the collapse of the country – although what action was not specified. Yeltsin called for a coalition government and there was talk of a senior army marshal and adviser to Gorbachev, Sergei Akhromeyev, being called in to preserve the Union. (Akhromeyev committed suicide after the coup.) All this led to Gorbachev being granted yet further powers as part of a fundamental restructuring of the presidential system which had only been in place since the spring. All organs of the central executive were now subordinate to the president. The ineffective Presidential Council was abolished, to be replaced by a *National Security Council* on which army, police and KGB leaders sat. Members were be nominated by the president, and its responsibilities involved 'implementing all-Union policy in the field of defence . . . and guaranteeing stability, law and order'. There was also to be a deputy president, but it required two votes in the CPD to get Gennadii Yanaev, a Communist Party official, approved.

The Council of the Federation was to have an enhanced role, aided by a committee of experts nominated by the republics. The president was in principle, bound by Federation Council decisions and members were responsible for putting its decisions into effect. Its main task was to maintain satisfactory relations between the republics and the centre. It was also intended to be an important advisory body and central to the policy-making process. In principle, therefore, the republics now had a much greater say in central policy-making. But since the autonomous republics were also represented it was probably too large a body for effective action. It seemed that the National Security Council was likely to be the main location of significant policy-making. The Council of Ministers was replaced by a Cabinet of Ministers subordinate to the president. The Cabinet included seats for republic prime ministers. This was not what many republics wanted. They preferred a horizontal structure, with republics having direct links with each other, and the centre having a co-ordinating role. Executive decisions would then be taken by the republics (Appendix C) (Rahr, 1991, pp. 1–4).

These constitutional changes were immediately followed by personnel changes which seemed to emphasize that Gorbachev was indeed moving away from the radicals towards a more conservative position. The relatively liberal Interior Minister, Vadim Bakatin, was replaced by Boris Pugo, a Communist Party official, and the First Deputy Interior Minister was to be General Boris Gromov. This reflected concern over growing disorder in the country and hostility towards the army in several republics. Most of Gorbachev's more radical advisers were replaced in January 1991. Several statements emerged from the army, the KGB and the leaders of the military–industrial complex which all expressed concern about the state of the country and their determination to prevent collapse. This was quickly followed by an appeal by fifty-three prominent public figures, including General Mikhail Moiseyev, armed forces Chief of Staff, senior Communist Party leaders and Patriarch Alexei demanding that Gorbachev take matters in hand if constitutional means failed to restore order. There was speculation about a declaration of a state of emergency or even a military coup, while at the December meeting of the CPD the Foreign Minister, Eduard Shevardnadze, resigned, protesting about the danger of the breakup of democratic processes and the imposition of a dictatorship.

Thus from November 1990 to the spring of 1991 Gorbachev had appeared to move decisively to the conservative side. His opinion poll approval rating went down to 10 per cent. Some felt he had been a Party bureaucrat all along, others that he had merely reverted to the traditional authoritarian behaviour of Russian and Soviet rulers, or was a hostage of the conservatives. Still others thought that the move to the right may have been tactical, if reprehensible. The conservatives were weaker in popular support than they claimed but the reality was that they controlled all of the main sources of power: the military, KGB, Party, industry and the mass media. Perhaps, faced with a collapsing country and the prospect that far-reaching reforms would cause social unrest, Gorbachev had to opt for stabilization and the support of the old establishment.

From Gorbachev's point of view, although he was under very heavy pressure from the conservatives, he was also failing to get constructive support from the disorganized radicals, who could not come up with a clear alternative programme. They had formed a number of groups – none of them nation-wide – mostly with vague programmes, while relations between the leaders of the groups were often quarrelsome. Where radicals gained power, as in Moscow and Leningrad, they were unable to make much impact on the chaotic property laws, the control of local markets by organized crime, and the deliberate sabotage of food distribution by Party-controlled farmers. Demonstrations of radical power had been patchy – in the Baltics and in the miners' strikes, for example. Shevardnadze stated bluntly that the democrats had always been too disorganized to give Gorbachev the support he needed. The radical Inter-regional Group of Deputies refused to form themselves into a party and were divided on political and economic issues. Some radicals also made sweeping attacks on Gorbachev. The death of Sakharov deprived them of their most distinguished leader and caused a severe loss of membership.

Gorbachev versus *Yeltsin*

Opposition from the republics was led by Yeltsin, in his capacity as Chairman of the Supreme Soviet of the Russian Federation, the most powerful republic. In fact, much of the response to the crisis in the Soviet Union could be understood as a power struggle between Gorbachev and Yeltsin and what they represented. The tension between them was heightened by the violence in Lithuania and Latvia during January 1991. Gorbachev offended many republic leaders by assuring them in the Federation Council, only a few days before it happened, that violence would not be used against the Lithuanians. Even more important, Yeltsin used the events as a major issue with which to attack Gorbachev and to express solidarity with the Baltic republics.

A publicity campaign against Yeltsin was in full swing in the early months of 1991 while he fought back with a television broadcast demanding the handing over of presidential power to the Federation Council. In another speech he argued that centralized power could not be reconciled with economic freedom. The Communist Party was showing signs of division. In the Russian CPD about 15 per cent of Party delegates supported a pro-Yeltsin reformist movement within the Party called 'Communists for Democracy'. It was led by an Afghanistan War veteran, Colonel Alexander Rutskoi, later to be Yeltsin's Russian Deputy President. He especially objected to the way in which decisions democratically taken by the soviets were openly wrecked or disregarded by Party officials in the regions and localities. At this time there seemed a possibility of radicals and reformist Communists uniting to form a centre-ground alternative to the Party.

The Povorot *(Reversal) in the Spring of 1991*

However, the conservatives were still putting pressure on Gorbachev, demanding a state of emergency, a ban on political parties, press censorship and even the resignations of both Gorbachev and Yeltsin.

Soyuz, the conservative group in the CPD, produced a declaration on a nation-wide 'third way' (between the Party and 'so-called left-wing democrats') based on 'all-Russian patriotism'. There was evidence that Soyuz did not have the extent of support that it claimed, and this may have caused Gorbachev to realize that he could safely make overtures to the radicals. By April it was clear Gorbachev and Yeltsin were prepared to move towards a compromise. In an unguarded moment Yeltsin had talked of a 'declaration of war' against Gorbachev (Rettie, 1991a). Now he was calling for round table talks involving the republics, the CPSU and other parties and movements. His position had grown stronger after the Russian Supreme Soviet gave him special powers and permission to hold a republic-wide presidential election. Gorbachev, on the other hand, needed to offer the country some positive political developments in the face of serious economic crisis and miners' strikes. On 24 April an event took place which indicated that a realignment of political forces had indeed taken place. *Pravda* published a 'Joint Declaration on Urgent Measures for the Stabilization of the Situation in the Country and for Overcoming the Crisis'. It was signed by Gorbachev and Yeltsin, together with the leaders of nine republics (not the Baltic republics, Georgia, Armenia or Moldavia). They admitted the gravity of the crisis, the need for co-operation to overcome it, and proposed a plan to begin the process. This included vague promises to improve the production and distribution of consumer goods. Equally vague was mention of a 'special work regime' in certain industries (that is, a ban on strikes) and a call for a ban on all acts of 'civil disobedience' – which some found rather sinister in view of the Stalinist past and the Soviet Union's very recently won rights of public meeting.

A significant passage stressed the need for greater independence and autonomy on the part of the republics. The republics which refused to sign the statement would be able 'independently' to decide whether or not they wanted to join the Union. Presidential elections were proposed in 1992 rather than 1995 as the existing constitution required. At the same time as this declaration was made, Gorbachev fended off strong attacks in the Party Central Committee and from Soyuz. He now appointed some radicals as his advisers and Yeltsin settled the miner's dispute (for the time being). Control of the Russian mines had been ceded to the Russian Federation. A month later it was announced that thirteen republics (remarkably excepting only Georgia and Estonia) had agreed to the 'special work regime' counterbalanced by incentives such as wage increases tied to higher productivity, and the right to sell part of their products on the open market. Simultaneously seven economists, led by the radical, Grigorii Yavlinsky, went to discuss an economic reform plan with economists at Harvard University in the United States.

Events Close in on Gorbachev

When Yeltsin was elected President of the Russian Federation on 12 June 1991 he demonstrated that power in the Soviet Union was now established on new foundations: on non-Party, republic-level popular election. Neither the Party nor the central government could find an effective candidate or muster much support against him. But his victory also illustrated the fragile nature of the new system, the lack of effective organization on which to base political power. In the summer of 1991 there was much talk of the need to form a nation-wide democratic party but such efforts failed, often because of differences over personalities. Some radical leaders, such as Landsbergis in Lithuania and Gamsakhurdia in Georgia, were accused of authoritarian tendencies, while Yeltsin was sometimes accused of being an irresponsible populist. In June a determined attempt was at last made to form such a party, backed by big names such as Shevardnadze and the mayors of Moscow and Leningrad. Gorbachev immediately gave his approval and perhaps thought it could give him the political strength further to marginalize the conservatives. However, events overtook this initiative.

In spite of his increased formal powers, Gorbachev had become weaker, seeing many of his decrees ignored and being unable to contain the forces he had unleashed. For example, the decrees for joint police –military controls in cities and the right of the KGB to enter businesses suspected of 'speculation' and inspect the books, appear soon to have lapsed. He was probably attempting a delicate balancing role, pushing reform forward step by step at a pace which would not provoke too strong an opposition from conservatives or a total loss of patience by radicals, but this could look like vacillation. The problem was that ever greater powers would be ineffective because either the administration was likely to block any significant initiatives or the essential channels of communication did not exist to ensure implementation of his decrees. In addition, the Supreme Soviet was not effectively controlled either by Party discipline or by practical working arrangements between assembly and executive. While he was accepted as the only possible president for the time being, the crisis over relations between the centre and the republics grew, and was not likely to be helped by the result of the national referendum on the Union which, while showing overall support, illustrated wide divergences between regions, republics, and urban and rural areas.

6

The Decline and Fall of the CPSU

The Party's Development

The official view of the Communist Party's role had been that it was the vanguard leadership in society's drive towards full Communism. It admitted no division of society into rulers and ruled: politics and government involved all the people. It decided questions of ideology and policy and considered itself sensitive to the opinions of the public and state institutions. In its relationship to the rest of society the Party was monopolistic, embracing all social and economic interests. But modifications in ideology, generational changes and factors such as the state of the economy, social developments and global politics, were fundamentally altering this relationship. As the Soviet economy developed, even before the extensive Gorbachev reforms, there had been a growth of special, influential interests in the Soviet Union and the CPSU had to take account of them. Repression was ruled out in a technologically sophisticated, industrialized society. Interests could have been allowed expression within the Party, or political structures could have been modified to allow the organization of some sort of Popular Front with the CPSU as leader. Contested elections had long been advocated by a few Soviet commentators, and this now seemed the inevitable course as the Gorbachev reforms developed, with the Party itself more and more being a party (albeit the major one) among other parties (Appendix A).

General Secretary Mikhail Gorbachev

With Gorbachev as Party Secretary a new and dramatic period in the history of the CPSU seemed at hand. He told an audience in Warsaw in July 1988 that he came late to the idea of political reform and it was only when his economic reforms began to slow down that he realized the need for them to be allied with political change. The record of his career suggests this is true. His generation understood that change was needed, but he came to power without a plan. Neither conservatives nor radicals were too sure about him. He seemed to be advocating democratic changes but at the same time insisting on one-party rule. He soon began substituting his own supporters for the former leaders – all this before consolidating his power at the regional and lower levels of the Party hierarchy (Teague, 1986). The Twenty-seventh Party Congress of 1986, fortuitously held a year after his election, confirmed Gorbachev's new appointments and heard of his intention to initiate reforms. Increasingly people saw the Party as the main obstacle to change, but Gorbachev's position was being challenged by alarmed conservatives who thought he threatened the 'socialist guarantees' of full employment, low prices and welfare benefits, while radicals were impatient at his hesitant moves towards a market economy and his retention of the Party's monopoly. Some thought he should transform the Party into a parliamentary party within a multi-party system before it was too late. Gorbachev considered this view unfair since, in his view, it was the Party, after all, which had started *perestroika*. But in reality, it was Gorbachev who had started *perestroika*, and the Party bureaucracy had only reluctantly followed him, even though he had much support among rank and file members.

The Nineteenth Special Party Conference

The Special Party Conference of 1988 was the first to be called since 1941 and was intended to give approval to the proposals for reforming the CPSU which Gorbachev had been so urgently advocating. Party *congresses* were called regularly every five years. A *conference*, on the other hand, was only called when the Party leadership deemed a situation to exist which justified it.[1] The failure of reform to make obvious progress, and the resistance of the Party bureaucracy were the reasons that made this conference necessary. In principle, it could take many vital decisions and some previous conferences had done so. The election of delegates to the conference was confused, as the method of election had not been laid down. Conservatives and progressives struggled for advantage. The conference itself was conducted with unprecedented freedom of speech and criticism. Among the resolutions eventually agreed were those to establish an executive style presidency, to limit Party executives to a five-year period of office, renewable once only (they would be also be appointed after contested elections), to enable members of the Central Committee to be replaced between congresses, and to reconstruct the organization of the Party so as to prevent it interfering in governmental and administrative areas beyond its responsibility or competence, ensuring greater real power to the popularly elected soviets.

Other resolutions welcomed the formation of new social groups in support of *perestroika*, but condemned 'any action aimed at destroying the socialist basis of society, inciting nationalism or racialism, or advocating war, violence or immorality'. Freedom of conscience, and the right to take part in decision-making were described as basic human rights. It was necessary to have an 'effective mechanism for free dialogue, criticism, self-criticism and self-control' (Steele, 1988). In his speech Gorbachev proposed basing legitimacy on the restoration of power to popularly elected soviets, but combined with the continued existence of the one-party Communist system. He wanted local Party secretaries to be chairpersons of the local soviet 'so as to give them authority'; this suggestion may have been a necessary concession to conservatives. It certainly was one that provoked vigorous criticism because some saw it as incompatible with the transfer of power from the Party to the soviets.

The Failure to Reform the Party

In the nation-wide elections for the CPD in March 1989 a large number of CPSU officials who stood as candidates were defeated. Nevertheless, a greater proportion of Party members stood for election than under the old quota system. In one sense, the elections legitimized open debate within the Party again. In another, they demonstrated that most people believed that the Party was still the most effective vehicle for reform. At this time many still felt it better to make the Party democratic from within rather than trying to develop alternative parties. It was also more realistic, given the strength of the conservative resistance within the Party's ranks. In April Gorbachev retired almost a quarter of the Central Committee, while promoting twenty-four of his supporters. The retiring members were largely 'dead souls' (that is, people who were members by virtue of high office previously but no longer held; they included eleven members of Brezhnev's Politburo). He spoke of 'a new type of working man' involved in all the economic and social processes 'so that he may feel like a human being' and criticized Party officials for failing to keep in touch with, and understand, the new mood in the country (Millinship, 1989).

By the end of 1989 the Party was experiencing the first signs of disintegration. At a Central Committee meeting in December Gorbachev reasserted the Party's leading role as a 'consolidating and uniting force'. He rejected the move to drop Article 6 of the Soviet Constitution, which guaranteed this role.[2] He was responding to the action of the Lithuanian Supreme Soviet which, a few days previously, had struck out a similar article from the republic's constitution, while the Lithuanian Communist Party was preparing to declare a breakaway from the CPSU. He said, 'We are duty bound not to cross the line beyond which the CPSU is threatened with destruction as a single political organization, and the vital consolidating force of the Soviet Union' (Cornwell, 1989).

Later, attempts by the Inter-regional Group to raise the question of Article 6 were defeated. Further difficulties arose, however, when the group threatened to set up an opposition party, 'a left-wing radical opposition to speed up *perestroika*'. Afanasyev, its leader, probably weakened his position by suggesting that it was time to consider a breakaway from the CPSU, of which most Inter-regional Group deputies were members. Such ideas were rejected because a majority thought that Gorbachev was already under heavy attack from conservatives (as had been evident in the Central Committee) and therefore should be supported even if he was not moving as fast as many wished. The bitter attack by conservatives on Gorbachev and the demands of the radicals indicated that the artificial unity which had stifled debate within the Party since Lenin's day had broken down. Different groups were now identifying themselves, demonstrating that the process of *glasnost* and open political activity could not be reversed.

A fall in Gorbachev's popularity among radicals began to show itself by the summer of 1989. His refusal to consider the abolition of Article 6 was unpopular and he was unwilling to formalize intra-Party democracy by recognizing the radical Inter-regional Group as an official lobby. Figes (1989) suggested that Gorbachev was like Stolypin, Prime Minister under Nicholas II, whose attempts to carry out reforms were doomed by lack of popular support. In Gorbachev's case much of this loss of popular support could be explained by his firm adherence to the leading role of the CPSU. Figes argued that Gorbachev should have split the Party and led the reforming wing. The left would have been more easily controlled and would have provided a base for building popular support. However, the reality was that ineffective organization and the vague policies of the radicals prevented Gorbachev identifying with them. The conservatives appeared to have no convincing leaders or alternative economic ideas, but there was clear evidence that they were able, behind the scenes, to water down or delay the government's economic reforms.

The Party Begins to Lose its Grip

Some members wanted the forthcoming Twenty-eighth Party Congress brought forward to a date even earlier than had already been decided (it was originally scheduled for 1991). The Central Committee meeting of February 1990 had previously been postponed, a sure sign of conflict. Rumours of a move against Gorbachev by senior ranking regional Party officials were heard. Certainly, these people seemed to be the core of resistance to him; they were afraid of suffering the same fate as the Eastern European Communist officials and for the same reasons: economic failure, resentment of privileges, collapse of belief in Communism. Unable to gain wide public support for their position, Communists hostile to reform thought of appealing to Russian nationalism and of forming an unholy alliance with those nostalgic for tsarist Russia. Therefore, the policy document to be submitted to the Party Congress was of great importance. It had to include more power for grass-roots Communists and less for fewer full-time Party officials, but without alienating them.

Gorbachev set two goals: the renewal of the Party not later than the Party Congress, now brought forward to July 1990 and an enhancement of the power of the soviets; he resurrected the revolutionary slogan: 'All power to the soviets'. The two aims seemed incompatible. Real power had to go either to the (albeit renewed and reformed) Communist Party or to the soviets and a system of political pluralism. This contradiction was at the root of Gorbachev's difficulties. In his various offices – Party Secretary, President, chair of the Defence Council – he had enormous theoretical power. In practice he was weak because he had no democratic mandate to take unpopular decisions. He was appointed Party General Secretary by the Politburo on a 5:4 vote (Gromyko broke the deadlock) and became president, not by popular vote, but by being elected in the Congress of People's Deputies. He had none of the authority which electoral victory brings, (unlike Boris Yeltsin with his 90 per cent of the Moscow vote in the March 1989 elections, and his popular election to the presidency of the Russian Federation in June 1991). He appeared to be hostage to the Politburo and Central Committee which installed him in office.

Gorbachev's long-awaited admission of the need for a pluralist party system was signalled in a new draft proposal entitled 'Towards Humane Democratic Socialism', prepared for the Central Committee meeting of February 1990; it called for a radical restructuring of the Party, which would no longer exercise any state or government powers. It would abandon its constitutional right to a monopoly on power and leave the door open for a multi-party system. This time Gorbachev told the Central Committee that the Party could no longer rely on a guaranteed leading role. If it was to have a leading role it would have to fight for it. In a radical departure from the Party's former position he said,

In a society undergoing renewal the Party can exist and play its role as vanguard only as a democratically recognized force. This means that its status should not be imposed through constitutional endorsement [a reference to Article 6 in the 1977 Constitution]. The Soviet Communist Party, it goes without saying, intends to fight for the status of being the party which rules. But it will do so strictly within the framework of the democratic process by giving up legal and political advantages, offering its programme and defending it in discussions, co-operating with other social and political forces, always working amidst the masses, living by their interests and their needs.

The extensive democratization currently under way in our society is being accompanied by mounting political pluralism. Various social and political organizations and movements are emerging. This process may lead at a certain stage to the establishment of parties. The Soviet Communist Party is prepared to act with due account for these new circumstances, co-operate and conduct a dialogue with all organizations that are committed to the Soviet constitution and the social system endorsed in that constitution. (Gorbachev, 1990)

He then went on to propose the modification of the principle of 'democratic centralism' under which Politburo decisions were binding on lower bodies, and which prevented open internal debate and grassroots initiative. He promised that Party branches would have the 'decisive role' in electing delegates to the Congress. But he did not make clear whether minorities within the Party would have the right to draw up their own platforms or whether 'factions' with their own rules, organizations and election manifestos would be ruled out.

Some saw Gorbachev's proposals as ambiguous. On the one hand there was the effort to create new pluralistic structures, but on the other there was a tendency to concentrate more power at the top, as in the proposal to create an executive presidency. A fierce debate, including criticism of the proposals, and of Gorbachev himself, followed. The Central Committee meeting was also marked by a huge unofficial demonstration outside the Kremlin walls in support of reform, which must have strengthened Gorbachev's hand. The march was organized by several progressive groups. Eventually, the Central Committee agreed to the creation of the executive presidency and to opening the Party to electoral competition. A law was drafted to lay down the rights and obligations of parties. The Politburo would continue to exist but only to deal with internal Party matters. The Central Committee also agreed to modify – not abolish – Article 6 of the Constitution. The revised Article 6 read,

The Communist Party of the Soviet Union participates in running the country and nominating candidates like other political and social movements. The Party does not claim full governmental authority. It aims to be a political leader but with no claim for any special position codified in the Constitution.

The main radical critic of these changes was Yeltsin, supported by many younger people and nationalists in the republics. He said,

The new draft platform does contain a number of progressive points. But the general impression is that it was written with two hands, the left and the right, both making a constant attempt to conciliate each other. (Rettie, 1990a)

On the conservative wing, the leading spokesman was Ligachev who articulated the feelings of the Party bureaucracy and many Russians. He claimed to be a supporter of *perestroika* but believed in Party unity, the unity of the Soviet Union and in socialism above all. He opposed talk of a federal Party, saying, 'The main dangers to *perestroika* and the Soviet Union are the powerful forces of a nationalist, separatist, and anti-Socialist tendency' (Rettie, 1990b).

Democratic Platform

Overall, the differing expressions of opinion, and the reference by the editor of *Pravda*, Ivan Frolov, to Gorbachev as 'the leader of the progressive forces in the Party' indicated that old ideas of monolithic Party unity were dead. The split developed further in March when *Pravda* published the programme of Democratic Platform (a radical ginger group within the Party) which demanded the renunciation of a single ideology, with Marxist works in future put 'alongside the entire treasure house of humanistic thought'. The Party should reject Communism as its goal. Instead, it should strive for a democratic society, becoming a parliamentary party among other parties based on principles of freedom, justice and solidarity. The group called for the Party to reject its monopoly on power by deed, not just by word, and start a dialogue with other progressive forces. It should give up democratic centralism and the principle of branches based on production units. The Politburo's response was to send an open letter to all members calling for an end to the forming of Party factions. It said it opposed Party splits and expected people who disagreed with the official line to resign. The letter particularly attacked Democratic Platform and its leading members were expelled. All this caused a furious reaction. Yeltsin demanded the formation of a new party in readiness for the failure of the forthcoming Congress to reform the Party. 'First the leadership calls on members to have an open discussion. Then when we have it they expel people from the Party', he said.

An open reply to the Politburo and Central Committee's letter, signed by Yeltsin and other deputies, commented,

The conservative part of the Party and state apparatus, which has brought the country to the edge of economic and political catastrophe, is making furious efforts on the eve of the Party Congress to bring about a coup against *perestroika* in the Party.

> We do not recognize the right of officials in the Party to impose their will on the rank and file. We appeal to Communists not to permit the persecution of Party dissidents and to divert the Party from the course towards democracy and renewal set out by Mr Gorbachev. We demand a Party-wide discussion on all the key issues of the country's development. (Steele, 1990b)

Many in the Democratic Platform now believed that the election of delegates to the Party Congress would be manipulated to prevent radicals getting a majority. Surveys showed that Democratic Platform had the support of up to 40 per cent of the Party members but would have only 2 per cent of the Congress delegates – about a hundred in all. A great debate occurred at their national conference over whether to leave the Party straight away or wait to see the results of the Party Congress. The purpose of waiting was to demonstrate to the public that the Party was beyond reform. It was assumed that many Democratic Platform supporters had left the Party already. In the event the conference decided to wait, but was generally pessimistic. Democratic Platform members would then consider forming a new party. Gorbachev found this perverse, which is why he wanted to expel them.

The Formation of a Russian Communist Party

There was a feeling among many that a renewed Communist Party must be Russian, because they felt that the Soviet Union was dead as a unified entity. The republics would either become independent or their political parties would want to operate within their own borders. Gorbachev had been hoping to stem the demands for a Russian Communist Party by maintaining the CPSU in being. He conceded that a conference should be held on the subject in June, although it was clear he was not in favour. Now he was faced with the threat that the conservatives might claim the title 'Leninist', while the Democratic Platform had the image 'democratic'. Conservatives did achieve the setting up of a Russian Communist Party (see pp. 180–2). They spoke the language of control – control over the criminal 'mafia', curbs on co-operatives, ceilings on prices, barriers against unemployment – without being clear how they would encourage growth. Their message of nostalgia and nationalism, and their appeals to order were bound to be attractive to many. The Democratic Platform issued a declaration that the setting up of a Russian Communist Party had 'ignored the real political situation in the country'.

The Twenty-eighth Party Congress

The Congress opened with the knowledge that it would be dominated by conservative Party officials. There was growing realization of the Congress's crucial role in deciding not only the future of the Party but also of *perestroika*. It was widely expected that the Party would split, with the Democratic Platform leaving, and possibly the centre and right dividing as well. The programme for the Congress provoked fierce debate, particularly over the phrase 'private property'. Conservatives were only willing to accept 'various forms of property'. At the same time the programme attacked the all-out free marketeers and those 'who want to transfer the bulk of public property into private hands, and who advocate the total commercialization of health and education'. Many members of the Politburo were given a rough time by delegates when forced to give individual accounts of their work. Gorbachev was overwhelmingly re-elected as General Secretary even though he had delivered a very strong attack on conservative thinking and 'those who came to this Congress hoping to take the Party back to the old conditions of commands and orders'. Although his speech won only lukewarm applause, he nevertheless demonstrated his political skills in retaining command of the Congress, in spite of strong opposition from right and left. He exploited the divisions on the left, and the lack of leadership and alternative policies on the right. The conservatives were shown to be without a viable alternative to Gorbachev or his policies. They could not face the internal political crisis or international repercussions of rejecting him.

In addition, Gorbachev achieved a rule change by which the Secretary would be elected by the Congress, and not by the Central Committee. This meant he could only be voted out by the Congress, and so could avoid the fate of Khrushchev who was dismissed by the Central Committee in 1964. A late challenge for the post of Deputy General Secretary from Ligachev, the leading conservative, failed when he obtained only 776 votes to Vladimir Ivashko's 3,109. Delegates appeared to realize that, although Ligachev had their support, the rank and file Party members in the country would resign in huge numbers if he was elected. The vote was a further victory for Gorbachev, in that it resulted in the election of his preferred candidate. Ivashko had been Ukrainian Party Secretary (replacing the hard-line Vladimir Shcherbitsky) until he became President of Ukraine a few weeks before his election as Party Deputy Secretary. However, a pointed comment was made on Ivashko's election by Mykhailo Horyn, leader of the Ukrainian nationalist movement, when he said 'Only a man who does not think about his future can abandon the post of President of a 52 million strong nation to become Deputy Secretary of a Party which is dying on its feet' (Millinship, 1990b).

Gorbachev's final speech was almost entirely an attack on the conservatives. He did not balance this by attacking the radicals. Rather, he appealed to them to join him in an alliance. Let there be no split, he said, 'among the democratic, progressive forces which are dedicated to carrying out transformations in society'. But this was not enough to persuade many radicals to remain in the Party. There was never much chance that the Congress would go far enough to satisfy them. One of the leaders of Democratic Platform, Vyacheslav Shostakovsky, announced the intention to split from the CPSU and form an 'independent, democratic, parliamentary party' (Steele, 1990f) while Yeltsin, Anatoly Sobchak (chairman of the Leningrad Soviet), and Gavriil Popov (chairman of the Moscow Soviet), resigned from the Party. This was the first split in the CPSU since that between Bolsheviks and Mensheviks in 1903.

Gorbachev foresaw some of this and created the executive presidency partly to have a power base if the CPSU were to be forced into a minority role. It was to be expected that he would devote most of his time to his presidential duties. He continued to be the Party leader and chaired the Politburo when it met – which had already become much less often than previously. It was now a Party Committee, not directly concerned with the state's policies. But the CPSU remained the most influential political body in the country. It had great power in the regions and in the military–industrial complex. It might have become a western-style parliamentary party, but to have moved too fast in that direction would have been to provoke massive and effective resistance from officials and hard-line members. On the other hand, many felt that the Party was becoming marginalized at an ever-increasing rate.

In June 1991 the former Foreign Minister, Eduard Shevardnadze, announced the formation of a new party of democratic reform to act 'in parallel' with the Communist Party. This led to attempts to discipline him by the Party's Central Control Commission. However, he declined to attend the disciplinary meeting and instead resigned from the Party. Whether this meant a new major split, with radicals leaving to support the new grouping, was uncertain. Further tensions were caused when Yeltsin banned Party organizations in Russian workplaces. Significantly. Gorbachev did not take any action against this move. In any case it was soon to be overtaken by events.

One of the final straws which caused conservatives to attempt a coup were the dramatic proposals in a new draft Party Programme presented by Gorbachev to the Central Committee in July. This in effect advocated the abandoning of Marxism-Leninism as the Party's platform and the dropping of its role as the party of the working class. Instead it would become a liberal, social democratic party. Although the programme was carefully worded so that almost anyone except hard-line Communists could have subscribed to it, the direction in which it was pointing was clear. The Party would have to accept the market economy, privatization and the competition of other parties. The Central Committee accepted that the programme would be discussed by a Party Congress in the autumn. This would have been a tense gathering and might well have resulted in further splits. The attempted coup meant that the Congress would never take place.

The End of the Communist Party of the Soviet Union

All the leading members of the abortive coup were prominent in the CPSU. Further, the Party Politburo did not denounce the coup until it was clear that it had failed. When he returned to Moscow after his temporary imprisonment, Gorbachev at first was unable to comprehend the extent to which the situation had changed. He defended the Party, and argued that it still had an important role to play. It was very soon brought home to him, both by politicians and advisers together with demonstrations in the streets, that the Party was finished; its opponents would not tolerate its influence any longer. As a result, Gorbachev resigned as Party Secretary. It was announced that the activities of the Party were suspended, and that its assets were to be transferred to temporary control of local authorities. Some officials committed suicide, most noticeably Nikolai Kruchina, chief of the Party's business management department. This preceded the revelations of the existence of large-scale secret Party funds and that the Party had transferred huge sums to bank accounts abroad.

In spite of such a dramatic collapse, it was clear that ex-Communists were still in, or had regained, power in Soviet Central Asia, Azerbaijan and elsewhere. Fears remained that Communists (even if now calling themselves by some other name) retained control in many towns and cities, as well as rural districts. Many officials remained in place, putting a brake on reforms either by their opposition or by ignorance of what was entailed. In November Yeltsin formally banned the Communist Party throughout the Russian Federation. This provoked protests from those who considered such a move undemocratic, and also from loyal Communists, who demonstrated in protest on 7 November when, in past times, the celebrations marking the anniversary of the October Revolution would have been held.

Conclusion

Since the start of the Gorbachev secretaryship the CPSU had undergone the most stormy period in its history since the Revolution. It lost its leading role and many of the regional and local secretaries felt betrayed by the centre. They were determined to hang on to their power and privileges. But the Party membership was split between conservatives and radicals and there was a real possibility that the radicals would decide to leave. The conservatives had been vociferous, but were weakened by their failure to find a leader to replace Gorbachev and their lack of convincing alternative policies, except a reversion to authoritarianism. The weakness of their support among the public and also among the Party rank and file had become evident.

It was uncertain whether the radicals could get their act together in order to provide a united and convincing national electoral alternative to the CPSU. Throughout 1991 they were leaving the Party in increasing numbers, while attempts were made to organize a democratic party for Communists. The new draft Party programme signalled a social democratic future with the abandonment of Marxism-Leninism. All these possibilities were brought to an abrupt termination by the failure of the coup attempt. Within a few days the Party had effectively ceased to exist as a political force, although ex-Communists remain influential or in control in many areas.

Notes

1   See Service, R. (1988) 'The history of the party conference', *Independent*, 24 June.
2   The constitutional basis of the CPSU's unchallenged rule was Article 6, one of the major innovations of the Brezhnev Constitution of 1977, which replaced the 1936 Stalin Constitution and formalized the leading role of the Communist Party in Soviet society. The 1936 Constitution referred to the Party as the 'leading core of all the organizations of the working people, both governmental and non-governmental'. Article 6 of the 1977 Constitution replaced this with a much more definite and wide-ranging definition:

> The CPSU is the leading and guiding force of Soviet society and the nucleus of its political system, of all state and public organizations . . . armed with Marxist-Leninist teaching, the Communist Party shall determine the general prospects of society's development and the line of the domestic and foreign policy of the USSR. (Roberts, 1990)

7

Political Action from the People

Introduction

Overt political action 'from the grass roots' was ruthlessly suppressed during Stalin's time. After his death, organized group activity up until the time of Gorbachev was very limited in scope but did exist. The most obvious politically significant points of pressure towards which groups had to direct their attentions if they were to have influence on policy decisions were the Communist Party leaders, appropriate Party divisions or government ministries, and the Supreme Soviet. Mostly people found indirect ways of expressing discontent, such as complaining about specific issues to imply a more general grievance, publishing unwelcome or controversial data, or writing and speaking in a 'coded' manner. The Soviet Union was *not* a pluralistic society, but a society of pluralistic-type interactions. Groups did not always succeed in gaining meaningful influence but the setting out of alternative solutions may have had some effect. Examples of group opposition to official proposals were sometimes evident (as in Khrushchev's educational reforms and anti-parasite laws). Direct access was not always necessary; informal contacts and the use of the mass media were widespread. It was often difficult for varieties of opinion to coalesce sufficiently for effective action. Wider and larger groups such as workers and peasants had very limited opportunities for expressing their views, although they could sometimes use existing organizations like trade unions. It is therefore better, for the pre-Gorbachev period, to look for the effect of 'group-type activities' within the context of specific policy issues rather than pressure groups as such. In the Soviet context there was conflict of attitudes rather than conflict of organized groups.

Gustafson (1981) has pointed out the difficulties of the post-Stalin leadership in building agreement without being able to use great public mobilization campaigns or terroristic fear. Khrushchev's old-style methods of exhortation and pressure gave way to a greater emphasis on persuasion, debate, alliances and the identification of parallel policy interests. For some years there had been a growing realization that discussion of the pros and cons of an issue (and not simply an expression of will based on the principles of Marxism-Leninism) was necessary for realistic decision-making. There were also officially sponsored public discussions (such as that on the new Soviet Constitution of 1977) which, before Gorbachev, tended to touch on relatively superficial issues or be merely a formal manifestation of support. Within the official establishment signs sometimes emerged of debates and campaigns. Gorbachev's style and technique, therefore, partly emerged from a slow but significant change in the methods of Soviet policy-making.

In any complex, industrialized society policy-making institutions need the expertise and co-operation of other institutions. In the Soviet Union these included the Academy of Sciences, research institutes and standing commissions of the Supreme Soviet. Particular needs and problems of the state may on occasion have enhanced the status and influence of certain groups of experts where their advice was urgently needed or had been proved correct. This happened, for example, in connection with the defection of workers from the 'virgin lands', the declining birth rate in European Russia, and planning problems. In return for their co-operation they could exact some return. Before Gorbachev, virtually everyone was employed by the state. Specialists depended on politicians for employment, access, funding, ability to publish and professional standing. Thus it was very difficult for experts to have independent leverage. Technical and environmental experts, combined with support in the ministries, made an influential interest, but they, in turn, needed active support from above if they were to influence policy significantly. The more committed the political leadership the more limited the scope for independent criticism. As the *political* stakes rose experts could not easily maintain their influence. Much activity intended to influence policy-makers was more the opportunity to obstruct than influence policy outcomes. In any case, the poor quality of the economic and social infrastructure meant that, even if they won the argument, the specialists (managers, inspectors and so on) often could not deliver because of delays, inadequate resources, and the overcentralization and bureaucracy of the system. This weakened their position.

Before Gorbachev the Party aimed to have virtually complete control over the organized activity of the country. The official justification for this was that it ensured that collective rather than particular or individual priorities and values prevailed, and that the country's resources and energies were properly channelled towards common objectives. In fact, total supervision was never achieved. There were dissident groups of various sorts with political aims at variance with those of the state and Party, and also people who wished to carry on some activity (as did unlicensed religious groups) seen as socially or morally debilitating by the authorities. Cultural activities also gave rise to non-political organized groups which met with official disapproval. At one time it was jazz that was frowned on. Later, when this had come to be tolerated, various forms of contemporary pop music were forbidden or life made difficult for their practitioners. The history of Soviet pop is a remarkable story of survival under cultural rather than directly political oppression (Troitsky, 1987). The basic difficulty for political leaders before Gorbachev was to reconcile increasing interaction and co-operation with the maintaining of control over a problem which increased dramatically in extent in the very different situation of the 1980s.

Glasnost: *Informal Groups and Open Politics*

Gorbachev recognized the necessity, in a democratic society, for there to be free and open discussion, as well as involvement in policy-making. He may have been surprised by the torrent of opinion unleashed. After a hesitant start, the expression and organization of opinion under the new circumstances of *glasnost* became unstoppable. Far from having developed uniform views in the Soviet period, people came to welcome the opportunity to express themselves openly on manifold topics, not all of them by any means political. The media joined in enthusiastically and, instead of merely stating the official line with nuances, took up the journalistically far more constructive task of giving expression to many alternative views. At first these 'informal' groups (that is, ones unlicensed by the authorities) caused concern but eventually it became clear that the Party could not realistically hope to regain control of the situation; too many groups were being organized all over the country. Many had political aspirations (incipient political parties, nationalist groups, and so on) but were sometimes very small in numbers and funding. The position was very fluid and flexible and was inevitably going to take some time to settle down (Tolz, 1987b). A situation soon arose in which the Party could not simply tolerate such groups, but had to consider 'co-operation, partnership or even formal agreements' as Alexei Masyagin wrote in *Pravda*. He was the Central Committee's adviser on the Party's personnel and development policy and a liberal. But at the same time Viktor Chebrikov, Politburo member and former KGB chief, denounced informal groups for claiming to support *perestroika* while really damaging it and opposing the Party. The main target of these strictures were the Popular Fronts in the Baltic republics, which were already starting to modify the country's political arrangements.

Some Examples of Pressure Group Activity

The Churches

Religious practice never died out in the Soviet Union even during the severe persecution of the Stalinist period. (Gorbachev himself was baptized in the 1930s.) After the Revolution Patriarch Tikhon excommunicated the Bolsheviks and was imprisoned. By 1927, however, agreement had been reached between the acting Patriarch, Sergei of Nizhni-Novgorod, and the Communist Party, maintaining a tradition of Church support for the state that had gone back centuries. Since then the Orthodox Church had actively supported the Party and was assumed to have links with the KGB, which was confirmed when the KGB archives were opened. Many found this objectionable, but others saw it as the only way for the Church to survive. Stalin used the Orthodox Church to stimulate patriotism during the Second World War, but a second attack took place under Khrushchev, involving the closure of many churches. A number of the hierarchy in office during the 1980s had been appointed in the Brezhnev period and, under the freedom of *glasnost*, were criticized for the inadequacy of their leadership.

Serious attempts to improve relations with the churches began, particularly from 1988, including the return of the Moscow patriarchate to Moscow from Zagorsk, and the handing back of Vilnius cathedral to the Roman Catholic Church in Lithuania. Churches were reopened and new ones began to be built. Clergymen appeared on television. They took their seats as deputies in the Soviets. They were gradually allowed to resume charitable work in prisons and hospitals. In April 1988 Gorbachev met the Russian Orthodox Patriarch in the Kremlin, the first meeting between the Party leader and the Patriarch since Stalin in 1945. In his statement Gorbachev said that the new laws on religion would reflect the interests of religious organizations, that is, not simply Party interests. The millenium of the Russian Orthodox Church was widely celebrated later in the year (Antic, 1988a, 1988b). In September 1990 the Supreme Soviet at last gave outline approval to the new law. It denied the government the right to propagate atheism or interfere with religious activities, and gave religious organizations the same access to the mass media as any other public body. Churches and other religious institutions would be allowed to own land. People studying for the priesthood were guaranteed the same right to defer military service as ordinary citizens. Conscripts would be able to attend services in their free time. The tax rate on enterprises connected with religious bodies was cut from 69 per cent to 35 per cent.

In spite of this religious revival, the Orthodox Church was faced with problems within the community of believers. The extreme anti-

Semitic Russian nationalists identified themselves with Russian Orthodoxy. Liberals criticized the hierarchy for being too cautious and
started their own publications, schools and charitable activities. The
Patriarch of Moscow criticized both clergy and laity who devoted more
time to politics than to spiritual matters. There was particular trouble
in Ukraine where the Ukrainian (Greek) Catholic Church, no longer
proscribed, was demanding the return of its property. In Ukraine, too,
there had been a revival of the Ukrainian Autocephalous Orthodox
Church, albeit not recognized by the Patriarch of Constantinople (the
titular head of Orthodox churches). The Orthodox have a long history
of schism and there were parishes which had declared their adherence
to the Russian Orthodox Church in exile (whose headquarters were in
North America). Since the 1920s also, there had survived the 'True
Orthodox Church' which went underground in protest at Patriarch
Sergei's agreement with the state in 1927. It, too, was re-emerging
(Ellis, 1991). The Orthodox Church was also concerned with revived
activities of the Roman Catholic Church and the Pope's attempts to
strengthen the Catholic Church in Russia and in other republics. In
1991 Pope John Paul II appointed six Catholic bishops to cover the
whole of Russia, including a bishop of Moscow. Thus an ironic consequence of *glasnost* was a deterioration in relations between the Orthodox and Catholic Churches. When the Pope then called a
conference on the role of the Church in the changed conditions of
Eastern Europe, the Orthodox refused to attend.

Russian Nationalists

Glasnost also enabled right-wing movements to organize and publicize
their views (Ostrow, 1991). The best known of these was the National-
Patriotic Front or Pamyat (Memory), ostensibly a coalition of six
organizations with varying aims including the preservation of historic
monuments. In reality all were fervent Russian nationalists and anti-
Semitic, arguing the need for a religious and spiritual revival. These
nationalists interpreted the Revolution xenophobically, seeing it as a
result of the secular spirit which had spread from the West since the
seventeenth century. From this secularization, they argued, had come
the idea that, by the application of scientific principles, a better type of
human being and a perfect society could be created. At a moment of
crisis, according to these nationalists, a small group of fanatical
Bolshevik intellectuals gained control and destroyed all the things
which enable human society to operate at all (law, tradition, private
property, the market). This fanaticism was something liberals could
not withstand.

Pamyat not only hold Jews responsible for the worst violence of the
Revolution but for the terror and misery which followed. The ruin of

Russia is blamed, not on Communism as such, but on a deliberate 'Zionist–Masonic conspiracy' whose perpetrators infiltrated the Communist Party. This conspiracy has infected Russia with a western or 'cosmopolitan' virus which is intended to destroy Russia by such means as alcoholism and AIDS. In January 1990 a group of about a hundred invaded a meeting of April, a new independent association of progressive writers, which included the poet Yevgenii Yevtushenko. The invaders shouted Russian nationalist and anti-Semitic slogans. The incident followed several weeks of tension after attempts were made to sack Anatolli Ananiev from the editorship of *Oktyabr*, a leading literary magazine and an organ of the Writers' Union. Some writers also claimed that Jews had taken control of Leningrad's main journal and demanded that they should be allowed to set up a new Leningrad branch which would be 'free of Jews'. Many other manifestations of anti-Semitism occurred, including the publication of an article, 'Russophobia' in the journal *Nash Sovremennik*, by Igor Shafarevich, a leading mathematician and member of the Academy of Sciences. Gorbachev rather belatedly spoke out against anti-Semitism in April, while in October a notable event occurred: Konstantin Smirnov-Ostashvili, a leader of Pamyat, was convicted of anti-Semitism and stirring up racial hatred. In the previous January it was he who had led those who broke up the meeting of the April group. He received a sentence of 'two years under intensified regime' and later committed suicide in prison. It was claimed that this was the first time that a state body had openly condemned anti-Semitism.

Towards the end of 1990 the growing concern over the state of the country, with a food crisis and increasingly assertive demands by nationalists, led to a *de facto* 'law and order' coalition being developed on the right. It included the army, the Soyuz group of deputies in the CPD and a self-styled 'centre bloc' claiming to represent some twenty parties and movements and which wanted a 'Committee of Public Safety'. It demanded a return to strong, central, authoritarian government. The most assertive of these groups was Soyuz, whose main spokesman was a Latvian deputy, Colonel Victor Alksnis. Backed by the well-organized and well-entrenched Communist Party, elements in the army, the military–industrial complex and the KGB, the group proved an influential political force, especially from the autumn of 1990 to the spring of 1991, when Gorbachev turned to them for political support.

The Trade Unions

Traditionally, Soviet trade unions were merely social organizations and more interested in co-operation with management than workers' rights.

But numerous strikes began to take place as the political and economic crisis deepened. In October 1990 the trade union movement took steps to reform itself. It abolished the old-style central council in favour of a looser, federal structure. Individual unions could now join a General Confederation of Trade Unions. The new chairman of the confederation was Vladimir Shcherbakov, who saw the need to defend workers' interests at a time when transition to the market economy was likely to cause widespread unemployment. Shortly afterwards the leaders of the military–industrial complex formed a National Association of State Enterprises in Industry, Construction, Transport and Communications, to strengthen their bargaining power. Their president called for a three-year strike ban, high taxes on co-operatives and a very cautious approach to denationalization, with collective forms of ownership preferred.

Of all Soviet workers, the miners had a distinctive tradition of independent attitudes, it being easier to assert a degree of independence beyond the Urals, far from Moscow. In the Kuzbass region, one of the main areas of the industrial unrest which arose in the late 1980s, they had been troublesome to the authorities before and after the Revolution. A special feature was that Lenin encouraged enthusiasts from Britain, the Netherlands and the United States to go to the area and create an industrial base. But they encountered increasing obstacles from suspicious Communist officials. After Lenin's death in 1926 Stalin dissolved the colony and arrested many of its members as 'foreign wreckers', but they left their own imprint of free thinking and modern methods on an already independent-minded population. The area experienced considerable industrial expansion as a result of the massive removal of heavy industry east of the Urals in the face of the German invasion during the Second World War. This created an area ideal for organized industrial dissent. The Kuzbass strike committees grew in influence after the strikes of 1989, eclipsing the local Communist Party and challenging the soviets. They were supported by radical elements in the local media (Rettie, 1991b).

Perhaps the most significant trade union development was the formation of a new miners' trade union at a delegate congress in the Ukrainian mining centre of Donetsk, at the end of October 1990. It was organized by committees outside the official union structure and resulted in agreement with the government over wages, conditions of work, supplies and the organization of industry. But soon some were denouncing the union. They felt that important elements of the agreement were not being implemented and that the union should have been restricted to underground workers, instead of including management and engineers who were seen as sympathetic to the government. Opponents perceived it to be the result of manipulation by political parties and a government which wished to weaken the miners by dividing them. The official union still controlled benefits and facilities such as holidays and social insurance. There were also complications over association with international trade union organizations which were divided into the pro-western Miners' International Federation and the left-wing International Miners' Organization.

Nevertheless, the new union decided to test its strength by organizing protest strikes for higher pay. These were at first one-day stoppages but after 1 March 1991 they escalated and spread to many mining districts, acquiring the political dimension which had been a feature of the strikes of 1989, with demands for the resignation of Gorbachev and more autonomy for the republics. Special hostility was directed towards the Communist Party. Offers of millions of roubles to improve miners' working and living conditions were rejected on the grounds that the government had not honoured its 1989 promises. The government accused radicals of stirring up the miners and Gorbachev refused to see them but they did meet Yeltsin and government ministers. The strikes were very serious for the Soviet economy because even a small reduction in coal production had a damaging effect throughout industry. Lengthy attempts to end the strike failed until control of the mines was transferred to the Russian Federation, and Yeltsin was able to reach agreement with them. However, he now had responsibility for keeping the agreement and avoiding confrontation in the future. This meant that the miners' opprobrium might become transferred from Gorbachev to Yeltsin. Meanwhile steps were taken to get the Soviet Union's Supreme Soviet to ban political strikes, although this would have been difficult to enforce. A decree of May 1991 did ban strikes in key economic sectors and introduced a number of production incentives.

The Beginnings of Party Politics

As the organization of some form of group politics began, there was confusion over terminology, especially over the expressions, 'left' and 'right'. The Communists called themselves, 'left' while their opponents call them 'right'. The anti-Communists avoided the term 'left' – considered to have been tainted by the Communists – and used the term 'democratic'. The traditional right and left designations also implied an ideological context which the radicals wished to remove from Soviet politics. Hence when Democratic Platform decided to form itself into a party it eventually settled on the name Republican Party of Russia, which linked it with the non-ideological politics of the United States. At first the question was how far democratic groups were prepared actively to support reform of the political system. There was no open disagreement on aims. The differences were largely between personalities in what were little more than political cliques. But as the move towards a pluralistic society in some form developed the question of what form of pluralism was desirable arose, involving such issues as social choices in a market environment, the degree of regulation of a market economy, the activity of government, the control of factories, the role of trade unions and the purpose and extent of social welfare.

The Soviet election campaign of March 1989 had given grass-roots discussion clubs the opportunity to mobilize around the attainable short-term goal of defeating unpopular Party officials. Radical efforts managed to achieve considerable success and they were encouraged to move on towards attempting to agree on new political programmes. Gradually, a left–right division along more familiar western lines could be discerned. The liberals advocated the establishment of a free market as quickly as possible, and Yeltsin, as well as the chairmen of the Moscow and Leningrad soviets, leant in this direction. Gorbachev's supporters preferred to call him a social democrat, and felt that collectivist ideas ran deep in Russian social thinking, stemming from memories of the Russian communal village. They wanted a democratization of political life, which had been stifled at birth when the Bolsheviks dissolved the Constituent Assembly, and a market economy. They feared that the development of a Soviet middle class, with the inevitable extension of social inequalities, would create a great deal of social tension.

On the conservative side were the Communist Party, including the bulk of the Russian Communist Party, led by Ivan Polozkov, the military–industrial complex, and some of the military and KGB, who wished to maintain much of the existing status quo, including maximum state ownership, the collective farms (even if unprofitable) and severe restrictions on co-operatives. But, as we have observed (see pp. 101–2) even inside the Party some radicals and progressives were thinking of demanding an end of the ban on organized groups with their own programmes, which was imposed by Lenin at the Tenth Party Congress in 1921. The reason for these moves was widespread disappointment at the outcome of the early sessions of the CPD and Supreme Soviet. These sessions were remarkable in their openness and frank comment, which contrasted so strikingly with the Supreme Soviet of the past. But radicals emphasized that the conservative majority retained control and that they felt it was with the support of Gorbachev. The Congress, they believed, performed three important positive functions. It was a 'school of democracy' for the whole nation. It exposed the various interest groups within the establishment. Finally, it showed that the existing leadership was bankrupt, having no concrete plan for solving the growing economic crisis. Their conclusion was that Gorbachev's 'revolution from above' had failed. There had to be alternative programmes, and alternative groups to put them forward, ready for the next CPD elections.

Political parties were beginning to be formally registered in 1990 but not all would survive by gaining public support and electoral success. The end of that year saw the entrenched conservative interests reasserting themselves. Radicals realized that they were disunited, disorganized and inexperienced in the ways of politics. There were calls for a more united opposition to Gorbachev and the Communist Party, as well as support for the striking miners. Early in 1991 Valentin Kuptsov, a Party Central Committee secretary, reported that there were more than 500 political parties in the Soviet Union, and twenty had a republic-wide membership. He said that the Communist Party was ready to work with any new party which did not reject socialism, but, at that time, the new parties had no programme except opposition to the Communist Party. The Republican Party was able to organize huge demonstrations in support of Yeltsin on the eve of the national referendum on the Union in March 1991. Among other groups or parties which emerged there were none covering all republics. They were small and had not yet been able to compete in elections to the CPD or Supreme Soviet. Until the collapse of the Soviet Union they were looking to the country and republic-wide elections, due in 1994 but thought likely to be held in 1992, following the signing of the new Union treaty.

The only radical group which had tried to combine several parties in a large coalition was Democratic Russia, which included the Democratic Party, the Social Democrats, the Republican Party and the Christian Democrats. However, it saw itself not as a party but as a loosely linked movement. Right up to the end of the Soviet Union, all attempts to organize an effective democratic grouping failed. In January 1991 forty-one parties met in conference at a Congress of Democratic Forces in Kharkov, but only twenty-one (some extremely small) agreed to the final statement. Much difficulty arose from the differing aspirations of the various republics. Some anti-Communist leaders, such as Landsbergis in Lithuania, were accused of authoritarian tendencies, while Gamsakhurdia in Georgia was seen by many as an autocrat. One of the last attempts to form an effective radical democratic party came from present or former Communists led by Eduard Shevardnadze and Alexander Yakovlev, the latter still an ally of Gorbachev's (see p. 104). However, many radicals criticized it for having too many former prominent Communists among its leaders. It intended to hold its inaugural conference in September when its future organization and policies were to be decided – but the coup intervened.

Conclusion

Although there was a great burgeoning of active groups in the atmosphere of *glasnost* they revealed both the difficulties of forming politically salient groups in the situation then prevailing, and also the high degree of ignorance of the practicalities of group politics within a democratic context. By the time of the breakup of the Soviet Union party and group politics was still in a formative stage, and its future uncertain in all of the fifteen new republics. Those in government did not always appreciate the role of opposition, or understand the right and necessity of criticizing a legitimately elected government.

Part III

Economic and International Disintegration

8

Economic Disaster

The Economy Before Gorbachev

The centralized Soviet economic planning system was created at the end of the 1920s and the beginning of the 1930s. Before that there had been no developed scheme for the functioning of a planned economy; there was little help from the writings of Marx. In addition, the regime faced the urgent but difficult task of introducing planning into a poorly developed country while attempting to reach a high level of military power in the shortest possible time. Stalin relied on the intuition of those assumed to have the knowledge of the ultimate interests of the working class – the Party. The five-year economic plans were based on information gathered from research institutes, surveys, Gosplan and the Council of Ministers. Getting supplies to the factories was frequently a major problem. Ways round it included the system known as *tolkach*: people were employed (usually illegally) to facilitate the supply of materials to a particular factory, building up reserves of scarce resources (which caused more shortages), and the creation of 'closed circuits' (the factory making its own supplies or bartering with other factories, and the black market).

The factory was preoccupied with fulfilling the plan. The management was answerable to the relevant ministry and to the Party in the area. From 1981 productivity governed the allocation of profit-sharing funds but management was frequently reluctant to take innovatory risks. The trade unions had not been involved in the fixing of wages, and strikes were forbidden before Gorbachev's time. (Strikes did sometimes occur, however.) Unions had only a limited concern with conditions of work. Their main functions included ensuring compliance with laws and regulations; arbitration in disputes with the management; running the social security system and cultural activities; and representing the workers in collective agreement negotiations, that is, 'production commitments' in return for social benefits and amenities. With *perestroika* official trade unions declined and independent trade unions began to be formed.

The Failure of the Command Economy

It was said that in this 'command economy' most of the commands were in effect given by their recipients, because it was the managers who knew best what their factories were capable of. Co-ordinating plans was steadily becoming too great a task. There was a serious over-commitment of resources to too many investment projects, resulting in long delays and conspicuous waste. Pressures from ministerial and regional interests had overridden criticism for many years. Cuts in the programme were never sufficient to bring supply into line with demand. The 'second' economy (that is, elements of private enterprise, often technically illegal) had some beneficial effects; it supplied certain needs efficiently, at a price. However, the 'second' economy also encouraged over-centralization and rigidity in the economy because it covered up the deficiencies of central planning; that is, it was a corrective mechanism for the planned economy and reduced incentives for reform. The large numbers of people involved were officially categorized as criminals.

After 1965 there had been a streamlining of the existing system with real but modest achievements. In 1973 production associations were created – a combination of enterprises – with greater flexibility in research, development and import–export decisions, but the basic structure of the system remained. Some improvements became evident in the 1980s. There was a wider application of well-tried techniques and an improvement in equipment and structures. These were forced on managers by a tightening of managerial discipline under Andropov. Gorbachev clearly intended to continue this (including the removal of ministers and top officials who were deemed unsatisfactory) and to accelerate technological progress. The trouble was that major reforms in, for example, communications and information, needed political and institutional rearrangements, changes in traditional attitudes and shifts in status among different forms of management – all very difficult. In the Soviet Union there were no reliable statistics, and few possessed management and accounting skills or truly understood market economics. Many came to regard a planned economy of the sophistication required in the contemporary world as impossible, even with the use of the most advanced computers. Anyone who did succeed in rising a little above the 'dulling egalitarianism' was subject to envy and resentment, as the hostility directed towards co-operatives established under Gorbachev illustrated (Yasmann, 1987). An example of the bizarre state of affairs which could arise when there was a severe shortage of goods and widespread food rationing was that people fell back on the extortionate prices of the black market (with its criminal associations) or the trade unions. The latter played a crucial role in distribution of goods. Often goods were only available at work via the trade union but, when demand exceeded supply, they had to resort to a lottery.

The 'Novosibirsk Paper'

In the summer of 1983 the 'Novosibirsk Paper' was leaked to western journalists, the first example to become public of an attempt to deal realistically with the Soviet Union's economic and social problems. The fact that it was prepared at all shows that realization of the extent of the Soviet Union's crisis, and the need for a new approach, was rapidly gaining ground among experts and some politicians. It was largely the work of Tatyana Zaslavskaia, one of a group of social scientists in the academic city of Novosibirsk. The paper tried to relate economic policy to the fundamental social problems which had been officially ignored. It was a frank discussion of Soviet economic weaknesses and emphasized the need for independent enterprises, realistic price policies, market relations and more progressive forms of salary.

Hesitations about radical reform were not just the result of ingrained vested interests. Under the old system enterprises were informed who their customers and suppliers were and, in principle, deliveries were compulsory, whether or not the fixed prices enabled a profit to be made. As the economy collapsed the element of compulsion no longer operated but had not been replaced by a proper market-based contract. The Party's control weakened, republics and regions started to go their own way, and barter became widespread. There was nervousness in the face of the unknown, lack of training and experience, poor flow of information, and weak grasp of the still ambiguous details of the new system intended to be based on market principles.

What Gorbachev Inherited

In January 1989 Gorbachev called the budget deficit 'our gravest legacy from the past' and indicated that stark economic choices had to be made to reduce allocations in areas not having a direct bearing on people's social needs. The deficit had been carefully concealed from the public. The Minister of Finance, Boris Gostev, put it at 36 billion roubles, but this did not take account of 63.4 billions borrowed from people's savings in the state banking system. Thus the budget deficit was not backed by goods but by printed banknotes or the money borrowed from personal savings. As long as the rouble was not convertible, the Soviet deficit did not have the significance for the global economy as did that of the United States. Making an issue of it was largely political, enabling Gorbachev to blame the Brezhnev era for the slowness of *perestroika*, and to put pressure on the big spending ministries to cut their budgets. The rouble inspired no confidence and the Soviet Union had lost its grip on the money supply. The Soviet authorities said that they wanted to introduce partial and, eventually, total convertibility of the rouble. But the task would be formidable, given that the rouble was not even convertible into goods domestically, as evidenced by the numerous discrepancies between relative prices within the country (Hanson, 1987). However, the new rouble exchange rate which came into effect on 1 January 1991 partially alleviated some immediate problems.

Early Changes Under Gorbachev

A crucial question for *perestroika* was the ownership of property. The abolition of private property was one of the most significant measures taken after the Revolution to eradicate exploitation, and its full-scale restoration would have been too much to accept for most people. Eighty-five per cent of property in the Soviet Union was owned by the state and the aim was to get this down to about 30 per cent (a process called 'destatization'). The intention of the 1990 Property Bill which came before the Supreme Soviet was to legalize various forms of ownership. The Deputy Prime Minister, Leonid Abalkin, said that the bill 'stands firm on the inadmissability' of exploitation. Society had a 'negative attitude to the term private property', he said. The main sticking point seemed to be the actual employment of one person by another. A heated debate took place on the meaning of 'socialist property', 'exploitation of man by man' and the 'alienation of the worker from the means of production' in the preamble to the bill. Some feared changes in the law would lead to these dangers occurring, while others argued that there had been no greater exploitation and alienation of workers than that achieved by state industry. In the end a compromise preamble stated that alienation and exploitation should not occur under any form of ownership, and the expression 'private property' was avoided in favour of 'individual property' and 'socialist property'.

Achieving economic efficiency was an enormous task and the situation was deteriorating. Statistics were unreliable, there were black markets alongside rationing, and criminal activity. There was a need for improvement in quality as well as growth, with only 18 per cent of Soviet production up to world standards. Attempts were made to hold down wage increases with high progressive taxes on collectives which awarded wages above the rate of productivity. Thus the new co-operative movement was burdened with high taxes and, consequently, unpopular high prices. Reform was also inhibited by a fear of insecurity and unemployment. The breakdown of the centralized supply and distribution system had created one of the biggest problems for *perestroika*. By the beginning of 1991, in an attempt to alleviate this situation, there were about a hundred commodity exchanges either in existence or announcing their formation. The main initial problem was to find sufficient goods to exchange. But at least it was a development with potential to grow into a market-based alternative to the state system.

In June 1987 a Law on State Enterprise was introduced with the intention of reducing bureaucratic interference and increasing managerial freedom. But as the law was coming into effect Gorbachev admitted on television that the great efforts of 1988 had failed to produce the results that were needed. A government report published at about the same time said that farms and factories were not producing goods fast enough to satisfy growing incomes, and much of what they did produce was still of low quality. This was a major cause of inflation. New technology was being introduced too slowly. The 1988 grain harvest was the worst for three years, 195 million tons compared with 211 tons in 1987. The shortfall meant heavy buying of grain in the United States and having to use hard currency reserves, making it harder to buy consumer goods. Rationing had to be introduced in several towns in central Russia. Food distribution and storage remained chaotically inefficient. According to a Central committee estimate 40 per cent of food produced was lost between production and reaching the shops.

Suggestions for Reform

A turning point in Gorbachev's realization that the reality of *perestroika* was very different from the speeches and theories came during a visit to Siberia in September 1988. A walkabout in the city of Krasnoyarsk turned into a nationally televised display of discontent. There were loud complaints about, among other things, housing, lack of food, the co-operatives and the endless Party meetings which produced nothing. Many thought that Gorbachev was attempting to graft the structure of capitalism on to a system which it was intended to keep socialist. The western view had always been that the Soviet Union would not achieve a real economic breakthrough unless it accepted the political consequences: that economic monopoly cannot be abolished unless political monopoly is also abolished. So far, Gorbachev had talked of market socialism and socialist pluralism but had not embraced a real change in the one-party system, although this was beginning to happen anyway. He relied on monitoring and feedback but he risked getting the worst of both worlds. Whatever remained of central planning (and it could be a great deal) and a partial market economy together could result in permanent tension, generating muddle and conflict. Some argued that this was happening already. For example, the offer of fifty-year leases to farm workers went part of the way to restoring the link between the peasant and the land broken by Stalin. But not many took up the offer because Gorbachev continued to give priority to collective farms and would not admit that they had been a failure. Similarly, the co-operatives were told that the government would do everything to promote them but, in the face of restrictions and hostile public opinion, their scope was limited and they were highly taxed. In any case, they flourished in service areas (such as restaurants) rather than industry.

The crisis continued to grow steadily throughout 1989 with considerable discussion among experts and advisers about what to do. Price increases were rejected as too risky politically. The need to reduce the budget deficit was recognized; it would be done by cuts in defence spending and prestige projects and by raising money with new and unconventional methods such as issuing loan certificates for special projects. Leonid Abalkin advocated an end to all subsidies to loss making industries, which he said would save 20 billion roubles a year. The firms, he said, should go out of business or be handed over to their workers or co-operatives. The problem of food shortage could be met by an increase of imports from the West.

Ryzhkov's First Economic Reform Plan

Nikolai Ryzhkov, the Prime Minister, presenting his first economic reform proposals in 1989, said that the government had rejected both the idea of going straight over to a market economy and a return to centralized control. Instead, it had decided on a policy which provided for a huge increase in the production of goods and services in 1990, followed by a (very slow) stage-by-stage introduction of 'market relationships'. It seems that considerable conservative pressure had been brought to bear on Gorbachev at a Central Committee meeting a few days previously when regional Party chiefs denounced his policies. The Abalkin proposals of a few weeks before had, therefore, been watered down. Instead, emergency measures were to be taken to reduce the budget deficit from the existing 10 per cent of gross national product to about 2–2.5 per cent. Inflation was to be brought under control and the external balance of trade corrected. The government also drafted a set of measures to restrain the growth of wages in order to reduce the demand for goods. Ryzhkov told the CPD that he was against freezing savings accounts or monetary reform of a kind to devalue the internal rouble and cut the value of individuals' savings. He also rejected rationing as a backward step. Critics felt it was difficult to see how any of the proposals could be achieved under the existing rigid system.

Gavriil Popov, editor of *Voprosy Ekonomiki,* said the government's programme was still based on central planning. Throwing money at economic problems through 'administrative socialism' from the centre had not worked since Khrushchev's time and would not work now. It seemed that they were trying to move towards a market economy by tightening administration. Nevertheless the CPD approved the Ryzhkov plan, most of its members being representatives of conservative Party and management interests.

Ryzhkov's Second Economic Reform Plan

Reports on the state of the Soviet economy in the first half of 1990 were gloomy. The only bright spots were the declining budget deficit and the prospects of a big grain harvest – except that transportation problems would severely hinder the gathering of the latter. The first meeting of the new Presidential Council was told that drastic action was needed and new proposals were being formulated. The Ryzhkov plan of 1989 was judged a failure. The difficulty was in bringing in painful reforms without causing major public unrest, and by a government without a popularly elected mandate. Opposition to reform came, not only from the bureaucracy, but from the trade unions who insisted on the right to work, the protection of the poorer sections of the community (the lower paid, war veterans, large families and students) and the preservation of the real value of wages.

When the new reform proposals were finally published in May 1990 the main difference between them and the proposals of December 1989 was the scale and speed of price rises envisaged. On average, Ryzhkov told the Supreme Soviet, food prices would double from January 1991. The price of bread, so cheap that farmers fed it to cattle, would double on 1 July. The cost of many services, including transport, would also increase sharply. The transition to a market economy would happen in stages. First would be the preparatory period until the end of 1990, with legislation passed to establish a 'regulated market economy', together with banking, credit, tax and financial reform. The second stage, beginning on 1 January 1991, would start with a drastic price reform, and a 15 per cent bonus to all wage earners by way of compensation. Ryzhkov said that present prices reflected neither the cost of production, nor the relationship between supply and demand. Nor were they in line with world prices. In the third stage, 1993–5, the economy would be 'de-monopolized': some 60 per cent of state enterprises would become joint stock companies in market competition.

The proposals met with a storm of criticism from politicians and the public. Reformers opposed them on the ground that they did not go far enough. Officials had said that there would be no 'shock therapy' but when the plan was finally unveiled it was described as 'shock but no therapy'. The proposals, by envisaging a move to a market economy step by step, were 'rather like changing from driving on the left to driving on the right by stages, starting with trucks' as one commentator said. News of impending price rises caused widespread panic buying in Moscow and other cities in May, requiring Gorbachev to go on television to appeal for calm. The Moscow authorities tried to stop people coming into the city to buy goods by announcing that shops would only serve those with residence permits. Other cities retaliated by stopping, or threatening to stop, supplies of goods to Moscow. The reality was that the Ryzhkov reforms were dead even before the Supreme Soviet rejected them, and even though the government announced the postponement of the proposed increase in the price of bread. It instructed the government to come up with an alternative programme by 1 September. Nevertheless, some progress towards a market economy was made. In June the Supreme Soviet voted to ask Gorbachev to issue a series of decrees from July which would put into effect anti-monopoly provisions and freedom to start small businesses, although the Supreme Soviet had not had a chance to debate the corresponding laws. These and other requests that he issue decrees on de-nationalizing and de-centralizing ownership, and setting up joint stock companies, amounted to a very considerable programme of privatization and went beyond the second Ryzhkov plan just rejected.

Fundamental Problems

Many pertinent questions were now being asked. Was there a consistent and workable set of reforms? Was there the political will, legitimacy and authority required to impose a necessarily painful and unpopular series of measures? Was a market economy incompatible with a dominant role for state ownership of the means of production? Should there be a capital market in which shares in companies might be freely bought and sold? Should private entrepreneurs be allowed to employ workers and, if so, up to what limits? Should a foreign currency market be established?

Gorbachev now understood that raising all prices by an average of 50 per cent but keeping them controlled was not the same as a free market. Even with wage and subsidy compensation, the price rises would have meant a 16 per cent cut in real living standards. So the next attempt at reform had to try to bring in the structure of capital and labour markets while stabilizing the budget and the money supply more gradually. The Soviet Union badly wanted foreign investment, for the expertise as much as the foreign currency. Yet only about 200 of the

1,700 joint ventures authorized were operating, and all on a small scale. In foreign exchange allocation, as in other sectors, central planning had broken down. Before western banks would lend money the Soviet Union needed expert advice on economic policy, land tenure, industrial management, company law and financial systems.

The '500-Day' Shatalin Plan and Ryzhkov's Third Economic Reform Plan

At the beginning of August a further attempt to devise an acceptable economic policy was made. Gorbachev and Yeltsin agreed to the setting up of a high-powered twelve-member commission. It was not clear how the new commission would integrate with Ryzhkov's third economic reform plan due in September, when the commission was also expected to report. There was no indication of co-operation between the two: the commission was to base its proposals on the Russian Federation's '500-day plan' (drawn up by Stanislav Shatalin and Grigorii Yavlinsky) while the government's plan aimed to stabilize and restructure the economy, rather than moving cautiously in stages as envisaged previously. In the middle of August both Yeltsin and Gorbachev cut short their holidays to return to Moscow where a crisis had arisen in the commission. Yeltsin suggested that work should stop on Ryzhkov's third attempt to produce a viable reform package as he saw it as unnecessary duplication. When the Supreme Soviet convened in the second week of September it found that there was as yet no agreed plan to consider. The situation became even more confused when the Russian Supreme Soviet decided it would adopt the radical Shatalin '500-day' plan anyway, while Ryzhkov's position was further undermined by Gorbachev indicating that he preferred the Shatalin plan.

As well as the rivalry between Gorbachev and Yeltsin, the role of Ryzhkov was significant. Much vilified by radicals, he was an important figure in the military–industrial complex, within which he had made his career. These huge defence and engineering plants were the ones most threatened by privatization and were closely linked to the government and Party bureaucracies. It appears that they were imposing a veto on significant reform and the refusal of Ryzhkov to heed radical demands to resign was connected with this. He brought 3,000 managers to the Kremlin for a conference in which Gorbachev was fiercely attacked. They argued that the reforms would cause economic chaos. The problem with the Ryzhkov plans was that they were perceived as too cautious and too centralized, this making them unacceptable to the republics. The Shatalin plan advocated a rapid transition to a market economy, and a very loose relationship between the centre and the republics, with the centre having a bare minimum of powers. Shatalin proposed a transition to a western-style market economy in 500 days, by the end of which only 30 per cent of state enterprises would remain in state hands (Shatalin, 1990). This was probably unrealistic in the circumstances of the Soviet Union, unfamiliar as it was with private ownership and the workings of the market. It would prove difficult, first, to dislodge the old bureaucracy which would try to take over the new privatized enterprises, and, second, to carry the general public's support in the face of an inevitable period of disruption. Previous fierce opposition to price rises and to co-operatives illustrated this.

The Gorbachev Compromise Plan

By the third week in September Gorbachev seemed to be backing away from the Shatalin plan. Further delays occurred in the Supreme Soviet, which appeared reluctant to come to a decision. This indecision indicated genuine disagreement and concern, a power struggle between individual politicians and between the centre and the republics, and conflicting opinions among the population. It may be that, by assuming wide presidential powers, Gorbachev hoped to impose far-reaching reform and to break the veto of the military–industrial complex. But events in the latter part of 1990 indicated that he was more likely to compromise and in fact wished to do so. In spite of his previously indicated support for the Shatalin plan, Gorbachev suddenly announced that he had rejected it. There was much speculation on why he did this. Pressure from hard-line vested interests, the divided organization and hence weak political 'clout' of the radicals, fear of popular unrest getting out of control, and a realization that the Shatalin plan devolved most power to the republics were all put forward as explanations.

Whatever the reasons, Gorbachev's compromise ('Basic Directions for the Stabilization of the National Economy and the Transfer to a Market Economy') was published in mid-October. He admitted that the country's economy was in a grave state of crisis and that a transfer to a market economy was essential. The reforms would be carried out in four stages with no time-scale indicated. The first would be 'stabilization of the national economy' especially the control of prices. The second stage would involve the privatization of small businesses and the establishment of a market infrastructure within 'severe financial restrictions and a flexible price system'. Third would be the establishment of the market, with a housing market and wage reform, including a minimum wage. The last stage would be 'the completion of the stabilization period' and include the limited convertibility of the rouble (Rettie, 1990e).

These proposals were far closer to the third Ryzhkov plan (although the republics got more say than Gorbachev wanted) than to the Shatalin plan and were immediately denounced by Yeltsin. The Shatalin plan was much more generous to the republics than 'Basic Directions'. In 'Basic Directions' the centre would have power to delegate authority over the economy to the republics, not vice versa, and the amount of authority left in central hands was greater. Nevertheless, the Supreme Soviet overwhelmingly backed 'Basic Directions', although it was from the start going to be jeopardized by the reluctance of the republics to adopt it and by the immediate economic and financial difficulties, such as the budget deficit whose extent was disputed but colossal. By November 'Basic Directions' was being attacked as inadequate in the West, and also by some Soviet economists, including Shatalin. They said that the plan was merely Ryzhkov's in disguise and, in addition, the Shatalin plan was also not being implemented in the Russian Federation in spite of a decision to do so. As a result of delays the republics were taking their own measures, which complicated national unity. The increasing economic difficulties were highlighted by the introduction of rationing in some cities, including Moscow and Leningrad. There were calls for Gorbachev to exercise his powers to take decisive action or resign. It became clear that the government seemed to have neither the will or the capacity to implement 'Basic Directions'. The Soviet Union appeared to be without agreed or viable policies to reform the rapidly collapsing economy.

The Crisis of the Planless Economy

A month later the government presented its proposed budget and forecasts for 1991. There was confusion because of the inability of the Finance Minister to provide complete budgetary figures for the whole country; Russia and the three Baltic republics had refused to take part in budget discussions. Billions of roubles had not been received because of refusals to pay contributions from Russia, Ukraine, the Baltic republics, Georgia and Moldavia. At the end of December the Russian Supreme Soviet voted to cut its contribution to the country's central budget by more than 80 per cent. The Soviet Finance Minister, Valentin Pavlov, said that since most of the central budget income came from the Russian Federation 'we cannot guarantee regular payments of salaries, pensions and allowances'. The CPD gave the republics two weeks to reach agreement, which they did after considerable difficulties and delays.

Ryzhkov was finally compelled to resign, after a heart attack. He was succeeded by Valentin Pavlov. Meanwhile, forecasts of impending economic catastrophe continued into 1991, with suggestions of hyperinflation and policies which would hinder aid and credits from the West. Actions designed to deal with problems sometimes seem ill thought out. An example was the withdrawal of fifty and one hundred rouble notes with only a few days for citizens to exchange them at the banks, up to a limit of a half their salary and to a maximum of 1,000 roubles. It was aimed at hitting black marketeers and speculators but ordinary citizens were at first badly affected by inconvenience and uncertainty. Potentially it gave the authorities the chance to conduct an instant audit of all enterprises, a step towards a better taxation system. Enterprises had to account for their funds before being repaid in new money.

Large price rises were announced for 2 April, but still fixed by the state rather than market based. This time the rises were handled more sensitively than in 1990. More warning was given and some compensatory rises in wages, tax allowances, pensions, student grants, and child benefits were effected in advance. In spite of all this, significant strikes and protest demonstrations took place, especially in Belorussia and in the mining industry. In any case, higher wages would increase production costs and inflation was likely to be the result. Only higher productivity could prevent this, but output fell by 4.5 per cent in the first two months of 1991. Among reasons intended to pass the blame for the increases from the government to others, Gorbachev said that some enterprises and local authorities were independently buying from suppliers at the best possible prices rather than going through the established state distribution channels. Instead of pointing out that this was the essence of a market system – supply, demand and a price contract – he condemned the practice as 'extremely negative'. In April Prime Minister Pavlov produced yet another draft programme to deal with the crisis. It consisted of stabilization measures and proposals for the transition to a market economy. It was almost immediately withdrawn for further consideration after most commentators found its proposals inadequate.

The Economy after the Coup

The failure of the coup attempt focused attention on the continuing economic problems of the Soviet Union. The changes instituted by Gorbachev were essentially marginal. Soviet enterprises had become responsible for their own accounts and for foreign trade – which enabled them to grasp the idea of profit – but the centralized system was still in place, plagued by supply shortages. The changes had been piecemeal and complicated by moves to acquires more power for the republics. Although attempts had been made to make enterprises more commercially conscious, it was only at the margins – in small businesses, crafts and private food markets – that privatization had occurred. The co-operative movement had established a food distribution system, but was often involved in crime and charged very high prices. It was not surprising that the virtues of the free market were not readily perceived by the average citizen. The positive side had been a willingness to learn on the part of some Soviet managers, often by means of joint ventures with foreign firms. Large-scale foreign investment, however, was unlikely until acceptable laws on foreign investment, property ownership and contract had been established.

After the attempted coup a team of economists, led by Grigorii Yavlinsky, worked on a new economic treaty. But it soon ran into difficulties as some republics announced unilateral measures. A tentative agreement was reached at the Alma-Ata conference in October when the republics recognized their economic interdependence and the need for agreement. They agreed on free trade between republics, a common currency and the raising of taxes by the republics, which would then contribute to central funds. They would also share the resources and responsibilities of the old Soviet Union. However, the reality was that some republics – Russia, Ukraine, Belorussia and Azerbaijan – were in a much stronger position than the others, and it seemed unlikely that they could continue to charge prices below the world level in the long run. Eventually, eight republics signed the economic treaty, with Ukraine, Azerbaijan, Moldova and Georgia postponing their adherence. The sticking point was the proposal for a common financial and monetary system. There was an additional hurdle and delay in the requirement that republic parliaments ratify the provisions before they took effect. In the event, the treaty was rendered ineffective by the collapse of the Soviet Union in December.

Russia Goes its Own Way

The reluctance of Ukraine and others to agree made Russia again threaten to take unilateral action. In the middle of November Yeltsin announced the suspension of all Soviet oil export licences to protect domestic supplies, and the taking over of responsibility for Soviet gold and diamonds, most of which were found on Russian territory. Next came a unilateral Russian take-over of exchange rates, the money supple and wages. Soon after this, Russia, Kazakhstan, Ukraine and Belorussia repudiated the Soviet Union's agreements with the International Monetary Fund and the World Bank. They said that they would take joint responsibility for paying the Soviet Union's foreign debt but would not accept any commitment contracted 'after the Soviet Union ceased to exist as a single state'. Eventually, eight republics (not including Ukraine) agreed with the Group of Seven (the most economically advanced countries) to guarantee the foreign debt. The terms, however, were harsh and many thought the West was missing a significant opportunity to exercise 'self-interested generosity'.

At the end of November Russia engineered a financial crisis for the Soviet government by denying a quorum to the Council of the Union so that it could not approve a huge additional credit from the state bank (Gosbank) to finance the government. Later, Russia took over the state bank and provided the credit, so underlining the increasing weakness of the central government. As the Soviet Union formally came to an end, to be replaced by the loose and fragile Commonwealth of Independent States, Russia announced that it would start freeing prices and wages at the end of the year. This was a very risky action which could have resulted in hyperinflation and chaos. Almost all the former Soviet Union's gold reserves had been used in debt servicing so there would be nothing to stop the total collapse of the rouble when it became convertible. The other successor republics were still economically very interdependent, with all their economic problems unresolved. Even those republics with potentially strong economies faced a long period of economic and political crisis.

9

From Superpower to Supplicant

Principles of Soviet Foreign Policy

For understanding global issues the Soviet Union used a different set of
concepts and parameters from the West, based on its ideological
premisses: military strength, superpower status, and global interests.
The concept of the *dialectic*, an assumption of continuous change
brought about by conflict, meant that the western goal of 'working
compromise' was rejected. The West worked towards some sort of
agreement. The Soviet Union aimed at a favourable deal as a stage
towards the attaining of further advantages; global compromise was not
seen as realistic. The Soviets also emphasized the importance of *initiative*, especially in a nuclear age. There was a need to avoid simply
reacting to the actions of others, although the Soviet Union did, in
practice, do just this and had a tendency to minimize risks and to back
down in crises. There had been various setbacks since the Second
World War such as failures in the Third World and the breakup of
Communist unity after the death of Stalin.

The Domestic Context

Soviet leaders gave priority to domestic over foreign affairs. Stability in
Soviet foreign policy depended on perceived national interest, the
priorities of ethnic groups, and interests such as the military–industrial
complex and the bureaucracy. Relevant matters included economic
resources and demographic features, and there was a heritage of historical, ideological and cultural factors, including Marxist-Leninist
doctrines, the influence of Stalin and the development of new (especially nuclear) technology. The influence of the increasingly discontented military and industrial lobbies was undoubtedly important.
These were not pressure groups in the western sense but acted by
means of personalities, mutual obligations and loyalties. They had a

tendency to react to western actions or attitudes in order to enhance their domestic position. The failure of the economy weakened the Soviet Union's position in world markets and its ability to keep up with advanced technology. In addition, nationalist demands undermined the central government and attracted growing attention from other countries concerned about fellow nationals or co-religionists, or eager to take advantage of the Soviet Union's difficulties. Soviet domestic backwardness was increasingly causing pressure for more interaction between the Soviet Union and the 'developed' West. Improved contact with the outside world was often a way of postponing unpalatable political and social reform at home. The Soviet Union was torn between preserving the status quo and adapting to a changing world, both of which meant internal and external insecurity. These matters, as much if not more than, the policies of the West, decided the Soviet Union's relations with the rest of the world.

Foreign Policy Before Gorbachev

A new Soviet peace campaign in the early 1980s was part of a long-term offensive strategy but was also intended to consolidate gains made. The Soviet Union was still active in the Third World but had inadequate resources, so that involvement had to be low key. It offered military aid to Third World states and former western colonies to increase its own influence or at least prevent them from identifying with the West. The policy depended on helping clients maintain one-party states, after they had been established, through assistance in political and secret police techniques, arms sales, military training, and economic aid. These regimes were often brutal and artificial. The Soviet Union also tried to establish its influence through Communist or sympathetic client states such as Cuba, Nicaragua, Ethiopia, Angola, Mozambique, Afghanistan and Yemen. The intervention in Afghanistan, in order to sustain the Communist regime there, raised old fears in the West of Soviet expansionism. But only in Vietnam was there a significant Soviet input to help overthrow the previous regime. The more its military help increased the more its political influence declined. It was never able to give much economic aid.

Another group of allies was built out of various countries who were anti-American. The Middle East countries, who were anti-American because of American backing for Israel, came to be supported by the Soviet Union, even though they were often also anti-Communist. Eight of the ten biggest recipients of Soviet investment were in the Middle East, including Turkey, a member of NATO. The Soviet Union also tried to increase Soviet influence and security by a buffer of Communist states in Eastern Europe, linked by the military alliance of the Warsaw Pact. The aim was to maintain tight control over Eastern Europe while extending influence in Western Europe. It involved questions such as whether to woo West Germany or to isolate her, and whether to play off Western Europe against the United States and try to dominate the entire European continent.

Gorbachev Rethinks Foreign Policy

Under Gorbachev these policies were reviewed and perceived to be morally suspect and short-sighted, disastrous both to the countries concerned and to the Soviet Union. Eduard Shevardnadze, Gorbachev's Foreign Minister, said, 'It is time to realize that neither socialism, nor friendship, nor good neighbourliness, nor respect can be respect can be produced by bayonets, tanks or blood' (Shevardnadze, 1990). He argued that recognition of national sovereignty and non-intervention were principles not to be broken either in Eastern Europe or elsewhere. The Soviet Union's policy in the Third World was transformed. Almost the only Soviet commitments that remained were Cuba and Nicaragua, and in both these cases the level of engagement was much scaled down. The vital impulse to such changes was that the Soviet Union had realized that its long isolation from the rest of the world was a major cause of its present crisis. Shevardnadze indicated that refusal to look at the world objectively had led Moscow to ignore the revolution in science and technology and its impact on the world economy. It similarly failed to see the foolishness of basing its foreign trade on exports of oil and gas instead of producing manufacturing goods to sell on the world market. This blindness, he said, contributed to vast material investments in hopeless foreign policy projects.

Shevardnadze used the jargon of the past to demolish the foundations of traditional Soviet strategy. 'Peaceful coexistence', he told his Foreign Ministry, should no longer be understood as 'a special form of the class struggle . . . the struggle between two opposing systems is no longer a determining tendency of the present era' (Frankland, 1989). This meant that the Soviet Union should not see itself as pitted militarily, economically and ideologically against much of the rest of the world. Instead, there had to be strong diplomatic efforts to improve relations with many countries, including China, Japan and Israel. But disagreements continued within the Soviet leadership. Yegor Ligachev quickly contradicted Shevardnadze. International relations, he said, were 'particularly class in nature . . . any other way of putting this matter introduces confusion into the consciousness of our people and our friends abroad' (Frankland, 1989).

Europe

In a speech to the Council of Europe in July 1989 Gorbachev outlined his European policy. It was based on political reality and a doctrine of restraint, and targeted on the creation of a 'vast economic space from the Atlantic to the Urals'. He wanted to define the goals clearly enough to avoid chaos and to narrow the East–West economic gap. This required reconciling western interests with the Soviet Union's own. He emphasized that the West had to accept that the states of Europe belonged to different systems. But he insisted on 'the sovereign right of each people to choose their own social system at their own discretion' and said he envisaged 'a change in the social and political order in some countries'. East European states soon took him at his word and ended Communist control. Without Soviet support they were unable to prevent non-Communists (or reformist Communists) from taking power in the latter part of 1989 and into 1990. They had economies in varying stages of decline, in spite of cheap supplies of Soviet fuel and raw material. Comecon, the Soviet bloc common market, was in danger of impoverishing them all and could not remain as it was. The Soviet Union's good relations with Finland were now pointed to as a model of what the Soviet Union's attitude to its neighbours should be. (A new treaty was signed with Finland.) However, some felt that the Soviet Union's influence on Finland had been considerable and that the Eastern European countries were still heavily dependent on the Soviet Union for trade, including vital basic products such as oil. Some or all Eastern European countries might want to join the European Community at some time in the future, while events had created the need for some new all-European security agreement. Gorbachev was setting the tone for this by using such expressions as 'our common European home'.

The most significant development was the reunification of Germany. In a speech to the European Parliament in December, Shevardnadze outlined the Soviet position. He supported self-determination without interference from outside, and asked everyone to consider the security implications. The question of the existing European borders was also an important issue. The interests of other European states were vital in deciding the German unity issue, not least those of the Soviet Union, which had lost 20 million lives in the Second World War. On each of his visits to Western Europe Gorbachev insisted that there was no design to decouple Western Europe from NATO or detach West Germany from its western alliance. He made it clear that, while security issues had priority, he recognized that, for the Soviet Union, economic relations in Europe were equally important. He needed western capital and urged western businesses to take a more long-term view of investment in the Soviet Union.

Relations with Other Countries

A series of talks took place at the end of 1990 with a view to restoring diplomatic relations with Israel. These continued through 1991 with Alexander Bessmertnykh (Shevardnadze's successor) paying the first visit to Israel of a Soviet foreign minister since independence forty-three years before. Relations with Israel were closely related to the questions of emigration of Jews from the Soviet Union and the joint sponsoring, with the United States, of a Middle East peace conference. In Asia diplomatic relations were established with South Korea but there were continuing difficulties with Japan over the Kuril Islands (known in Japan as the Northern Territories). They had been taken from Japan after the Second World War and Japan was not prepared to sign a peace treaty or extend aid to the Soviet Union until they were handed back. The problem was not resolved by a visit by Gorbachev to Japan in April 1991.

The arrival of George Bush as United States President might have heralded a more pragmatic and cautious approach to Gorbachev as his domestic policies ran into difficulties. There were elements in Washington who did not regard Gorbachev as a good risk. Central Intelligence Agency (CIA) personnel and defence experts were often reluctant to admit that the Soviet Union could change significantly. The Pentagon did not want to hear that the Soviet military threat was lessened, entailing that the United States military budget could justifiably be cut. But undoubtedly a great rethinking of United States policy was necessary. For the sceptics Gorbachev's peace initiative was seen as a way of sowing discord among the members of the western alliance. The United states felt that Western Europe was too sympathetic to Gorbachev's Soviet Union compared with the caution of Japan, and compared with the fact that China only agreed to a conference after its three conditions of troop withdrawals from Afghanistan, Kampuchea and the Mongolian border were met. The United States preferred the Chinese approach to that of many West European politicians. Behind these suspicions was Robert Gates, formerly Deputy Director of the CIA, and then deputy at the National Security Council. His CIA internal survey of Gorbachev's position concluded pessimistically in the autumn of 1988 that Gorbachev was locked in a paradox: the more his reforms progressed, the more they destabilized the system and encouraged vested interests to stop the reforms to preserve their position.

Although President Bush did not write off Gorbachev, he was worried about the destabilizing trends and the possibility that Gorbachev or a successor could halt or reverse *perestroika*. He was concerned that Gorbachev and his two former closest Politburo allies, Alexander Yakovlev, head of the Central Committee's International Department, and Eduard Shevardnadze, the Foreign Minister, were preoccupied with foreign policy, while domestic affairs such as law reform, agriculture and ideology were run by conservative figures. As a precaution Bush cultivated direct contacts with the heads of the separate republics, a move Gorbachev did not approve of. Shevardnadze dramatically resigned on 20 December 1990, making it clear that he felt conservative critics were undermining foreign as well as domestic policy. In later speeches and interviews he said that he was criticized for almost every aspect of the new Soviet policies: disarmament without any real concessions to compensate for it from the West, German reunification, the ending of Communist governments in Eastern Europe and the collapse of the Warsaw Pact. He was accused, he said, of putting humanistic values before Marxist-Leninist class values and the national interest. He felt that he was not defended by Gorbachev or others and warned that an attempt by conservatives to halt these changes was likely, even to the extent of imposing a dictatorship.

The Gulf War

The months leading to the invasion of Kuwait by Iraq and the outbreak of the Gulf war in January 1991 saw constant efforts by the Soviet Union to obtain a peaceful settlement and growing concern about United States policy. The use of force would, in the view of the Soviet government, throw the Arab world into confusion and push the Soviet Union into a position where it would have to choose between a new *entente* with the United States and its traditional links with the Arabs. Force could only be acceptable if under a United Nations mandate. The Soviet military were afraid that United States troops would remain in Saudi Arabia after a Gulf war. There was a significant difference of emphasis between the Defence and Foreign Ministries, the former being more alarmist and anti-American. Soviet attempts to avoid a military conflict went on up to the outbreak of war, and diplomatic activity continued afterwards. On the Iraqi invasion of Kuwait the Soviet Union fully supported United Nations Security Council resolutions in spite of its previous close relations with Iraq. But it wanted Iraq's withdrawal by peaceful means, while accepting that force might be necessary. After leaving Afghanistan there was no support among the Soviet public for further military action involving the Soviet army. The Soviet military were also unhappy about endangering years of close co-operation with Iraq, and so the sending of Soviet troops to the Gulf was not possible.

The Council for Mutual Economic Assistance (Comecon)

Comecon (or CMEA) was the Soviet Union's response in 1949 to the West's Marshall Plan (economic and financial aid for recovery after the

Second World War from the United States to Western Europe). It demonstrated the economic subordination of Eastern Europe to the Soviet Union (as well as Mongolia, Cuba and Vietnam, while Yugoslavia and Nicaragua had special status). At first, after replacing their Communist regimes, the Eastern European countries said that they were willing to remain in the Warsaw Pact, but they reserved their position on Comecon. The Soviet Union was anxious to preserve both organizations. At the end of 1989 Gorbachev told the Central Committee that the Pact 'retained its value for all members' and that Comecon was needed to 'integrate the economies of our countries into an all-European and world structure'. However, in 1989 the summit conference and meeting of prime ministers were not held. Lower-level meetings of Communist Party secretaries responsible for economic affairs took place but then even they no longer existed as a group. At the same time the European Community began to offer more attractive bilateral concessions, acting for twenty-four western powers. A number of Eastern European countries, including the Soviet Union, signed up.

At the second meeting of the Congress of People's Deputies, Prime Minister Ryzhkov talked of 'the creation of a single market among Comecon member countries', but conceded that exchanges would have to be at current world prices and in freely convertible currency (dollars). A blueprint for reform was available for the Comecon meeting which finally took place in January 1990 but there seemed little agreement on reform or whether Comecon should not be replaced by a new and more realistic organization. Several delegations called for an end to central control over the industries of member states, for market based pricing and for trade to be in convertible currency instead of the existing barter arrangements. But they differed greatly over the timetable for these moves. Many members wanted to withdraw from some Comecon trading agreements – and, indeed, these had already been breached by some countries. The end for Comecon came in January 1991 when the organization finally decided to dissolve itself after forty years, and voted to set up a new body – the Organization for International Economic Cooperation (OIEC) – to promote the integration of the former Comecon economies into the world economic system, while exploiting the economic links between member countries. In future they would trade in dollars rather than roubles. Instead of co-ordinating central plans of member states as previously, the new body would build up market based links between firms across the region in an advisory rather than a prescriptive capacity. The transition was likely to be protracted and close links would be maintained with the Soviet Union, upon which they were heavily dependent for raw materials. The setting up of OIEC proved difficult. Disagreements over the free market arose between Poland, Czechoslovakia and Hungary (in favour) and Mongolia, Cuba and Vietnam (against). There were also clear differences between the Soviet Union and the Eastern European countries, several of the latter being more interested in joining the European Community in the long term.

The European Bank for Reconstruction and Development (EBRD)

The reluctance of western banks to grant credit to the Soviet Union in its existing parlous state was reflected in figures which showed that the commercial banks lent $8 billion in net credit in 1989, but withdrew $12 billion in 1990. Enterprises were hardly encouraged to indulge in foreign trade by the further fact that the Soviet government confiscated nearly all exporters' foreign exchange earnings. Worries about the growing need of the Soviet economy for western aid caused difficulties in setting up the European Bank for Reconstruction and Development, whose main aim was to promote economic recovery in Eastern Europe. Although there was agreement that the Soviet Union should be a shareholder in the bank, European governments could not agree on how much it should be allowed to borrow, although the NATO meeting in March concluded that the West might be forced to give massive aid to prevent the Soviet economy from collapsing.

Starting with a modest 10 billion ecus (£7 billion sterling) the bank intended to help finance the rebuilding of Eastern Europe's infrastructure. Its consultants would advise on the reform of banking, accounting and legal services. The differences between western and eastern legal and banking systems had proved major obstacles to joint ventures. The EBRD would offer merchant banking and development banking services, working together with the World Bank and the International Monetary Fund, and would aim to take a more long-term view than other lenders. It would be particularly concerned with promoting better environmental standards (among other projects, it was soon engaged on one to clean up the Baltic Sea) but it realized that quick, dramatic results could not be achieved. Improvements in living standards would only be seen in the long term.

The chairman of the Soviet central bank (Gosbank), Victor Gerashchenko, told the EBRD that he would like a new internationally backed Soviet bank to be set up to finance efficient public sector projects and seek out profitable exporting companies, or those capable of replacing imports, that were suitable for privatization. But he also complained that the Soviet Union was not being permitted to borrow more from the EBRD over the next three years than the value of its paid-in capital ($200 million). There was a hint of tension over the EBRD's role, with the United States Secretary to the Treasury emphasizing that 'free market and democratic principles are enshrined in its articles' while Geraschenko remarked that the biggest obstacle to developing a Soviet free market was 'political and economic separatism'.

Western Aid to the Former Soviet Republics

Further aid to the Soviet Union was proposed by West Germany and France, but the United States and Great Britain felt that it should not be given until there was clear evidence of economic reform and reliable information as to where the money could most effectively be directed. In June 1990 Gorbachev wrote letters to Chancellor Kohl of West Germany and the President of the European Commission, Jacques Delors, implying that aid would be welcome. This was discussed at the European Community meeting in Dublin and the meeting of the Group of Seven leading industrial countries (G7) in Houston, Texas, immediately following. It was agreed to make a thorough investigation of the Soviet economy and reform plans before deciding on what aid would be appropriate.

In July 1990, Jacques Delors, visited Moscow to discuss an agreement on trade and co-operation and economic aid to the Soviet Union. The aid was envisaged to be in the range of the $15–20 billion regarded as essential by Soviet leaders. Shevardnadze also made it clear that the Soviet Union wanted full membership of the International Monetary Fund although this would almost certainly result in harsh conditions being imposed. It would, however, contribute to the integration of the Soviet economy into the world economy. The future of western aid to the Soviet Union was again complicated early in 1991 by the use of Soviet troops against the citizens in the Baltic republics.

The 'Grand Bargain'

As the G7 summit (which Gorbachev was to attend) approached a comprehensive plan for massive aid to the Soviet Union was developed unofficially between Soviet economists such as Yavlinsky and United States economists based at Harvard University. It became known as the 'Grand Bargain' and envisaged the West backing political and economic reform in the Soviet Union with a $150 billion aid package over five years. It would start with the signing of a new Union treaty and then an inter-republic economic treaty to establish a common currency, sharing of foreign debt and the restructuring of businesses. There would be an inter-republic economic council, privatization and price liberalization, together with associate membership of the International Monetary Fund and World Bank. Large amounts of foreign technical aid and investment were envisaged. But many questions remained, such as: how much aid was required; how should the aid commitment be shared out among western countries; should it be linked to other issues, such as the resolution of the Kuril Islands dispute with Japan; and, last but not least, was the capital available on the scale envisaged in the face of the West's own economic difficulties? Competing demands of debtor countries such as those of Latin America who were co-operating with IMF and World Bank adjustment plans, not to speak of the urgent needs of the poorest countries, also had to be considered. Many felt that it was more realistic to use the IMF and World Bank for the gradual integration of the Soviet Union into the world economy. The United States clearly preferred this option and rejected the massive aid envisaged in the 'Grand Bargain'.

The Group of Seven Summit and the Yavlinsky–Primakov Plan

Gorbachev decided to focus his campaign for western aid on the G7 meeting in London in July 1991. He set out his proposals in a plan devised by two of his economic advisers, Grigorii Yavlinsky and Yevgenii Primakov. In their letter to the G7 leaders they outlined the difficulties which the Soviet economy faced within the context of the transition from authoritarianism to democracy, and the nationalities problem. They pointed out that there had been a collapse of the Soviet monetary system, as well as its consumer and capital markets. There was a crisis of management with no clear decision-making structure. A straightforward 'path to economic reform throughout the entire economy' was needed, and there were signs that the republics were moving towards this with their agreement of April 1991 (see p. 92). However, the necessary far-reaching reforms would inevitably create tensions, with major risks for the Soviet Union and the entire world. Meanwhile, the Soviet Union had suffered a serious decline of production and was in danger of hyperinflation. Poverty was increasing and the country was having growing difficulty in paying for imports. The collapse of the Soviet Union would create serious geopolitical problems and raise grave issues regarding its large nuclear potential.

The proposals aimed at making the rouble convertible, encouraging direct foreign investment and the conversion of defence industries to consumer goods production. The main priorities were relief on the foreign debt and a stabilization fund for the rouble. Gorbachev did not specifically ask for financial aid. There was a firm commitment to democratization and human rights in the context of the new Union treaty then being negotiated. Yavlinsky and Primakov wanted the drafting of a plan to enable effective interaction between reformist forces in the Soviet Union and G7 countries. This would be initiated in the

Soviet Union but would involve G7 experts in its final stages. Once the G7 countries had examined this plan they should prepare a parallel plan of action to formulate the scale, time limits, and forms of their economic assistance. The letter continued by listing the conditions and factors which the G7 plan might take into account and pointed to the London summit as an opportunity to reach agreement and sustain the momentum of reform.

The G7 remained sceptical, and made no commitment to substantial financial aid. The talk was more of membership of the IMF and World Bank, and of the granting of Most Favoured Nation trading status by the United States. However, they agreed to keep in close contact with Moscow and to monitor developments. The most sceptical nations were Japan, the United States, and Britain, while Germany was the most in favour. In October, the Soviet Union was granted associate membership of the IMF. In spite of serious differences, the aid proposed by the United States and the European Community was modest, and Japan was constrained by the Kuril Islands dispute. Merely servicing the Soviet debt required $5 billion a year, and two-thirds of that debt ($39 billion) was owed to European countries (especially Germany). Rescheduling the debt was dependent on agreement between the republics about sharing liability for it, but many republics resented repaying a debt which was incurred without consulting them. Agreeing on, and co-ordinating, immediate humanitarian aid to see the republics through the winter of 1991–2 also proved very difficult, because of distribution problems and the uncertainty over whether it could be ensured that aid would reach the destination intended without being stolen by criminals or diverted by officials. Long before the end of the Soviet Union in December it was clear that the republics saw the centre as an irrelevance. This made it necessary for the western powers to envisage aid being channelled through the republics – an additional reason for uncertainty, but at their Bangkok meeting in the same month such conditions were agreed.

The Declining Power and Influence of the Soviet Union

The summit between Presidents Bush and Gorbachev, held in the summer of 1991, highlighted the dramatically changed relations between the two states. The Soviet Union had ceased to be a superpower, and its negotiations with the United States did not have the significance they once had. The summit was described as the first of the post-Cold War era, but in reality it was the end of a period of United States–Soviet Union rivalry and co-operation which had dominated world affairs. Contacts with foreign leaders was no longer doing Gorbachev's domestic prestige much good. People complained that it did nothing to improve the situation at home. The invitation to Presidents Yeltsin of Russia and Nazarbaev of Kazakhstan to join the talks with the American President underlined the changed relationship between the centre and the republics. Bush further emphasized this by visiting Ukraine. In the event, Yeltsin turned down the invitation to the talks, not wanting to be upstaged, although he saw Bush separately. Bush was in a strong position to put pressure on the Soviet Union, and he did so. While Gorbachev was privately trying to persuade the United States not to use further force against Iraq, he was at the same time resisting United States pressure on the Soviet Union to reduce its links with Cuba as the price for western aid. Bush also pressed for the independence of the Baltic republics, and the resolution of the Kuril Islands dispute.

After the attempted coup it became possible for Gorbachev to deal with the Cuban issue by announcing that he would soon begin talks on removing the Soviet 'training brigade' from Cuba. He said, 'we want to modernize our relations with Cuba and bring them into line with those we have with other countries'. Such a move would not have been possible before the attempted coup destroyed the influence of the conservatives. The Kuril Islands had been bedevilling Soviet–Japanese relations since they were seized by Stalin after the Second World War. For Japan their value lay in the fishing grounds and potential mineral wealth. For the Soviet Union their importance was mainly strategic, since they provide ice-free access from the Okhotsk Sea to the Pacific Ocean. Half of the 25,000 Soviet citizens who settled in the Kurils since 1945 were military personnel and most wanted the islands to remain as part of the Soviet Union. In 1956 the Soviets offered to return Shikotan and the Habomai group to Japan once a peace treaty had been signed formally ending the war. Japan held out and the offer was withdrawn four years later. Gorbachev, under pressure from conservatives and Russian nationalists, made no progress in resolving the issue. After the failed coup, the initiative passed to Yeltsin, with the prospect that substantial Japanese aid could come to Russia rather than to the Soviet government. Yeltsin seemed to be proposing a stage-by-stage return of the islands over a number of years, but any such move was likely to be opposed by Russian nationalists (Foye, 1992, pp. 34–40).

Last Initiatives by the Soviet Union

Gorbachev was still trying to assert his authority on the world stage. The Soviet Union and the United States took major steps to end their differences over Afghanistan by agreeing to end arms supplies to the warring factions by 1 January 1992 as well as urging other couhtries such as Pakistan, Iran and Saudi Arabia to do likewise. Gorbachev attempted to mediate in the Yugoslav crisis, to be involved in the Middle East Peace Conference and in nuclear arms control negotiations. But after the attempted coup it had become more and more clear that the outside world would have to deal with the republics separately, as well as, or instead of, the central government in Moscow. In September Germany, the firmest supporter of Gorbachev and the Soviet central government, recognized reality and announced that it would open diplomatic relations with the republics.

The West wanted a central authority to deal with such questions as arms control and Eastern Europe. Shevardnadze resumed the post of Foreign Minister, apparently in an attempt to give weight to the central government and to reassure the West. But the republics were determined to have their own separate relations with the West on trade and investment. There were already incipient foreign ministries in the republics which were intended to have close reciprocal links with the central foreign ministry. The European Community also began to envisage a future community, not only embracing countries at present seeking to join but also the states of Eastern Europe and the former Soviet Union. Inside or outside the European Community, the countries of Europe seemed likely to agree and to co-operate on many issues, from security to human rights and the environment. People began to envisage the merger of the Conference on Security and Co-operation in Europe (CSCE) (thirty-five nations) with the Council of Europe (twenty-four nations) together with its Court of Human Rights.

Up to the last minute most advisers to President Bush in the United States had been assuming that Gorbachev would continue to play a crucial role and that they should use their influence to hold the Soviet Union together. Bush had been playing it both ways by supporting Gorbachev but announcing that he would recognize Ukrainian independence after its referendum on 1 December. With the final collapse of the Soviet Union the world found itself faced with fifteen new republics. Diplomatic recognition came quickly for most of them (with the exception of Georgia) together with seats at the United Nations. It was accepted that Russia would take on most of the international functions of the former Soviet Union. It was also accepted that the republics showed sufficient democratic foundations to be received into membership of international organizations.

Conclusion

In September 1991 The International Institute of Strategic Studies devoted its annual conference to examining 'new dimensions in international security'. Zbigniew Brezinski spoke of the end of the Cold War

as the third great transformation this century of the 'organizing structure and the motivating spirit of global politics'. The transformation, at
the end of the First World War, was caused by the collapse of the
European balance of power and its position in the world. After the
Second World War Europe ceased to be the effective centre of world
politics and became the main area of ideological and military (nuclear)
competition between the superpowers. Now that the Cold War had
ended a new structure was needed which would provide political
stability. But this might be threatened by nationalist rivalries and ethnic
tension, or by Russian imperialism. Such an outcome might provoke
large-scale emigration from the Soviet republics. The response of the
West to this situation was crucial and centred on questions of giving aid
and expertise to the former Soviet republics and ensuring that nuclear
capacity was either eliminated or at least not misused.

Gorbachev's policies may have arisen out of necessity but he also
had vision. He used the expression 'new world order' at the United
Nations in 1988 and envisaged greater powers for the United Nations,
a huge programme of Third World debt relief and an attack on poverty
world-wide. The West did not respond in kind. Now there were to be
fifteen republics where formerly there was one Soviet Union, each
competing for loans and investment from the West. They would try to
associate with, or join, the European Community and even NATO.
The Central Asian republics looked towards Turkey, although Iran was
trying to gain influence.

10

Military Confusion

The Principles of Defence Policy

After the Second World War there was a huge buildup of Soviet forces with varied world-wide capability. Historical experience was very relevant, and the Soviet experience was that the Second World War showed the need for well prepared, well equipped and well led formations, as well as the crucial role of Party personnel in building morale and unifying objectives. There was always dispute in the West over whether Soviet military policy should be interpreted as essentially defensive (as the Soviets claimed) in spite of its apparent offensive postures. Thus the military alliance of the Warsaw Pact in Eastern Europe was sometimes justified by the Soviet Union as a defensive barrier. Defending the Soviet Union was also said to require a pre-emptive nuclear strike capacity with many powerful first-strike weapons. To win or survive a world war required the conquest of Western Europe. Western analysts argued that such policies could not realistically be interpreted as defensive, that the Soviets had deluded themselves and failed to acknowledge understandable scepticism in the West. There was also a school of thought which believed that the United States had always overestimated the Soviet threat, sometimes deliberately, so as to further its own ulterior purposes. For them, the Soviet Union had neither a 'grand global design' nor simply responded to 'targets of opportunity'. Rather it was modest in aim and opportunistic.

The West relied on a *balance of power* concept based on military and economic factors only. The Soviet doctrine of *correlation of forces* meant that defence policy was not just a matter of military priorities but of reliable allies, favourable public opinion and the support of groups and classes. The balance of power could be produced by deliberate policy. The correlation of forces was regarded as the result of social and historical processes, forming a basic substructure upon which the international system rested. Policies were shaped by the changing correlation of forces. Thus the Soviet Union distinguished its attitude to capitalism from its relations with capitalist states. Events such as the invasion of Afghanistan were explained as acts of deliberate policy resulting from the underlying objective course of history.

Problems from the Soviet point of view included the enormous military potential of the United States and her allies, and of China. There was also the fear that the United States might stop treating the Soviet Union as an equal. There was much resentment over American moralistic lectures on Soviet internal policy and the attempts to 'punish' the Soviet Union after the invasion of Afghanistan. By the mid-1950s the view was that availability of nuclear weapons required some sort of accommodation with the West. The United States had not used its superiority in weapons or intervened in Eastern Europe and so was no longer seen as a threat to basic Soviet security. The world-view was no longer one of capitalist encirclement but of there being an opportunity for internal development in a climate of international stability. An even more pragmatic and less ideological approach to policy developed under Brezhnev and a more flexible understanding of the foreign policies of other countries, especially that of the United States. The United States effort (especially under President Reagan) to gain military superiority instead of parity was very worrying not least because it involved serious economic consequences for the Soviet Union at a time when they were changing political leaders, and affected relations with client states. The conclusion must be that the Soviet Union had a global policy based on capability and ideology. In spite of its intentions, it reacted to events rather than fomenting or manipulating them. It intervened to help allies or 'sympathetic' forces (by 'invitation') but had no special areas of interest. It aimed to replace the United States as the main manager of international affairs in the three spheres of the Communist world, the capitalist world and the Third World.

Détente

Détente was the main concept underlying Brezhnev's foreign and defence policy of the 1970s. It aimed to reduce East–West tension and the arms race. There was, however, a contradiction between *détente* and the continuing massive Soviet military buildup. From the Soviet point of view this was seen as enabling them to deal with the United States on equal terms. In the West it made lesser states very uneasy and led the United States to make frequent accusations that the Soviet Union was overtaking it in military potential. In the Third World there was more success in the avoidance of war and crises, although a vigorous Soviet–United States rivalry remained. In the 1970s Soviet setbacks in the Third World were set against what was perceived as the relative military decline of the West. There was more emphasis on military rather than socio-economic influence in the Third World (sometimes using Cuban or East European proxies). This culminated in Afghanistan where local advantage was given priority over a deteriorating global relationship with the United States.

The basic Soviet aim was to have its cake and eat it, for example, by retaining control in Eastern Europe with the Warsaw Pact while increasing influence in Western Europe, conducting a bilateral dialogue with the United States but rival ones with Western European states, and increasing military power while conducting an arms control dialogue and economic co-operation. There seemed to be more and more difficulty in pursuing these goals. In the end, *détente* meant that the area of co-operation widened but rivalry remained. There was strong domestic pressure for military buildup but it was justified as a means of improving the Soviet bargaining position and so as contributing to *détente*, which would lead to better East-West economic relationships. However, it all tended to postpone the necessary major political and economic changes in Soviet society.

Policy on Nuclear War

The Soviet assumption and emphasis was on fighting a nuclear war and being prepared for it, rather than the western reliance on the deterrent effect. For the Soviet Union deterrence meant the acquisition of superior war fighting capabilities with the aim of prevailing in a nuclear war: deterrence first, then maximizing the chances of national survival and securing the optimal outcome. The United States policy in the 1970s of mutually assured destruction (MAD) was not formally accepted by the Soviet Union, which looked for superiority (if only marginal). The insecurity of the Soviet Union's enemies would, it was thought, encourage 'reasonable' behaviour by them. The increasing awareness of the devastating effects of a nuclear war cast doubts on the standard Soviet view that a progressive war must be more efficient than peaceful means in attaining victory over capitalism. Hence nuclear war came to be perceived as a last resort. A war between the Soviet Union and the United States was seen as inevitably becoming nuclear. Confrontation between the great powers had to be avoided, but in lesser confrontation the Soviet Union would support the 'anti-imperialist' side while emphasizing peaceful coexistence and arms limitation (as in the Strategic Arms Limitation Treaty (SALT) negotiations).

In the early 1980s there emerged a disagreement over nuclear policy in articles by the then Soviet Minister of Defence Dmitrii Ustinov and the Chief of Staff Nikolai Ogarkov. Ogarkov was arguing that the huge destructiveness of nuclear warfare required material reserves sufficient to exploit the Soviet Union's own nuclear strikes.

The underlying issue was one of military expenditure. But Ustinov (reflecting Brezhnev's views) rejected the ideas of military superiority, first strike and predictions of military victory. Although Ogarkov later modified his views he was demoted under Andropov and his successor Marshal Sergei Akhromeyev followed the Ustinov line (Weikhardt, 1985, pp. 77–81).

The Military in Soviet Society

The military–educational complex tried to instil an identification with the military and a military consciousness in the whole population. They wanted shared ideals and attitudes between the civilians and the military. The military, therefore, were an educational and socializing agent, an integrating and Russifying institution. In the 1970s there was a growth of military and military-related education outside the army. Basic military training began at the place of study or work before military service but was combined with a reduction in the length of military service. Civil defence programmes were much developed and integrated under the Defence Ministry. The head of civil defence had special troops at his command. A serious effort was made with elaborate training exercises. Voluntary support for the armed services was encouraged through 'patriotic education' (especially of the young). The Voluntary Society for Assistance to the Army, Air Force and Navy (DOSAAF) aimed to give moral and active support to the armed services. It was financed by, among other things, donations, an annual all-Union lottery and state grants. It had some difficulty raising the necessary funds and was subject to criticism about the quality of its activities. It was sometimes suggested that the Soviet Union was a 'militarized' society, but it is possible to overestimate the impact of all these organizations and activities. It is necessary to consider, not just the quantity, but the quality and effect of the programmes which were often criticized by Soviet sources. There is little evidence that the programmes of the 1970s increased the political power of the military. Educational activities and DOSAAF were not directly controlled by the military. In this, and in civil defence, local Party control was more evident. At best the military were partners in a programme dominated by civilians and using military values to achieve largely civilian ends.

We can summarize the role of the military in Soviet society by saying that the army was an important socializing agent because of civilian acceptance of many of the ideals it embodied. The military–industrial complex was of major significance in Soviet politics because politicians gave it significance. If military advice was taken seriously by the Communist Party it was because its leaders took seriously the goals officers pursued. There was a general belief that strong, powerful armed forces were necessary to further the best interests of the whole of Soviet society.

New Thinking under Gorbachev

A fundamental reappraisal of defence policy began after Gorbachev assumed office. He worked in conjunction with the Foreign Minister Shevardnadze. The Chairman of the Soviet Pugwash Committee,[1] Vitalii Goldansky, said that Soviet defence policy was 'ruinously costly' and bound to fail, especially in Europe, given that the gross national income of NATO alone was four times that of the Warsaw Pact. Soviet military programmes had a grave diplomatic cost. The deployment of medium range SS20 missiles not only 'intimidated' West Europeans, but diminished Soviet security by provoking NATO to deploy Pershing and Cruise missiles. Similarly, the huge Soviet chemical weapons programme created a very bad impression. Vyacheslav Dashichev remarked in a *Literaturnaya Gazeta* article that,

> The major goals of Soviet policy were correct, aiming at peace, security, disarmament, co-operation, non-interference in internal affairs and so on. But what were lacking were any thought out and sensible and scientifically grounded acts. And we were wrong in assessing the global situation, and the correlation of forces, and not making any serious effort to settle the fundamental political contradictions with the West. (Walker, 1988)

The result of this 'new thinking' was that Gorbachev initiated far-reaching changes, including the withdrawal from Afghanistan, the intermediate-range nuclear forces (INF) agreement reducing superpower nuclear arsenals for the first time, and ending thirty years of estrangement with China. Gorbachev had the ultimate aim of abolishing nuclear arms altogether. He decided to halt the production of enriched uranium in 1989 and phase out the production of fissionable materials for nuclear weapons. But this aim was not received entirely favourably in the West. Margaret Thatcher, the British Prime Minister, in particular, regarded the total abolition of nuclear weapons as unrealistic. Gorbachev did indeed recognize that, for the foreseeable future, the elimination of nuclear weapons was not feasible. He was prepared to accept an interim stage whereby 'the Soviet Union remains faithful to its non-nuclear ideals and the West replaced its strategy of flexible nuclear deterrence with the strategy of minimum deterrence' (Pick, 1989). At least Gorbachev was firm in calling for the scrapping of short-range nuclear weapons. The only people threatened by these weapons, he said, were European countries who have no intention of waging war against each other.

At the Paris international conference on chemical weapons in January 1989 Shevardnadze announced that the Soviet Union would begin destroying its stocks of chemical weapons without waiting for a new Geneva Convention to ban them. As soon as the chemical destruction plant was ready, foreign representatives would be invited to inspect it. His speech showed the contrast between the old secretive Soviet style and a new desire for openness. Shevardnadze also announced at the Vienna CSCE that tactical nuclear weapons would be included when the Soviet Union began to put into force its promised unilateral force withdrawals in Central Europe. He said that the common ceiling of conventional arms in Europe should only be sufficient for defence, and not for offence. Western countries played down these proposals, saying that they were mainly political and did not significantly change the huge Soviet surplus of weapons of all kinds in Europe.

Gorbachev could argue that the collapse of the Stalinist system in Eastern Europe was a benefit. It removed unreliable allies. It improved the Soviet Union's international image. It ended Moscow's subsidies to weak economies, and provided a huge hard currency dividend by allowing the Soviet Union to sell oil to Eastern Europe for dollars instead of roubles. But the military high command wanted evidence that the West was changing its own security policy to match or at least take account of the changes in the East. Some officers might have been satisfied with a NATO review which produced a slimmer western military machine in Central Europe: a reduced Bundeswehr, fewer United States troops in Germany, and a withdrawal of all tactical nuclear weapons. Others would have preferred moves towards a new European collective security system to replace NATO and the Warsaw Pact. Gorbachev made it clear that the Soviet Union was still very concerned about a united Germany joining NATO's military command.

Although Gorbachev had replaced almost the entire high command after taking office in 1985, the new men were not much more progressive than their predecessors. Middle-ranking officers were more enlightened, but many of the younger, more able officers were asking to be demobilized. The flight of Mathias Rust in a small plane from Finland to Moscow, unspotted by new expensive equipment designed to detect low-flying aircraft, gave Gorbachev the opportunity to replace the Defence Minister Sergei Sokolov with Dmitrii Yazov (later a coup plotter) (Clarke, 1987; Rahr, 1987a). There were practical and psychological problems involving the army and the dramatic changes in Eastern Europe. The collapse of Communist control meant that the Warsaw Pact no longer existed as a military organization and the army started withdrawing from Czechoslovakia, Hungary, Poland and East Germany. A major housing problem was created in the Soviet Union (in addition to the endemic one) by the return of such large numbers of troops. Many were forced to live in barracks separated from their families and pay was low. Moreover, the army reluctantly became involved in dealing with civilian disturbances within the Soviet Union itself. A small group of officers set up a union called 'Shield' to defend their interests. They stated that they felt they had joined the army to defend the motherland, not to police their own people. Draft resistance and evasion grew, especially in the Baltic republics, Armenia, Georgia and Azerbaijan. The standard argument that Communism and Stalinism, whatever their faults, enabled the country to achieve victory in the Second World ('Great Patriotic') War no longer had the same impact as formerly.

The Conventional Forces in Europe Treaty

The negotiations on the Conventional Forces in Europe Treaty (CFE) were concluded in November 1990. The Soviet Union agreed to give up its numerical superiority in conventional arms. Only modest reductions in United States and other western forces were required by the treaty to meet the aim of parity on both sides. Problems arose because many of the Soviet arms were not to be destroyed but simply moved to east of the Urals (and so beyond the ambit of the treaty). Others were categorized by the Soviet military authorities as naval weapons, and so outside the scope of the treaty. Although questions were asked, NATO eventually accepted Moscow's assurance that it was not trying to circumvent the treaty. With its signing the recognition of the division of Europe into spheres of influence had gone. But the Soviet Union felt that it had not gained as much as the West in these changes. NATO still existed and the CSCE had not yet become a new all-European security organization to replace the two alliances. The Soviet Union would have liked regular meetings of the thirty-five political leaders every two years with foreign ministers meeting every six months. The political leaders would have formed a three-person committee consisting of the former, current and future rotating chairmen of the thirty-five nation group, holding urgent consultations when necessary. There would have been a permanent secretariat.

Moscow also wanted to see a European Security Council developing out of a conflict prevention and resolution centre. It would have co-ordinated the regular inspections of military manoeuvres and exercises, which had already taken place on an *ad hoc* basis, between members of NATO and the Warsaw Pact. Any CSCE member state, including neutral states, could have asked the council to monitor unexplained troop movements. The council could also have had political functions, as an agency which tried to prevent political conflicts or which mediated on conflicts between contending parties if they arose.

The Defence Budget

The Soviet military found themselves having to face significant cuts. The budget of the Defence Ministry was reduced by 14.2 per cent and spending on arms production and military technology by nearly a fifth. Gorbachev announced all this at the United Nations on 7 December 1988. Defence Minister Yazov was told to make do with a 'reasonable sufficiency'. The Central Committee's military expert, General Batenin, explained the meaning of the phrase by pointing out that what mattered in contemporary circumstances was not the capacity to wage all-out war but the ability to ensure a country's security. Within the armed forces everything had to be reoriented towards the *prevention* of war, which differs from the theory of deterrence in that it rules out making mass demonstrations of force. In other words, the doctrine of 'reasonable sufficiency' was a way of telling the other side, 'Keep out of our territory'.

Addressing the Supreme Soviet in May 1989 Gorbachev revealed for the first time realistic details of the Soviet defence budget, which was four times higher than previously admitted. He said that for 1989 defence spending totalled 77.3 billion roubles, still well under the amount the United States was spending annually on defence ($300 billion). The Soviet Foreign Ministry spokesman, Gennadii Gerasimov, said that low pay for Soviet conscripts was one of the factors explaining the difference between the Soviet and United States military budgets. The Soviet Deputy Chief of Staff, Colonel-General Vladimir Kuklev, said that he believed the figures cited by Gorbachev included purchases of military equipment, expenditure on production and research and development, items not included in earlier official figures. Some western experts still doubted that these official figures gave an accurate estimate of the Soviet defence establishment. They believed that many costs were hidden in the budgets of other ministries and departments.

Conservative Influence on Defence Policy

The sudden and dramatic resignation of Foreign Minister Shevardnadze in December 1990 highlighted the tensions in the Soviet government between those who wished to move on from the authoritarianism of the past, and more conservative forces. The latter were clearly gaining in influence from the autumn of 1990. The Soviet military had much to upset them during the policy changes of the Gorbachev period. The principle of 'reasonable sufficiency' in defence illustrated the lessening military role in the forming of defence policy. This led to uncertainty over what the military might do. Could there be a military take-over, with or without Gorbachev, in spite of the lack of a history of military intervention in the Soviet Union? Would the military try to reverse Soviet defence and foreign policy? The resignation of Shevardnadze created a sense of foreboding in the West in spite of Gorbachev's assurances that Soviet policy would not be affected. The West would now have to take seriously the hard-liners in Moscow who resented German unification, who criticized the Conventional Forces in Europe Treaty as a defeat for Soviet security interests, and who saw Soviet support for American policy in the Gulf as an attempt to get favours from Washington.

The biggest worry was the fate of the Soviet nuclear arsenals should the country disintegrate. Nuclear missiles had been shifted out of the Baltic states into the Russian Federation and Ukraine, but it could not be certain what Soviet leader would be in control. The Strategic Arms Reduction Treaty (START), which would involve massive cuts in Soviet and United States nuclear arsenals, was expected to be signed in the spring of 1991, but increasing procrastination on the Soviet side (reflecting the growing influence of conservatives) and uneasiness about the Soviet honouring of the Conventional Forces in Europe Treaty in the spirit as well as the letter, postponed this to later in the year.

The military intervention in Lithuania early in 1991, the inability to complete negotiations for the Strategic Arms Reduction Treaty, and the preoccupation with the war in the Gulf made it necessary to postpone the summit talks between Presidents Gorbachev and Bush due in February 1991. Some people saw the West, and especially the United States, turning a blind eye to events in the Baltic (as it did when over 150 people were killed in Azerbaijan in January 1990) because so much had been invested in support for Gorbachev. The two arms reduction treaties were apparently considered to be of overriding importance. Others felt that there was less reason to tolerate repressive measures in the Baltic now that Gorbachev could no longer be seen as a reformer.

In June 1991 the head of the KGB argued that western intelligence services were working out plans 'for the pacification and even occupation of the Soviet Union under the pretext of establishing international control of its nuclear potential'. Thus some pressure was brought to bear on Alexander Bessmertnykh, the new Soviet Foreign Minister following Shevardnadze's resignation, when he visited Washington. The NATO countries warned Moscow that they expected the Soviet

Union to observe the Helsinki Final Act and the Charter of Paris (a document signed in November 1990 which symbolized the new era of pan-European co-operation). It was noticeable, however, that President Bush avoided criticizing Gorbachev by name.

The growing influence of conservatives throughout 1990 led to a significant change taking place in the budget for 1991. The total defence spending agreed was 96.5 billion roubles, compared with 71 billion in 1990. This large increase caused consternation among radicals. Until early in 1990 it appeared that defence policy was increasingly in the hands of the Foreign Ministry and civilian specialists working in think tanks linked to the Soviet Academy of Sciences. But the Defence Ministry and the military had reasserted themselves. Radicals said that the trend towards conservative policies in many areas was greatly influenced by the military. Even before *perestroika* they were concerned at the number of conscripts, mainly Central Asian, who spoke poor Russian and resented their Russian superiors. Now they were very exercised by unrest in the republics, increasing draft evasion, public protests about underground nuclear tests, huge problems in housing soldiers returning from Eastern Europe, economic reforms that implied higher prices for goods and technology bought by the army and, not least, attacks on the military by the reformist press and politicians. In April 1990 Marshal Akhromeyev denounced *Ogonyok*, a leading radical magazine, for 'systematically blackening the names of Soviet generals and admirals and portraying them as egoists and career nitwits'.

A decline of the influence of conservatives was signalled in July when the United States and the Soviet Union agreed on the Strategic Arms Reduction Treaty, which had been under negotiation for some ten years. The talks had seemed stalled since the beginning of the year as the power struggle continued in Moscow. It involved major reductions in long-range nuclear arsenals by 25 per cent for the United States and by more than 35 per cent for the Soviet Union. The two powers would now be at roughly the level they were at the start of the negotiations in 1982. These developments were followed by an announcement by President Bush that the United States would unilaterally get rid of multi-warhead nuclear missiles. He clearly wanted to build on the successful conclusion of the START negotiations. It put pressure on Gorbachev to eliminate the main part of the Soviet nuclear force, its SS18 multi-warhead nuclear missiles. In the event, Gorbachev did reply in kind by announcing the elimination of tactical nuclear weapons, cuts in the strategic nuclear arsenal exceeding the reduction targets in the START treaty, a one-year moratorium on nuclear testing and cuts of 70,000 in the Soviet army. These moves by Presidents Bush and Gorbachev showed that they had come to adopt the view of western peace movements throughout the 1980s, that competitive step-by-step cutting of arms was more effective than lengthy negotiations and delays in ratification.

After the Coup

With the breakup of the Soviet Union into, at best, a loose confederal association, it was clear that strategic policy on both sides would again have to be drastically rethought. There was much division in the former Soviet armed forces themselves over their future organization and role. Immediately, there was the question of who controlled them and to whom were they answerable. A salient fact was that there was not enough cash to allow military expenditure on the scale experienced in the past. Associated with this was the question of how to convert the vast military–industrial complex to civilian use. An immediate problem for both the Soviet government and the republics, as well as the western powers, was the location and control of the Soviet Union's nuclear weapons. These were still in place in Ukraine, Kazakhstan, and Belorussia as well as in Russia itself. There were fears that tactical weapons could be stolen by, for example, the militias being formed in many republics, such as Georgia, Armenia and Moldova. By early September 1991 Yeltsin announced to the Russian CPD that all strategic nuclear weapons would be moved into the Russian Federation. He pointed out that the other republics were willing to declare themselves nuclear-free zones. The United States began to consider financial aid to the former Soviet republics to help them to dismantle their nuclear weapons.

But in October a further crisis was caused by the announcement that Ukraine intended to form its own armed forces and would not be handing over nuclear arms on its territory for the time being. It was, however, seeking some form of joint control of all Soviet nuclear weapons. Kazakhstan also announced that it would retain its nuclear weapons for the time being, although President Nazarbaev tried to reassure western leaders by saying that they were under the joint control of a general staff which included the defence ministers of eight republics. The question of control was seen as crucial by the West, although there was the possibility that many weapons would become inoperable because of inadequate maintenance. The final transfer of power from the remnants of the government of the Soviet Union involved a negotiated handover of nuclear control from Gorbachev to Marshal Yevgenii Shaposhnikov, a former Soviet Defence Minister now representing the Russian Federation. This took place on 25 December. Anxiety over the question continued after the creation of the Commonwealth of Independent States, in spite of frequent reassurances by presidents and defence ministers.

Defence Policy in Fifteen Republics

NATO came to recognize the need to deal directly with the separate republics as well as with the centre. It more and more seemed likely that it would be necessary for each republic to sign arms control agreements such as the Nuclear Non-proliferation Treaty, and to agree to abide by the Conventional Forces in Europe Treaty. Future treaties would have to be negotiated with individual republics. They would be able to join the Conference on Security and Co-operation in Europe and NATO's new East European organization, the North Atlantic Co-operation Council. The council, set up on 20 December 1991, originally included the sixteen NATO states, nine Eastern European states, and the three Baltic republics. Its main purpose was to have regular consultation on security issues and to help East European countries and the former Soviet republics with the restructuring of their defence industries.

In June 1991 the role of the CSCE was enhanced when it was agreed that it could meet at short notice, at the request of twelve of its thirty-five members, in response to emergencies, defined as major human rights violations or 'major disruptions endangering peace, security or stability'. Germany wanted the CSCE empowered to intervene in disputes by sending observers and, in the last resort, using force to deal with conflicts which breached the Helsinki or Paris agreements. The Soviet Union reluctantly agreed to these arrangements but retained the right to veto any action resulting from such meetings. A speech by the United States Secretary of State James Baker at this time clearly envisaged the CSCE as a major institution in a future 'Euro-Atlantic community' which would embrace the former Soviet republics and Eastern and Western Europe, as well as the United States and Canada. More and more, NATO also thought of the CSCE as the body capable of political (and possibly military) intervention to prevent civil strife threatening European security. The similar membership of the North Atlantic Co-operation Council and the CSCE pointed to an eventual merger between the two organizations. These ideas did not get universal support from other European countries and the future role of the CSCE was not yet agreed between the main powers.

Notes

1   Pugwash: an international scientific conference held at intervals to discuss the problems and dangers threatening the world.

Part IV

Fifteen New Republics

The Nationalities Reject the Union

The Nationalities after the Revolution

A most important and (until the last years) neglected fact about the Soviet Union is that it was a country of many nationalities (well over a hundred). Although a large number of these had very small populations, a wide variety of languages and dialects were spoken, and many different cultural and historical traditions expressed. Lenin wanted the new state to be composed of proletarian republics based on nationality, and administrative divisions reflected this, although the understanding and consciousness of nationality varied greatly from area to area. However, the republic frontiers were often relatively arbitrary, suited to the convenience of the centre rather than the actual distribution of ethnic groups. But in any case it was envisaged that these proletarian republics would eventually be replaced by a united community of Soviet people. Lenin placed Stalin, a Russified Georgian, in charge of nationalities policy. As a result, his plan for a 'national contract' between free and independent Soviet republics was transformed into a Soviet empire dominated by Russians and terror. The republics' indigenous cultures and economies were repressed and their national Communist leaderships frequently purged. Whole peoples (for example, Crimean Tatars, Volga Germans, Kalmyks, Chechens) were deported from their homelands as 'Nazi collaborators'. Although millions of non-Russians had fought in the war, not all Soviet citizens fought on the Soviet side, so that Stalin celebrated victory in 1945 with a pointed toast to the *Russian* people, and subsequently increased repression in Ukraine and the Baltic republics. Half the population of Soviet prison camps during the post-Stalin period had been imprisoned for trying to preserve their national language and culture against what they saw as increasing Russification. A brief period of relative liberalization after Stalin's death was followed under both Khrushchev and Brezhnev by an offensive against 'nationalist deviations'. Thus most of the nationality problems of the 1980s and 1990s had long been simmering under the surface. Gorbachev's policy of *glasnost* and *perestroika* dramatically revealed the fact that nationalism was still a potent force in many parts of the Soviet Union.

Nationalism could be divided into two kinds, although they were often closely linked. The first, cultural nationalism, centred on the strength of interest in the language and artistic and literary heritage. Other factors included the degree of geographical concentration of the nationality (and the location of members of the nationality in other parts of the Soviet Union), links with fellow nationals abroad and the relationship with the relevant wider culture (Islamic, Asian or western). The second, political nationalism, involved factors which caused disputes and tensions to a greater or lesser degree in many parts of the Soviet Union. They included central–local relations, Russian immigrants in the nationality's area (including types of work done and the location of immigrants relative to the indigenous nationality), the question of Russification (that is, the degree to which Russian language and culture replaced and dissolved the indigenous language and culture, with or without official encouragement), the tradition and history of independence and dissent (with the emphasis on recent events), the importance of the local economy to the central authorities and, last but not least, the overall nationalities policy of the Soviet Union.

Nationalities policy was concerned with such questions as the extent of Party membership in particular nationalities (that is, the proportion and rate of increase in a given nationality) and also membership of the Central Committee, the deliberate policy of encouraging Russians to emigrate to the nationality's territory, education in the native language, the teaching of national history, and the amount of television, radio and printed material allowed in the national language, or produced locally. In 1962 the central authorities complained of too much 'localism' (for example, too many local radio programmes). It was certainly the case that conditions varied in different republics. For example, Lithuania had a very high percentage of printed material in the local language in spite of having a much smaller population than Ukraine (but only 20 per cent of the Lithuanian population was not Lithuanian).

The success of Russification, insofar as this was a goal of the central authorities, seems to have varied among different nationalities. There has been no universal agreement on the indicators to be used as a measure. Among those that were used we find the extent of intermarriage between nationalities and the proportion of the nationality habitually using its own language. In use of the local language there was often a significant difference between urban and rural dwellers, with the latter using it more frequently than the former. Another factor was the existence of non-nationals (usually Russians) in the higher posts of the republic, such as second secretary of the republic Communist

Party. The head of the republic government traditionally tended to be an indigenous inhabitant of the territory, but Russians often occupied a significant number of important posts. Nationals who did rise to high Party or government office in the republic had often been Russified, with little more than their surnames to indicate their national origin.

The National Economies

The occupations and functions of each nationality were closely related to the social and demographic circumstances. These factors included the proportion of urban dwellers and children in the population, and the proportion of women with more than elementary education. In addition, it was necessary to consider wages and per capita income, together with what nationalities held the higher paid jobs. Of primary importance was the fact that nationalism had been sustained by competition for resources between the different republics. This created a problem for the central authorities of maintaining a satisfactory balance, from their point of view, between national and republic needs. The republics were regarded as contributors to the whole rather than territories with individual needs. The uniformity of the national economic plan required the predominance of the central agencies. All taxation was regulated by the central authorities and there was little scope for raising local taxes on their own account although there were plans to change this. The all-Union budget determined the proportion of taxes to be allocated to each republic (that is, how much could be retained by each republic). However, the republics did have very limited opportunities to participate in the compilation of the budget (through the Supreme Soviet commissions). More decentralization was permitted after the death of Stalin. Khrushchev set up the Councils of National Economy responsible to the republican governments, and republics were allowed to control the allocation of revenue between the autonomous republics and the local authorities in their area. But after Khrushchev's fall the councils were abolished. A minor protest took place when, in 1965, some speakers at the Supreme Soviet called for more involvement of local soviets in deciding economic matters.

Unrest among the Nationalities

The relaxation engendered by *glasnost* increased emigration from the Soviet Union by some ethnic groups. The expansion in the number of Jews arriving in Israel was already causing political problems there. Similarly, German immigrants, with little remaining cultural or linguistic links with Germany, were creating difficulties for the West German government. Less well known was the emigration of ethnic Greeks (known as Pontian Greeks) from Uzbekistan and Kazakhstan to Greece, settling mainly in the Athens area. This group was expelled from Turkey at the beginning of the century, and later Stalin exiled them to Siberia and the Islamic republics. The Greek government had difficulty coping with the influx and it was already causing tension, not helped by the fact that the immigrants spoke an old dialect influenced by Turkish and Russian. This example epitomized the many complexities of the nationalities issue in the Soviet Union, complexities exposed when they were no longer suppressed or ignored.

Minor nationalities often perceived a greater threat from the local major nationality than from the Russians. There was clearly a possibility that national passions would eventually give rise to disturbances in some areas. Serious inter-ethnic violence finally broke out in 1988 and 1989. In the eighteen months up to July 1989 some 200 people were killed and 2,000 wounded in Armenia, Azerbaijan, Georgia, Uzbekistan, Kazakhstan and Tajikistan. Hundreds of homes were destroyed and 250,000 people became refugees. The disturbances resulted in a new law of April 1989, which included a clause against premeditated actions aimed at arousing ethnic hatred or discord, and with heavy prison sentences on conviction. Later in the year things were considered sufficiently serious for a nation-wide broadcast by President Gorbachev (on 1 July) when he warned of the consequences if unrest spread from relatively confined areas to areas where millions of people of different nationalities lived side by side. He acknowledged that the causes of the violence included the unlawful deportation of peoples by Stalin and economic and cultural stresses. There had to be a profound transformation of the federation of Soviet republics. He promised to do everything possible to ensure the security of national groups and to protect their languages and culture. A special plenum of the Central Committee would consider these issues. Meanwhile it was important for everyone to obey the law if rights of minorities and all citizens were to be guaranteed. What he did not say was equally important. He did not mention the right of self-determination or the possibility of confederation. Rather, he emphasized the links between the nationalities.

There was a point of view that the major nationalities should be given the opportunity to secede – there were good reasons why not all might choose to do so – and that the resulting federation would be stronger as a result. There had long been a formal right in the Soviet Constitution for any of the all-Union republics to secede from the Soviet Union, but this was not taken sufficiently seriously for procedures to be laid down to effect such a secession. However, the reformed Supreme Soviet did have submitted to it a law setting out secession procedures. It would have required a referendum in the republic concerned, called by the republic Supreme Soviet or by one-third of the citizens. A two-thirds majority of registered voters would have been required for it to pass and at least three-quarters of the electorate had to vote. Then a result in favour of secession would have to be submitted for approval to the all-Union Supreme Soviet in Moscow. These requirements would have been very difficult to achieve, bearing in mind the large minority of non-indigenous inhabitants in the republics, many of whom might well have opposed secession. In any case, a further complication was that some nationalists (as in the Baltic republics) did not recognize the legality of their annexation to the Soviet Union in the first place, and thus regarded the law as irrelevant.

The Republics Assert Themselves

By the middle of 1990 there were signs that the republics were beginning to take things into their own hands. Not only were they, in some cases, recognizing each others' declarations of sovereignty and other aspirations, and signing treaties of friendship and co-operation, but administrations in various regions of the country were retaining their produce for their own populations. Some reduced supplies to Moscow in retaliation for its regulations restricting the purchase of food to its own residents. In May Popular Fronts from eight Soviet republics formed a joint action committee aimed at helping them leave the Soviet Union. At a conference in Kiev they decided to work together 'to ensure the Empire's peaceful disbandment'. Representatives from Armenia, Azerbaijan, Belorussia, Georgia, Latvia, Lithuania, Ukraine and Uzbekistan as well as democratic Russian movements adopted a resolution calling for round table talks between the Soviet government and the Popular Fronts. They set up a Union of Democratic Forces coalition with a consultative committee to meet monthly. But in August Gorbachev denounced the attempt of those who were 'working directly or indirectly for the breakup of the Union'. Although he admitted that violations of federal principles in previous years had caused damage, the 'unitary nature of our state led to a very high degree of economic integration. To destroy these ties would be a reactionary move directly opposed to growing trends in the world economy, especially in Europe'. The Soviet Union was a nuclear power with a highly complex and integrated defence system, so it made no sense to 'start dividing up nuclear weapons or the system of national defence management'.

Meanwhile, the issue most concerning the central authorities was the proliferation of armed groups in various republics. At the end of July the Interior Minister, Vadim Bakatin, said that illegally armed groups were operating in Moldavia, Georgia, Latvia, Lithuania, and

Estonia as well as in Azerbaijan and Armenia. Gorbachev issued a decree banning the creation of armed groups and ordered the confiscation of weapons. It also stated that action would be taken against illegal groups within fifteen days if they were not disbanded. There was a reluctance to intervene by means of the army – the Interior Ministry troops – after the violent suppression of protesters in Georgia had evoked world-wide criticism. There was a need to maintain some common ground between the army and the civilian population, and to acknowledge the growing demands in some republics for 'national' armies serving within their own republic boundaries. Several republics at once defied the decree's provisions. The Armenian Supreme Soviet voted twice to suspend application of the decree to its own republic, and also declared that the decree was not valid in Nagorno-Karabakh (the Armenian enclave in Azerbaijan), over which Armenia had no legal authority.

Evidence of anti-Russian feeling came from many areas. For example, the Tass News Agency reported that 3,000 Russian speakers had fled Tuva in Siberia after a campaign of intimidation by local people. Factory workers were threatening to strike unless they were protected against stone-throwing, armed robbery and anonymous death threats. The imposition of presidential authority was expressed by the creation of joint army–police patrols in major cities, and the use of the KGB, in conjunction with the Interior Ministry, to crack down on large-scale organized economic crime. But the central government was concerned that, in some republics, KGB, police and interior ministries had broken away from central control.

The New Union Treaty

In June 1990 Gorbachev called a meeting of the Presidential Council of the Federation to discuss fundamental questions on the relationship between the republics and the central government. The effort to draw up a new Union Treaty was part of the political struggle between Gorbachev and Yeltsin. The latter was aiming to enhance the powers of the Russian Federation and was the main champion of the autonomy of the republics, if not their outright independence. He had long been calling for a drastic review of the federal structure of the Soviet Union, favouring 'a strong Union' but one resting on 'firm horizontal ties among the republics'. These would first establish a network of bilateral treaties between themselves on trade, finance, cultural co-operation, protection of minorities, etc. The Union Treaty would come later.

The proposals made by Gorbachev involved a Union of Sovereign Socialist States. Each could have its own link with the centre and its own degree of freedom to decide what issues to leave to the centre's control. There would be a new Union Treaty, replacing that of 1922, 'to guarantee the republics' real economic and political sovereignty and their effective interaction'. Republics could have a federative or confederative link with the centre, just as Finland or the Khanate of Bokhara had in tsarist times. It was up to the republics' parliaments to decide among a multiplicity of options, taking historical, cultural and economic circumstances into account. This was not likely to go far enough for many republics, while the Baltic republics maintained that only total independence would satisfy them.

When the first draft of the treaty was published late in November it retained powers for the centre which the republics were unwilling to accept, even where they were not seeking full independence. The proposed central powers were defence (including command of the armed forces and the right to declare war and conclude peace), conduct of foreign policy, economic policy (including conducting financial, credit and monetary policies based on a single currency for the whole country), and definition of republic borders. It did declare that 'republics are owners of the land and natural resources on their own territories' which many republics had claimed, but the declaration was limited by, for example, the use of gold and diamond reserves having to be agreed with the Union government and other republics. This could have led to conflict between, say, the Russian Federation and autonomous republics within its borders. Taxation was mentioned only briefly and vaguely, while there was no mention of any procedures for the withdrawal of a republic from the Soviet Union.

Another difficulty was that the draft treaty stated that the treaty could be signed by the autonomous republics and autonomous regions within their borders. This would have allowed an autonomous republic such as Abkhazia in Georgia to have stayed in the Union even if Georgia decided to leave. Rafik Nishanov, chairman of the Supreme Soviet's Council of Nationalities, also suggested that 'peoples who have no statehood will be able to take part in the Union Treaty. They can be represented by their national associations or other organizations.' This would have permitted minorities such as the Gagauz in Moldavia to have had a direct link with Moscow even if they were not recognized in the existing constitution. The same would have applied to Russian minorities in the various republics.

The draft treaty was not well received by those republics already hostile to the Union. The Baltic republics and the Belorussian Popular Front were meeting at this time to discuss the formation of a Baltic Sea region with talk of national armies and mutual aid in the case of economic blockade from Moscow. As well as the Baltic republics, Armenia, Georgia and Ukraine said they would not sign the treaty, either at all or as it stood. The Russian CPD delayed accepting the treaty by voting for an exchange of opinions. President Nazarbaev of

Kazakhstan pointedly remarked at the all-Union Congress of People's Deputies that it was for the republics to decide what powers to give the centre rather than the other way round. He was echoed by Islam Karimov, President of Uzbekistan, so making it clear that opposition to the draft treaty was not confined to those republics seeking independence. But Gorbachev emphasized the dangers of a breakup of the Union and made it clear he was prepared to introduce direct presidential rule if trouble continued in some areas. At this time he was seeking far-reaching presidential power to deal with the economic and social emergency, moves roundly condemned by Yeltsin. In the event, imposition of direct presidential rule did not occur, partly as a result of climb-down (in Moldavia) or international opinion (in the Baltic republics).

The issue of military conscription was of great concern to the centre. Many republics showed increasing reluctance to allow their nationals to serve in the Soviet army either at all or outside the republics' territory. Some devised alternative forms of national service. Although 79 per cent of the quota for 1990 was met, it fell to as low as 28 per cent in Armenia, and 12 and 10 per cent in Lithuania and Georgia respectively. This issue was the pretext for paratroopers being sent into Lithuania in January 1991. They were there ostensibly to round up defaulters. As negotiations went on it became clear that nine republics were prepared to be involved in the proposed treaty, while six were not. The Soviet government took the view that these six (the three Baltic republics, Georgia, Armenia and Moldavia) would have to have a special dispensation to remain in the Union, or would have to invoke the secession procedures. Their independence movements formed the Assembly of Popular Fronts and Movements in Republics not Joining the Union Treaty (or the 'Kishinev Forum') to enhance political and economic co-operation between them.

A revised draft of the Union Treaty was published in March. It demonstrated the growing pressure from the republics for initiative and control to emanate from them. The revision provided that 'Constituent republics shall retain the right to independent action on all issues of their development.' But the central government would have retained responsibility for defence, borders and co-ordinating law enforcement and foreign policy. The republics would have been able to establish direct diplomatic and trade ties with foreign states, sign international treaties and join international organizations. They would have been able to secede from the Union 'in accordance with the order established by the parties to the Treaty'. But, as we have seen, the prevailing conditions for secession were extremely restrictive. In this second draft other major changes were that the republics would have had the ownership of land and natural resources and joint control even over Union matters; there would be no exclusive Union rights.

The Referendum on the Union

In an attempt to strengthen his hand against the pressures from the republics, Gorbachev decided on a nation-wide referendum on the Union, which was duly held on 17 March 1991. The six republics who refused to sign a union treaty also refused to take part in the referendum. The Baltic republics had previously held their own referendums, which registered large majorities for independence. The somewhat loaded referendum question was: 'Do you think it essential to preserve the Union of Soviet Socialist Republics as a renewed federation of equal sovereign republics, in which human rights and liberties will be fully guaranteed for all nationalities?' Some republics added further questions. For example, in the Russian Federation people were asked to vote on the idea of an elected executive president for the Federation (at the time Yeltsin was chairman of the Russian Supreme Soviet), and in Ukraine people were asked if they wanted to stay in the Union on the basis of the republic's declaration of sovereignty. With such additional questions on the ballot paper the result was likely to be less than decisive and to be claimed as support by both radicals and conservatives. Television was used by the government to put forward pro-Union views while opposition leaders such as Yeltsin were restricted in their appearances and had to rely on radio and printed media. Overall, 80 per cent of the electorate voted and of this 76 per cent were in favour of the Union – but that amounted to only 58 per cent of the total electorate. The majorities varied widely from place to place. The Central Asian republics had well over 90 per cent of voters supporting the Union to 71 per cent in the Russian Federation and 70 per cent in Ukraine. Some major cities could muster only modest majorities for the Union – or even rejected it (as in Kiev). In Russia the vote for a directly elected president was almost as high as that for the Union, while in Ukraine large majorities voted for the sovereignty of the republic.

The Agreement of Novoye Ogarevo

In April the Agreement of Novoye Ogarevo was reached between Gorbachev, Yeltsin and representatives of eight other republics, so disarming the conservative opposition which Gorbachev anticipated at the impending Communist Party Central Committee meeting. The agreement specified a major role for the Union republics (with the nine signatories having 'most favoured' status) and envisaged the signing of the treaty being followed by a new constitution and elections to the Congress of People's Deputies, as well as direct elections for the presidency - probably in 1993. The new state would be called the Union of Soviet Sovereign Republics, dropping the word 'socialist'.

By the end of June another draft had been drawn up, providing for a two-chamber Union parliament, with each republic having only one vote in the upper house, so meeting the objection that otherwise the Russian Federation could outvote all the others. The most important issue still remaining by this time was that of taxation. The centre wanted taxation rights while the Russian Federation and Ukraine wanted the republics to collect taxes and from them to provide for the Union budget. This latter arrangement would have left the centre very dependent on the republics. Other republics, such as Kazakhstan, preferred Union taxes from which they, as poor republics, could be subsidized. Increasingly, the treaty looked confederal rather than federal, and elected bodies such as the Russian Supreme Soviet were ensuring delay by insisting on discussing and approving the treaty before signature.

Just before the Communist Party's July Central Committee meeting Gorbachev managed once again to disarm criticism, as he had in April. He announced agreement on the Union Treaty, except for the question of federal taxation which he expected to be resolved within twenty-four hours. He ignored the necessity for republic soviets to approve the treaty, but highlighted the fact that, although conservatives strongly disapproved of it, they had no alternative which would get the agreement of the republics, as Gorbachev had done. He named 20 August as the date from which republics could start signing the treaty. Further hard bargaining between Gorbachev, Yeltsin and Nazarbaev produced an agreement on federal taxes. They would not be mentioned in the treaty but the republics would agree that a certain percentage of republic taxes would go to the centre, subject to periodic renegotiation depending on the level of taxes in general. Thus both sides made compromises. All this was thrown into the melting pot when the attempted coup occurred on 19 August, the day before the signing of the treaty was to begin. Clearly the impending signing was one of the major factors which precipitated such drastic action by conservatives.

The Republics after the Failed Coup

The immediate response to the abortive coup from leaders of the republics varied from outright condemnation (in the Baltics and Kazakhstan) through sitting on the fence (in, for example, Ukraine) to support (in some of the Central Asian republics). Later, when the coup had failed, some leaders changed their tone, and there was a rush of declarations of independence in the hope of strengthening their negotiating positions *vis-à-vis* the centre and the Russian Federation. The unexpected declaration of independence in such a hitherto relatively acquiescent republic as Belorussia was an attempt to distance the republic from Russian-dominated reforms and, they hoped, to retain Communist power under another name. There was apprehension, no longer of an army-backed coup, but of a nationalist civil war which could have fascist overtones. Some smaller ethnic groups also supported the failed coup and in turn tried to declare independence when the coup attempt had obviously failed. Western states now felt able to recognize the independence of the three Baltic republics. The suspension of the Communist Party provoked various reactions. Some republic Communist parties attempted to disassociate themselves from the CPSU and local leaders resigned from the Politburo or Central Committee. In some places the Party was banned and in others its property was confiscated.

The main question was the future of the Union Treaty. It was obvious that the already highly decentralized draft treaty would have to be revised in an even more decentralized direction. At the beginning of September Gorbachev, at a meeting with leaders of ten republics, suggested that there could be a three-tier system. Some would sign the Union Treaty (probably Russia, Ukraine, Belorussia and the Central Asian republics), others would be associated through various agreements (possibly Armenia, Azerbaijan, Georgia and Moldavia), while others would have economic links only (the Baltic republics). Negotiations on an economic union soon started. It was clear that any such union would of necessity be dominated by the Russian Federation and Ukraine. There was real fear of a new Russian domination, exacerbated by Yeltsin's talk of renegotiating the Russian Federation's boundaries. The transition possibly to some association analogous to the European Community would be painful and there would have to be a central authority to arbitrate the many likely conflicts.

The Realities of Independence

There were certainly reasons why many republics might have hesitated to insist on full independence. For many, their economic viability as independent states was questionable. In the past they had paid wholesale prices for power, oil and raw materials from the rest of the Soviet Union. If they became independent, and had to buy such imports on the world market, many of their factories would go out of business. With western aid they could rebuild their economies, but only after a transition period of high inflation and mass unemployment. The Soviet Union had been organized as a centralized economy, taking little regard of the republics' specific interests. It would be extremely difficult to disentangle this economic structure and not necessarily advisable to do so. There had been a monopolistic concentration of industry in particular areas, which meant that no republic had a completely viable industrial infrastructure. All were dependent on other republics for vital supplies and none could compete with the West. The European areas of the Soviet Union accounted for three-quarters of industrial employment, which meant that the relationship with the underdeveloped south and east closely resembled a colonial type. On top of all this, there were widespread environmental problems and such immediate questions as how to apportion the Soviet Union's foreign debt among the republics. Thus there did seem to be a strong case for some political co-operation related to their economic interdependence. For the West there was the likelihood of having to deal with a number of very fragile economies with weak currencies, still very dependent on the Russian Federation, with the possibility that the region might destabilize. Meanwhile, it was difficult to know who, if anyone, was in control, politically and economically.

The Economic Treaty

The twelve remaining Soviet republics signed a declaration of civic and inter-ethnic concord in Alma-Ata at the beginning of October. In the declaration they agreed, among other things, not to question each others' borders for the next fifty years and signed a declaration of economic intent. It was a vague document and did not make clear how far the republics were willing to integrate their economies. This became an economic treaty which was signed on 18 October 1991, but by only eight of the twelve republics. The non-signers were Ukraine, Azerbaijan, Georgia and Moldova. Later, all except Georgia said that they would sign in due course. The treaty provided for an economic zone with a single monetary and banking system, joint customs controls and tariffs and co-ordinated energy, transport and communications policies. Up to twenty further agreements had to be reached before ratification.

Towards the end of 1991 it became clear that the republics were extremely lukewarm about the economic treaty and increasingly reluctant to sign any sort of Union Treaty. The last straw was the Ukrainian referendum vote on 1 December in favour of independence. No union without Ukraine was considered viable so the idea of a union was abandoned and the Commonwealth of Independent States was formed by the three Slavic republics. Other republics soon joined this initiative, which clearly did not envisage any role for the old Union centred in Moscow. Nevertheless, independence, when it came, was unexpected in some republics and not really welcomed in others. They remained interdependent with many economic, social and nationalist problems with which to face an uncertain future.

Conclusion

The idea of 'new socialist man', a citizen with common socio-political values and goals, although with continuing cultural diversity, had long been officially envisaged as a logical and desirable outcome of the progress towards full Communism. The differences and antagonisms between nationalities were to be removed in a merger of nations, but this was not understood to mean a crude uniformity. Although some small nationalities had become merged in their nearest large neighbour with whom they had some affinity (and this process was continuing), nationalism in various forms continued to be of major political significance in the area before and after the collapse of the Soviet Union. Previously, demographic or ethnographic phenomena had only become significant to the Soviet authorities when they affected overall policy goals. All Soviet policies had ethnic consequences, but the authorities tried to suppress the influence of nationalist factors and usually (with their greater resources) could do so. The era of *glasnost* and *perestroika* released a new upsurge of nationalist feelings in all the republics. A variety of factors influenced this and affected policy.

Gorbachev stated the main principles upon which he considered nationalities policy should be based. The first, 'a strong centre and strong republics' seemed contradictory unless an acceptable distribution of power could have been agreed. The second, that every Soviet citizen should feel at home anywhere in the Soviet Union regardless of his or her origins, would have taken time, education and a change in attitudes and habits to achieve. In his Nobel Peace Prize speech in June 1991 Gorbachev again emphasized his oft-repeated view that withdrawal from the Soviet Union could come only through 'the framework of a constitutional process' as laid down by the Soviet Congress of People's Deputies in Moscow. But the complex procedure was seen by nationalists as designed to obstruct secession and it did not meet the objection of the Baltic republics, Moldavia and Georgia, that they had been forcibly incorporated into the Soviet Union against their will and, therefore, were not legally part of it.

In the end the republics showed that they had no trust in the centre. With their achievement of total political independence, formidable economic problems still existed, and tension between nationalism and democracy came to the surface. Democracy came to be associated by nationalists with pressures towards disintegration. The result was that general dissent and intolerance of minority ethnic groups became evident, such people being regarded as disloyal to the new nationalist regime. Democracy in a form recognizable in the West was by no means certain to prevail in many of the former Soviet republics.

12

Russia and Belarus Accept the Inevitable

Russia

Introduction

The Russian Soviet Federated Socialist Republic (RSFSR) was central to the existence of the Soviet Union. It was by far the largest all-Union republic. Many of the Soviet Union's ethnically based autonomous republics lay within its boundaries, with their own actual and potential ethnic tensions. The federation consisted of almost three-quarters of the Soviet Union's land mass, just over half the total population, and much of its raw material wealth, especially those commodities such as oil, gas, furs and precious metals which earned most of the hard currency. It was the centre of Soviet heavy industry, with a dominant position in the supply of energy and industrial raw materials. It also possessed the core of the Soviet Union's scientific potential, employing almost 70 per cent of scientists and, to an even greater extent, it contained the country's military–industrial sector. The true pattern of economic relations between the Russian Federation, the other former Soviet republics and the rest of the world was concealed by the distorted system of domestic rouble prices, above all by the extremely low prices for energy resources. A transition to prices more in line with those of world markets would have greatly enhanced the federation's economic position, to the disadvantage of the other republics.

In spite of this dominant position, the provinces of the Russian Federation were often very backward. There were serious environmental problems, inferior housing and social provision, and, in many areas, a depopulated and very poor countryside. During the Gorbachev period unrest among workers, and threats of strikes, indicated increasing dissatisfaction. There was a growing feeling that the Russian Federation must reassert itself. Russians often complained that the federation subsidized the other republics and did not get the full benefit from its exports abroad. But, while it was within the Soviet system, what it could do about this was limited. Most of the Soviet Union's industrial and scientific potential was located in the federation, but only a small portion was directly administered by the federation's institutions. Almost all heavy industry and much research was controlled by all-Union ministries. Under Soviet arrangements, the federation could not change the prices charged by industries under central control, and it had little chance of securing control of the hard currency export earnings of the oil and gas industries. It had direct control only over its food and light industries and some other economic activities not of strategic importance.

The Nationalities in the Russian Federation

It had sometimes been suggested that there should be a reduction in the size of the Russian Federation because it embraced many small nationalities having quite different backgrounds and histories from the Russians – and often from each other. Yeltsin suggested that the various national minorities should have greater rights to create their own autonomous areas. But, with the position of the federation becoming crucial after the failed coup (which some minorities supported) and the formation of the Commonwealth of Independent States, the Russian centre was more likely to assert itself over the minorities, and Yeltsin himself caused concern by talking of revising the republic's external boundaries. Another aspect of the growing nationalistic ferment was the emergence of Russian or Slavic nationalism, which often had neo-fascist overtones (including anti-Semitism). Adherents to organizations such as Pamyat argued that the nationalities, inside and outside Russia, had already been indulged too much and that it was time they were firmly put in their place (by the Russians, of course). But aside from this extremism, before the failed coup consideration had been given to revising the constitutional place of the federation within the Soviet Union. After it, nationalism received an even greater emphasis.

The Russian Supreme Soviet

In May 1990 the federation held the first meeting of its newly elected Russian Congress of People's Deputies (RCPD). Because of its size Russia was the only republic to elect a CPD, which then chose a Supreme Soviet. All the other republics elected their Supreme Soviets directly. The Russian Supreme Soviet was split almost equally between conservative and radical forces. Many delegates were employed by organizations subordinate to the central authorities and were likely to be reluctant to back measures provoking direct conflict with the centre. Attention was concentrated on the efforts of Yeltsin to get the RCPD to elect him President of the Russian Federation. This election was an attempt to gain a strong power base from which to conduct his campaign against both conservatives and what he considered to be Gorbachev's inadequate policies. The other main candidate was the outgoing Prime Minister, Alexander Vlasov, who was thought to be supported by Gorbachev. He delivered a 'state of the Russian Federation' report to the Congress which was notable for a strong call for the federation to have 'the exclusive right to own and dispose of all its natural resources'. In his speech, Yeltsin went further and demanded that the laws of the Russian Federation should have precedence over the laws of the Soviet Union itself, a demand similar to that made by the Baltic republics and rejected by Gorbachev.

Yeltsin was finally elected Chairman of the Praesidium (President) of the Supreme Soviet of the Russian Federation on 29 May after two indecisive ballots and strong attempts to prevent it by Gorbachev. However, he promised to work co-operatively with Gorbachev. Subsequently, a Yeltsin supporter failed to get elected as Prime Minister. Instead, the Russian Supreme Soviet elected Ivan Silayev, a moderate reformer. But they did declare that the federation's constitution and laws took precedence over Soviet laws. Any Soviet legislation in conflict with Russian sovereignty would be suspended in the territory of the federation. This could have undermined the entire Soviet Union. Gorbachev said that he believed the Russian Supreme Soviet would not, in fact, 'approve any laws that damage the development of a new federation of republics'. The vote, by a large majority, was indeed taken on only one article of a draft declaration on Russian sovereignty. Any disagreement between the federation and the Soviet Union was to be resolved in line with the existing Union Treaty. But radical critics said this was a contradiction since the Union Treaty gave supremacy to Soviet law. For them the contradiction made the declaration of sovereignty empty. In any case, these declarations of sovereignty made by various republics did not mean any immediate practical change. They were really establishing their position for the forthcoming renegotiation of the Union Treaty. The reality was that the central authorities still had control of supply lines and transportation. As it was, the final version of the declaration contained a clause preventing it from having immediate effect.

Yeltsin also announced that the federation would have a multi-party government, the number of ministries would be halved and the government team include non-Party people and the chairmen of the Moscow and Leningrad soviets. There would be a defence minister to work with the Soviet Defence Ministry on conscription and troop movements. It would have its own foreign ministry, foreign trade ministries and bank. The federation had already started talks with the Baltic republics, Moldavia, Ukraine and Kazakhstan on forming direct political, economic and cultural links.

Within the Russian Federation itself Yeltsin drastically cut back on privileges previously enjoyed by Party officials, and introduced for approval by the Russian Supreme Soviet the Shatalin–Yavlinsky economic plan to be introduced in four stages over eighteen months (see pp. 129–30). The plan was too radical for some. Early in July 1990 the Russian Communist Party leader, Ivan Polozkov, gave an interview to *Sovetskaya Rossiya* in which he talked of 'comradely dialogue' but opposed any rush towards creating a labour market. He wanted the immediate formation of a consumer market and a gradual move to a capital market, but a labour market was 'connected with private ownership, hired labour, unemployment and ultimately with the departure from socialism'.

The Revival of the Russian Communist Party

The federation had not had a Communist Party of its own since 1992, presumably because of a fear by Lenin of extreme Russian chauvinism, but Russians predominated in the CPSU anyway. With the changes in the Soviet Union and the resurgence of Russian nationalism, pressure to review this situation was strong. This time the intention was to help placate the Russians, who felt they had been neglected by *perestroika*. Accordingly, the Central Committee set up a 'Russian bureau' at the end of 1989 to look after the interests of the Russian Federation. This was the beginning of a move to establish a separate Russian Communist Party (RCP) although Gorbachev was, in the first instance, opposed. The bureau was chaired by Gorbachev to enable him to monitor events in the federation, which contained 60 per cent of Party members.

The initiative for the recreation of the Russian Party came from a group of ultra-conservatives whose programme made it clear that they wanted a return to authoritarianism. They seized on the idea that the Russian Federation was the best endowed republic but the worst off, since, they argued, it gave way to and supplied the others. They reconstituted the RCP Conference in June 1990, which was dominated by conservatives and was seen as a dress rehearsal for the CPSU Congress the following month. The election of delegates was ostensibly democratic, that is, genuinely contested at grass-roots Party branches. But, crucially, regional Party conferences then had to whittle down the list of successful candidates to the right number. These conferences were packed by Party officials who ensured that they and their sympathizers got elected. As a result, only 11 per cent of the delegates were workers, and 43 per cent were officials from the Party bureaucracy who felt most threatened by the proposed reforms.

Gorbachev's opening speech to the RCP Conference was coolly received, although he attacked the Democratic Platform as well as the conservatives. He warned against conflict between the Russian Federation and the Soviet Union. In a dig at Russian chauvinism he stressed that the aim of the RCP was to revive Russian culture and that of other nationalities in the federation. He defended *perestroika*, saying that it had achieved more in three years than all the attempts at reform since Stalin's death. Calling for 'the fastest possible switch to the market economy', he implicitly attacked Yegor Ligachev who had demanded a referendum on whether *perestroika* was leading to capitalism:

Somebody is trying to impose the idea that the movement towards a market is a step back towards capitalism. It is difficult to think of anything more absurd. The market came with the dawn of civilization and it is not capitalism's invention. (Steele, 1990d)

Conservatives who wanted to return the Party to old-fashioned methods had 'lost touch with reality'. Other speakers won more support. An official, Ivan Osadchy, said,

Instead of strengthening the Party, the leadership has reduced it to crouching unarmed in the trenches under massive shelling by anti-socialist forces. We reject the removal of ideology from Soviet society. We want a Leninist Party with a communist perspective. (Steele, 1990d)

On the second day of the conference there was a call from Ligachev for Gorbachev to resign as Party Secretary. Colonel-General Albert Makashov spoke for many in the military high command when he criticized reforms for leaving the country open to attack:

Germany is reuniting and will probably become a member of NATO and Japan is becoming a decisive force in the Far East. Only our learned peacocks claim that no one is going to attack us. Because of the so-called victories of our diplomacy the Soviet army is being driven without combat out of countries our fathers freed from fascism. (Steele, 1990e)

Although the conference adopted resolutions acknowledging the reality of a multi-party system and the moves towards a market economy, Gorbachev suffered defeat when he failed to get one of his preferred candidates to lead the RCP. Ivan Polozkov, a leading conservative who had criticized Gorbachev at the conference, was elected on the second ballot. Polozkov had been Party Secretary of Krasnodar, in south-west Russia, where he had closed down numbers of co-operatives. Before the conference ended Gorbachev stated that he intended to fight to retain the leadership of the CPSU. Polozkov made conciliatory moves and supported Gorbachev's retention of the Party leadership. He said that the new Party had to be 'thoughtful, moderate, democratic and realistic'. Polozkov also promised to work closely with the Russian President, Yeltsin, and the distanced himself from General Makashov and his criticisms of defence policy. The Democratic Platform issued a declaration that the RCP Conference had 'ignored the real political situation in the country'. Many Party progressives were shocked by the hard-line tone of the conference debates, which it was felt did not reflect rank and file opinion. Thousands of members resigned and others tried to undermine the RCP by insisting that members must register formally, instead of being included automatically by virtue of their membership of the CPSU.

The Confrontation between Yeltsin and Gorbachev

Throughout the autumn of 1990 the rivalry between Yeltsin and Gorbachev continued. In spite of some expressions of the need to co-operate, the Russian Federation continued to challenge central power by publishing a draft constitution for itself which did not mention socialism or the Union. By January 1991 the question of a popularly elected executive presidency for the federation was being actively discussed. If elected to such an office, Yeltsin's authority and legitimacy would be greatly enhanced over that of Gorbachev, who was not popularly elected. By March the conservatives in the Russian Congress of People's Deputies (RCPD) were responding by trying to move a vote of no confidence in Yeltsin. With the conservative–radical division in the RCPD finely balanced this could have been a big threat. As the time for these decisions approached Gorbachev banned demonstrations in Moscow. A dramatic confrontation occurred, with a huge demonstration near the Kremlin during the RCPD's session being faced with considerable police and military force.

In the event the conservatives did not press their no confidence vote, apparently feeling that attacks on Yeltsin tended to increase his support in the country. They did delay the vote on the principle of an elected presidency but in the end Yeltsin achieved this also, the election to be held in June 1991. The opposition of the Communist Party was countered by a new organization – Communists for Democracy – with the aim of supporting Yeltsin. There were about 800 Communists in the RCPD but only about 240 supported the RCP leader, Polozkov. In April Yeltsin challenged the Communists by demanding and getting new powers to end the miners' strikes, which were seriously threatening an already very weak economy, to enforce a crisis economic programme and to enable the Russian Supreme Soviet to pass laws without the delay of seeking subsequent RCPD approval. He had often been criticized for being something of a populist politician, whose weaknesses would be evident when he had to take responsibility for decisions, instead of simply opposing those of others. In April, to counter this accusation, he appointed a team of advisers with many radical members, illustrating that much intellectual support was moving away from Gorbachev and towards Yeltsin. Many of the new team were formerly advisers to Gorbachev. As rivals, and yet forced into necessary co-operation, Yeltsin and Gorbachev continued to play a complex game. Gorbachev spoke sympathetically of the problems of Russia and its many minority nationalities. By breaking up Russia, regardless of who does it, we break up the entire Union, he said. He did not support some of his own followers who were encouraging Tatarstan, Bashkortostan and other autonomous republics to break away from the Russian Federation and become republics in their own right.

The Russian Presidential Election

Yeltsin faced a Communist Party challenge in the presidential election. The Party adopted as its candidate Nikolai Ryzhkov, the former Soviet Prime Minister, although it did not officially endorse him. Another more liberal challenge came from Vadim Bakutin, former Interior Minister, and a member of the Security Council. He was thought to be Gorbachev's favoured candidate. Both Yeltsin and Ryzhkov chose military figures as their running mates for deputy president, although Yeltsin's was a liberal member of Communists for Democracy (Air Force Colonel Alexander Rutskoi) while Ryzhkov's was the conservative General Boris Gromov, Deputy Interior Minister. Altogether, there were six candidates. Although supported by organized groups (in Yeltsin's case, Democratic Russia) none of the main contenders represented a political party or had a developed programme. It was therefore an election about personalities rather than policies. The leaders of the Moscow and Leningrad city soviets also ran for election in their respective cities. In the event they were elected, as was Yeltsin, with well over the 50 per cent needed to avoid a run-off. Yeltsin did particularly well in the towns and cities but less well in the countryside where the Communist Party often still had firm control. The result confirmed his new power and greatly enhanced his legitimacy as a democratically elected leader, in contrast to Gorbachev.

Communists in the Russian parliament continued to make trouble and were strengthened by divisions among the radicals. Much of this trouble was concentrated on a long-running dispute over the election of a chairman for the RCPD. Yeltsin responded to Communist obstruction with a decree banning the organization of political parties in executive branches of government at all levels as well as in state institutions and other organizations in the federation. In effect this applied to the Communist Party's network of cells through which it controlled society. In spite of a furious dispute over the legality of this decree, Gorbachev went on holiday without attempting to have it rescinded.

In the days just before the attempted coup, the struggle for power between conservatives and radicals, and between Yeltsin and the Russian parliament continued. A new party of Russian Communists supporting democracy – the Democratic Party of Communists of Russia – was founded. Leading members such as Alexander Rutskoi, Yeltsin's deputy, were expelled from the RCP but the RCP tried to retain moderate support by dropping its hard-line leader, Ivan Polozkov, and replacing him with a more moderate colleague of Gorbachev's, Valentin Kuptsov. Finally, a week before the attempted coup, Yeltsin announced plans to introduce presidential direct rule, in an attempt to bypass the Communist-dominated RCPD and Supreme Soviet. He created four councils answerable to him: a State Council, a Security Council, a Federation Council and a Council of Ministers (to concentrate on economic matters). He also intended to send prefects to the provinces to ensure that decrees were carried out. Eventually they would be elected, but it was clear they would be supporters of the Yeltsin government; there was no room for opposition. The real power centre was to be the State Council – a revival of the old tsarist name. The day to day business of the council would be the responsibility of the State Secretary (Gennadii Burbulis), a more important post than that of vice-president or prime minister. However, he was responsible to Yeltsin who held the ultimate power. Parliament, with its large number of Communists, was weakened by these arrangements as were the local soviets, which would not like the appointment of presidential prefects who could interfere with their activities. Some radicals were afraid that Yeltsin's plans had authoritarian overtones, with no effective constitutional restraints on the president.

Russia During and After the Coup

Yeltsin took the leading part in denouncing the attempted coup, and concentrated Moscow opposition in the Russian parliament building, the 'White House'. He had the legitimacy, being the one republic leader who had been popularly elected. Demonstrations and strikes occurred in other parts of Russia although positive opposition was by no means universal; Yeltsin's call for a general strike did not get a widespread response. Afterwards, there was a strong feeling that Gorbachev owed his survival to the Russian stand, and especially to Yeltsin. Yeltsin used his enhanced position to take many executive actions, including the suspension of the RCP, seizure of some of its property and temporarily forbidding the publication of some Communist publications, including *Pravda*.

The period following the failed coup was one of internal crisis in the federation government. There was a struggle in the bureaucracy over access to Yeltsin and a prolonged dispute over the appointment of a new Prime Minister. Disagreements emerged between Yeltsin's executive institutions and the Council of Ministers (the Russian government) about their respective powers, while parliament complained that it was not being consulted. A major disagreement was over economic policy: whether the federation should work with other republics in an economic community as envisaged by the Alma-Ata talks on a new Union Treaty, or 'go it alone' and charge other republics hard currency. At the end of October the decision to 'go it alone' was announced when Yeltsin took the big political risk of announcing far-reaching economic reforms. This involved freeing most wages and prices at the end of the year, land reform, and the rapid privatization of the economy. Major cuts were to be made in defence spending, industrial subsidies and support for all-Union ministries. Credit and money supply would be strictly limited. He also announced the takeover of the Soviet state banking system. He warned that there would be a very difficult time in 1992 but put himself and his political future on the line by assuming the vacant post of Prime Minister himself. The Russian parliament overwhelmingly supported these moves but only on the significant condition that it had the right to approve or reject presidential decrees for a week before they could come into effect.

As attempts to agree on a new Union Treaty faltered, Yeltsin continued to assert the power and authority of the Russian government by encroaching on central authority. In December he bailed out the state bank (Gosbank), which had run out of money, in return for a 'consolidated budget' between the federation and the Union government in which the federation would clearly be dominant. This crisis had in a sense been created by the federation because it arose when the lower house of the all-Union Supreme Soviet failed to muster a quorum to approve a Gosbank credit to the central government of 90.5 billion roubles. Federation deputies had stayed away in protest at what they considered the reckless printing of money to finance unproductive bureaucratic, military and other activities. With the creation of the Commonwealth of Independent States, in which the federation took a leading part, the Soviet Union and its central institutions were finally abolished and the federation became an independent state, negotiating economic, military and other agreements with other states in free association. It took over most of the former Soviet government's responsibilities and obligations, including its adherence to disarmament treaties, and its seat at the United Nations. This move was the logical conclusion of the progressive encroachment of the federation on central power over previous months.

The Future for an Independent Russia

The Economy

In the new situation of independence, the Russian Federation was in a very strong position in the long term. It was self-sufficient in energy and had the major part of the former Soviet Union's industrial capacity. If it charged world prices it would enjoy a large trade surplus. In the short and medium term there were the disruptive effects of a transition to a market economy and difficult negotiations ahead with other republics. Proposals were put forward in September 1991 to the World Economic Forum in Moscow to get round western reluctance to fund projects, by giving western investors a stake in the country's huge reserves of oil, gas, timber and other natural resources, but there was confusion over the rouble's convertibility and no coherent financial policy. Private capitalism might create new divisions and dangers such as exploitative monopolies. Civil society would have to develop to resist this and there would be a need for a political labour movement, and a democratic opposition which could be constructive but, on the other hand might, given a serious economic crisis, collapse into narrow authoritarian nationalism.

Russians in Other Republics

Even greater difficulties related to the position of Russians living in other republics and of the ethnic minorities in the federation itself. Many argued that some sort of close agreement was necessary with the other republics in order to retain the integrated communications and energy structures and to safeguard the 25 million Russians living elsewhere. (The federation recognized Russian citizenship for all Russians living outside its borders.) Some Russians had worked in other republics, in manufacture, mining and transport, since before the Revolution, but the greatest migration had taken place since 1929 with the huge industrialization programme of the five year plans. At the time of independence, while many emigrant Russians were manual workers, others were part of the political or managerial elite. Many Russians had already left Central Asia since troubles began there, while there had been talk in Estonia and Georgia of restricting citizenship rights to those living there before the annexation and their descendants. Problems of Russians being disadvantaged by not knowing the local language also caused tensions, while Yeltsin's mention of renegotiating Russia's borders created anxiety in republics such as Kazakhstan, where Russians were almost as great a proportion of the population as Kazakhs, and widely distributed throughout the republic.

In Ukraine there were problems in the Crimea, which was heavily populated by Russians and was part of the Russian Federation until it was transferred to Ukraine in Khrushchev's time. In the Donbass mining region of the Ukraine the population was mostly Russian or Russian-speaking Ukrainians. They had supported the independence movement, Rukh, but were hostile to the replacement of the Russian language by Ukrainian. To alleviate fears of Russians, and after Yeltsin's talk of redrawing boundaries, a joint agreement between the federation and Ukraine at the end of August 1991 established the principle of economic and military alliance without the involvement of President Gorbachev and the central government. There were further difficulties in the Baltic republics where, although some Russians backed independence, others were very hostile. Moldavia, too had an aggressive Russian minority who were trying to declare independence.

The Nationalities in the Russian Federation

On the announcement of the coup some of the local soviets in industrial cities of the Urals and Siberia pledged loyalty to Yeltsin. But many Russian autonomous republics and regions came out in support of the coup and called for the state of emergency to be confirmed by the all-Union Supreme Soviet. Many wanted to enhance their political position and sixteen declared sovereignty, mainly as a move by local Communists to preserve their position and cause difficulties for Yeltsin. A number of these autonomous republics (for example, Buryatia, Karelia, Mordovia, Udmurtia and Komi) had Russian majorities in their population. The level of economic development and the cultural cohesion of the local nationality were just as, if not more, important than mere numbers. Further difficulties existed among the Muslim population of the North Caucasus and in Tatarstan. The Tatars had a well developed industrial base and believed independence was a viable proposition. Their government had refused to take part in the Russian presidential election in June.

Events were particularly dramatic in Checheno-Ingushetia where a power struggle and demands for independence by the Chechens led Yeltsin to make the mistake of sending troops, which then had to be withdrawn when the Russian Supreme Soviet refused to endorse the decision and told him to proceed by negotiation. This particular crisis highlighted the potential troubles to come. Still other nationalities, deported from their homelands by Stalin, were conducting vigorous campaigns to have their rights and homelands restored. These included the Crimean Tatars and Volga Germans. The economic problems facing the federation, and the relatively low level of political sophistication among the nationalities, meant that the resolution of these difficulties might well be long and acrimonious. At one time Yeltsin was promising the autonomous republics 'as much sovereignty as you can swallow'. But by November he was saying, 'We cannot and will never allow a disintegration of Russia into dozens of feuding fiefdoms; we already had such a period in our history and it cost us dearly.' People pointed out the resemblance to Gorbachev's attempts to save the Union.

Russian Nationalism

Before the coup, Russian nationalism had largely been the preserve of conservatives. But during the coup radicals appropriated it to help focus resistance. The older generation believed in the Russian dominated, imperialistic Soviet Union and blamed Gorbachev for its downfall. Others realized that only after the dissolution of the empire was real reform possible. For them, the empire was associated with totalitarianism, the KGB and the ruin of the economy. The popular election of Yeltsin and the opinion polls showed that authoritarianism was no longer acceptable to the great majority of people, especially to the younger generation. Yeltsin courted the Russian Orthodox Church in a populist appeal to Russian traditions. Because of previous repression, religion was now fashionable and was idealized as having been part of the state in old Russia. The Orthodox Church wanted to return to its previous important position in the state, but was hesitant in condemning ultra-nationalist groups in St Petersburg and elsewhere. There were, of course, many other churches and religions in Russia. Slavophile writers claimed that they were purely cultural and religious, and not opposed to other nationalities, although they opposed westernization. However, the Russian Federation was no longer the agrarian village society they harked back to and, with industrialization, a degree of westernization of culture was inevitable. The nationalists were certainly capable of causing trouble. The extreme nationalist candidates got 10 per cent of the vote in the Russian presidential election, which some felt it would be possible to expand if the groups became united. Anti-Semitism was often implicit (and sometimes explicit, as in the Pamyat Society) and could be exploited in a search for scapegoats to blame for the country's troubles.

Conclusion

As the largest, best armed and potentially richest state in the region, the Russian Federation was bound to have a profound influence. It was clear, for example, that much policy in Ukraine was governed by near paranoia about the influence, threat or even domination of the federation. To overcome these fears Russians would have to set aside centuries of imperialist thinking. Internally, the economic and social problems were very severe. A period of hardship and difficulty for the population was inevitable, exacerbated by corruption and criminality. Reaching satisfactory agreements with the ethnic minorities would be a long and difficult process. It was by no means certain that democratic thinking and practices could take firm root in these circumstances.

Russia's relations with the rest of the world centred on questions of economic aid and security. Both questions were far from being resolved as the country entered on post-imperial independence. Of the major economic powers, only the European Community showed real sympathy for giving substantial economic aid. The United States and Japan, for their own separate reasons, held back. Great concern was expressed in the West about the security arrangements for the region, especially with regard to the huge nuclear arsenal. Assurances that the nuclear weapons would remain under joint and effective control did not entirely allay western unease. A major problem also arose over the control of conventional weapons, with quarrels over joint command and the formation of separate armies in the republics; these quarrels were especially virulent between Russia and Ukraine.

Belarus (Belorussia)

Belorussia, one of the three Slavic republics, was once part of Kievan Rus and then came under the influence of Lithuanians and Poles. It passed under Russian rule when the area was partitioned in the eighteenth century and suffered greatly during Russo-Polish wars and Napoleonic invasion. After the October Revolution it was nominally independent for less than a week, and became a Soviet republic in 1919. Subsequently it was considerably increased in area, notably in 1940 when parts of eastern Poland, predominantly Belorussian in population, were added. Some hundreds of thousands of Poles still live in what is now western Belorussia and there are a sizable number of Ukrainians in the republic. Potential disputes existed over the border with Lithuania, because an area of present-day Lithuania was part of

Belorussia between the two World Wars. Doubts always existed that Belorussia had a real sense of national identity. There had been a high degree of Russification. Julian Birch characterized Belorussia as 'quintessential border country' (Birch, 1991, p. 74).

With the advent of *glasnost*, attempts to form a Popular Front along the lines of the nearby three Baltic republics ran into considerable opposition from the Belorussian Communist Party. The founding conference had to be held outside the republic, in Vilnius. A few months before, a demonstration in the capital, Minsk, calling for a memorial to the victims of Stalinism was broken up by the police. Nevertheless, in the March 1989 national elections a number of prominent Party candidates were defeated, including the Party Secretary in Minsk. This did not stop the Party from trying to prevent the holding of Popular Front meetings. By July 1990 events in Belorussia had developed sufficiently for the Belorussian Supreme Soviet to do what some other republics had already done, namely to declare sovereignty. The sovereignty declaration proclaimed the republic to be a neutral state and a nuclear-free zone (it had nuclear weapons on its territory), with the right to raise its own army and security forces. As had other republics, it declared that the republic's laws took precedence over the laws of the Soviet Union. It also claimed the right to 'voluntary unions with other states, and free withdrawal from such unions'.

Nevertheless, Belorussia was considered politically the most docile of the republics and well under the control of the Communist Party. Even serious fall-out over the republic from the Chernobyl nuclear disaster in Ukraine did not provoke significant public reaction. This is why Gorbachev chose Minsk for a speech on the occasion of the Union referendum in the spring of 1991, when he denounced 'neo-bolshevik' tactics and those creating an unsettling atmosphere. But, unexpectedly, within a few weeks of his visit, major industrial unrest broke out, centred in Minsk. These strikes started as protests against price increases but soon became political, demanding the disbanding of Communist Party cells in factories and the resignation of Gorbachev. Some factory managers were sympathetic to the protest against price rises, but disapproved of the political demands. Further one-day strikes followed, in spite of a ban on strikes by Moscow.

The failed coup threw the hitherto firmly based Belorussian Communist Party into disarray. To general surprise, and in spite of a majority in the republic's Supreme Soviet, the Party at first separated from the CPSU and its leader, Anatolii Malofeyev, resigned from the CPSU Politburo. Eventually it was outlawed altogether (to be revived under another name). At the same time the Communist President, Nikolai Dementei, was made to resign the republic declared independence and the name of the republic in the national language, Belarus, was adopted. Many felt that these moves, far from being a genuine rejection of Communism, were essentially intended to retain as much influence as possible for *de facto* Communists. But these and other events drew attention to deep hostility in the republic to the old centralized system.

The disgrace of the Communist Party and the impending investigation of many Communist deputies for allegedly supporting the coup gave a fillip to the hitherto rather weak Popular Front, led by Dr Zenon Poznyak. (It had one tenth of the seats in the Supreme Soviet.) There was an increasing upswell of nationalism in the last months of 1991. Although Belarus joined the other Slavic republics in forming the Commonwealth of Independent States, the leader of the Supreme Soviet, Stanislau Shushkevich, was almost immediately forced by the Popular Front to go to Moscow to try to water down the agreement. The republic was now talking of its own currency, army and a share of the Soviet Union's gold and currency reserves. For the first time, as the Soviet centre collapsed, independence seemed both possible and desirable but with an uncertain future. Belarus was dependent on the Russian Federation for vital resources such as coal, iron and steel and felt threatened by Yeltsin's announcement of the freeing of prices in the federation. With no real tradition as an independent entity, the republic looked to links with neighbouring republics, from Lithuania to Ukraine – perhaps as a bridge between the Baltic and the Black Sea. While the sense of national identity had hitherto been weak, the collapse of the Soviet Union certainly gave people a feeling of new possibilities.

13

Ukraine and Moldova Break Free

Ukraine

Recent History

Ukraine has an area of some 603,700 square kilometres (larger than any other European country) and a population of over 50 million. It is rich in minerals and agriculturally advanced by Soviet standards. Its history shows that it has never attained more than semi-autonomous status at best. The original ninth-century Rus was based in Kiev, uniting eastern Slavonic tribes centred on Kiev in the south and Novgorod in the north. As Russia emerged, there were rivalries between its princes and they were unable to resist the invasions of the Mongol-Tatars in the thirteenth century. Kievan Rus was destroyed and a stronger Russia grew around the principality of Moscow while the people of Kiev came to be regarded (although not by themselves) as provincials. Russia and eastern Ukraine were formally united in 1654 under the Pereyaslav agreement.

Eastern Ukraine has much stronger links with the Russians than the western areas, going back centuries to the time when Christian Slavs united to protect themselves against the Turks. There had also long been a tension between, on the one hand, identifying with the Russians in defeating the invading Poles and, on the other, consciousness of a distinctive Ukrainian identity. Ukrainian nationalism grew in the nineteenth century, especially in Galicia. At the time of the Russian Revolution and the end of the First World War Ukrainians fought against both the Bolsheviks and the Germans. The Soviet army conquered them and a civil war developed in which, with the help of the Poles, they tried but failed to expel the Soviets. From 1918 for three years Galicia formed the Republic of West Ukraine but it collapsed through lack of international support and inability to resist the better equipped Polish forces which attacked it. Poland then assimilated western Ukraine and, while the urban and landowning classes became predominantly Polish, the majority in the countryside was Ukrainian. Supported by the country dwellers guerrilla forces existed, especially the semi-fascist Organization of Ukrainian Nationalists (OUN). These guerrillas split into the Bandera (hard-line) and Melnyk (moderate) factions. In the Second World War they again fought against both the Soviets and the Germans, and the OUN became more liberal democratic in outlook. There was a brief eight-day period of nominal independence in 1941. After the Second World War western Ukraine was incorporated (with other territories) into the Ukrainian Soviet Socialist Republic. The role of the OUN was inherited by the Ukrainian Insurgent Army[1] which broadened its popular base in the 1940s.

Soviet Policy towards Ukraine

Soviet policy in Ukraine was comparatively liberal in the 1920s, but became repressive in the 1930s when Stalin's purges were at their height and Khrushchev was First Secretary of the Ukrainian Communist Party (UKP). Much terror resulted and there was a famine of massive proportions. Russification was suspended during the war but revived again afterwards with new signs of Stalinist repression. Under the influence of *glasnost* and the efforts of Memorial (the society for commemorating Stalin's victims) many graves and skeletons of secret police victims were found all over Ukraine. There was little resistance to the integration of western Ukraine from the wartime allies of the Soviet Union. Many Poles were deported to Poland. The minority but indigenous Greek Catholic Church in western Ukraine was abolished. A hurried sovietization programme was undertaken and collectivization of agriculture pushed through. More important, the area was industrialized and, as a result, there was an influx of Russians which had an effect on educational and cultural life, the socio-economic position of the peasants and remaining tacit support for the Greek Catholic Church.

On Stalin's death there were attempts by UKP leaders to win greater freedom of action, linked to socio-economic development and their own personal advancement under Khrushchev. Khrushchev was not prepared to use terror against the politically loyal leaders of the UKP or against the intellectuals – they too were now more assertive. Khrushchev, because he had been UKP First Secretary, promoted some of its officials to high levels in the CPSU, but there is little evidence of pro-Ukrainian influence in central policy-making. All this was short-lived and, by 1958, assimilation was being re-emphasized. Some UKP leaders were accused of undue nationalism and the First

Secretary Shelest was dismissed in 1972 when there was a shake-up in the Party, state and cultural apparatus.

The Greek (Ukrainian) Catholic Church

The Greek Catholic Church (although with a relatively small membership of about 4 million) had close links with the nationalist movement. It is a uniate church, that is, in communion with the Pope and the Roman Catholic Church, but with its own rites. Uniate churches have for centuries acted as a buffer between the Orthodox and Catholic Churches. The Greek Catholic Metropolitan Andrew Szepticki was hostile to the Russians and when the Nazis invaded Ukraine in June 1941 he wrote a pastoral letter declaring, 'We greet the victorious German Army as a deliverer from the enemy.' He may have thought that the Nazis would guarantee an independent Ukraine but they had no such intention. Supported by Metropolitan Andrew they set up the so-called Galician Army Division in 1943, made up of Ukrainians. The Ukrainians have argued that they needed a military force of their own to defend the interests of their country when the Germans were defeated. But, at the time, their uniate leaders openly supported the Nazis against the Soviets. In June 1944 the Galician Division was defeated as the Soviets advanced westwards across Ukraine. Its members dispersed, some becoming emigrés in Western Europe and North America, others being forcibly repatriated to their probable deaths in the Soviet Union.

Having driven out the Nazis from Ukraine and Poland, the Soviets arrested the new uniate Metropolitan, Bishop Slipyi. Accused of collaboration with the Ukrainian nationalist movement, he was tried and exiled to Russia (although later released by Khrushchev) along with most uniate priests and bishops. In 1946 a 'synod' was held in Soviet controlled Ukraine. The uniate church, accused of collaboration with the enemy, was dissolved (by 'its own free will'). Its churches, monasteries and libraries were handed over to the Russian Orthodox Church. Until recently it continued actively to exist only in Ukrainian communities in the West and has been renamed the Ukrainian Catholic Church.

The policy of *glasnost* saw a growth of religious toleration, which meant a resurgence of the uniate Ukrainian Catholics in western Ukraine. In spite of their relatively small numbers they were significant because of their association with Ukrainian nationalism and their links with exiled Ukrainians abroad. In the spring of 1989 the Ukrainian Catholics increased their campaign for legalization. Hitherto they had been forced to hold their services outdoors or in private homes. That summer some 100,000 people demonstrated in Lvov, the main centre of the Church, to demand legalization. In the autumn they started seizing Orthodox churches which they claimed had been taken from them when they were forcibly dissolved by Stalin. They felt that the Orthodox Church was reluctant to recognize their case. Legalization was granted by the Ukrainian government in December 1989 and the Orthodox Church also recognized their existence.

The passage of time and the advent of Gorbachev created a climate in which a new generation was prepared to seek reconciliation. At the beginning of December 1989 the Ukrainian Catholic leader in exile in Rome, Cardinal Myroslav Lubachivsky, issued a statement saying that his Church was prepared to extend its hand to the Russian Orthodox Church 'as a sign of peace, Christian love, forgiveness, reconciliation and respect'. He returned to Ukraine on 30 March 1991 to be the first Ukrainian Catholic patriarch since Stalin's forced abolition of the Church to celebrate mass in their Cathedral of St George in Lvov. Both Gorbachev and the Pope were anxious for the Catholics and the Orthodox to reach an accommodation, sharing church buildings, etc. But centuries of division and conflict would have to be overcome and relations between the churches were not good.

An additional factor in the religious situation is the revival of the Ukrainian Autocephalous (Independent) Orthodox Church, giving Ukrainians another opportunity to assert their sense of national identity. The Church (which is not recognized by the Orthodox Patriarch of Constantinople, the nominal head of Orthodox churches) has some strength in western Ukraine. In October 1990 there were incidents when the Autocephalous Patriarch, Mstyslav, returned to Kiev after forty-six years exile in North America to preach at St Sophia's Cathedral and claim it for his Church. A few days later, Alexei, Patriarch of Moscow and All Russia, came to celebrate the liturgy there on behalf of the Russian Orthodox Church. Angry demonstrations against his visit did not succeed and Rukh (the Ukrainian Popular Front) claimed that Patriarch Alexei's visit was 'a spiritual assault on Ukraine by Moscow'. Thus further emphasis was given to the volatile religious situation in the republic. The pressure of nationalism was later demonstrated when the Orthodox Church in Ukraine decided to break away from the Russian Orthodox Church and requested permission from Patriarch Alexei to appoint a separate Ukrainian patriarch. It also called upon its members to vote for independence in the referendum of December 1991.

Perestroika *in Ukraine*

When Gorbachev tried to get *perestroika* moving he encountered opposition from the UKP, and especially from the Party Secretary,

Vladimir Shcherbitsky. The UKP had long had a reputation of being particularly oppressive and the elections in March 1989 saw the defeat of Party leaders in several Ukrainian cities. The third anniversary of the Chernobyl nuclear disaster[2] was marked by big demonstrations in Kiev, the capital, demanding new safety standards. This grass-roots protest movement gained much of its initial impetus from the environmentalist Greens, who, some time before, had set up a movement called Green World. At their rally in November 1988, on ecological and nationalist themes, ten thousand people were present. The Ukrainian radicals were lagging behind those in the Baltic republics. The Writers' Union drew up a programme for a Popular Front Movement (known as Rukh and led by Ivan Drach); it was published in February 1989 although not without encountering difficulties from the authorities. Its original aim was basically a call for decentralization, that is, more control by the republic of its own affairs. The main active supporters were the intelligentsia, engineers and scientists who wanted increased contact with the outside world, managers who wanted greater independence from the centre, and a small number of workers who wanted independent trade unions and more control over their workplaces. But over time the tendency was to move towards demanding independence.

The UKP was originally unenthusiastic about Rukh, branding it as an intellectuals' movement, suggesting it was anti-Soviet and anyway unnecessary because the Party was dealing with ecological and language issues. Party members were discouraged from joining. There were no high Party officials prepared to take a radical line, as happened in the Baltic republics. There was, however, a difference between eastern and western Ukraine. In Lvov in western Ukraine the Communists were steadily forced on to the sidelines, while in Kiev in eastern Ukraine the Communists were still so strong that, until the collapse of the coup, pro-independence demonstrators were not allowed to gather in the city centre. Gorbachev visited Ukraine in February 1989 and heard much criticism of his economic reforms, which had failed to relieve shortages. He wanted to urge the UKP to show more enthusiasm in backing *perestroika*, and spoke to a meeting of reform-minded UKP members, encouraging them to work for democratization, elected bodies and to pay more attention to rank and file Communists. He told workers on the streets of Kiev that they should get rid of bosses who did not perform well. But the UKP was dragging its heels over issues such as the examination of Stalin's crimes and the establishment of private co-operatives.

In March 1990 Rukh declared its intention to become the republic's first fully-fledged opposition party, campaigning for independence from the Soviet Union. However, the move was not supported by the full leadership. Those who did support it wanted complete independence and for the UKP to take full responsibility for the 1932 famine, the politics of Russification and the liquidation of the Ukrainian intelligentsia. One fifth of the delegates at the founding Rukh Congress were Party members, indicating that the UKP was seriously split. Numbers of Rukh supporters were elected to the Ukrainian Supreme Soviet, which was also split between pro-independence groups and those loyal to the Soviet Union. Rukh won many seats in local elections, especially in western Ukraine. But the authorities were still taking a hard line. Nineteen students were gaoled in February 1990 after there were widespread strikes demanding the abolition of Marxist-Leninist ideology courses and Party cells at the universities. In December Rukh formed the Democratic Party of Ukraine.

Sovereignty and Independence

In July Ukraine followed other republics in proclaiming sovereignty, under which Ukrainian law was to take precedence over Soviet law in its territory. It also claimed the right to raise its own army and issue its own currency, but a majority of deputies maintained that Ukraine should stay in the Soviet Union and develop, rather than break, 'the existing social, economic, cultural and other links' with other Soviet republics. They also voted for a 'permanently neutral state, not participating in military blocs' which enjoyed the 'supremacy, independence, absolute authority and indivisibility' of its power on its own territory (Rettie, 1990c). The campaign for independence and breaking away from the Soviet Union began to spread from western to eastern Ukraine. One impetus for this was dissatisfaction with the proposals for economic reform, even the Shatalin '500-day' plan being seen as not radical enough because it still preserved too strong a centre. This view came to be held both by the UKP and by the Democratic Bloc, the main opposition in the Ukrainian Supreme Soviet representing about forty groups. Support for the market economy was often mainly political. It was seen as the best way to break up the old system and the Communist Party organization which was still strong in industrial areas.

The most remarkable turnaround was the support for the nationalist cause by the UKP. The leadership seemed to have decided that its only chance of retaining political influence was to lead the nationalist movement and to control the process of privatization. The Ukrainian Supreme Soviet passed resolutions in favour of its own national army, banned the deployment of conscripts in areas of inter-ethnic tension and demanded that all Ukrainian conscripts serve only on Ukrainian territory by 1 December 1990. None of these resolution had the force of law but they were symbolic of the republic's aspirations and understanding of itself. They suggested that only a very loose federation would satisfy them, even with the other Slavic republics. Demonstrations against Ukraine's Communist-dominated government started early in October, including a hunger strike by some 350 students at Kiev University, and these gradually grew in numbers and significance. After a week, in which the demonstrations spread to Kharkov and other cities, the Communist Prime Minister, Vitaly Madol, resigned. Radicals were disturbed in November by the arrest of Stepan Khmara, leader of the radical Republican Party, after a scuffle with a policeman. His trial was suspended indefinitely in May 1991, and he was given bail, although five others arrested with him remained in prison. Charges were finally dropped after the abortive coup. There were fears that the police were to get sweeping new powers. At the same time the Ukrainian Supreme Soviet adopted a decree banning demonstrations during working hours and limiting them to designated areas. These events led to the temporary suspension of the Supreme Soviet, because of a boycott by the entire opposition, and the breaking up by the police of pro-Khmara demonstrations. However, the Supreme Soviet did vote to add questions to the referendum on the Union concerning the acceptance of the republic's sovereignty.

The All-Union Referendum

The all-Union referendum recorded a vote of 70 per cent for a renewed Union in the republic but 80 per cent of these voters said yes in answer to the question whether Ukrainians wanted 'Ukraine to be in a union of Soviet sovereign states based on the declaration of sovereignty'. The vote for the latter was, as expected, much heavier in western Ukraine. The Supreme Soviet voted to adopt a new constitution in the republic and to hold a referendum on independence in the autumn. There would be a popularly elected president and Ukrainians would have a right to private property. They adopted a market reform plan which assumed 'the Ukraine's complete economic and political independence'. The republic also planned to take the military complex under its control from 1 January 1992. A major issue was whether to sign Gorbachev's Union Treaty before deciding the question of the new republican constitution. Old-style Communists wanted the treaty signed straight away, but other Communists were split between progressives who advocated delay, and the uncertain, illustrating the increasing political ineffectiveness of the UKP. In the event the Supreme Soviet voted to postpone a decision on the Union Treaty until after the adoption of a new constitution, a move which had wide popular support. Increasingly, leading spokesmen, even the hard-line Communist Party leader, Stanislav Gurenko, emphasized Ukraine's sovereignty and need to control its own resources. Leonid Kravchuk, Communist chairman of the Supreme Soviet and head of state, worked hard to create a consensus between Communists and the pro-independence groups. Meanwhile the republic more and more tried to go its own way in economic and financial matters, setting up checkpoints on its borders to prevent agricultural products being smuggled in from neighbouring republics to be sold at higher prices, turning over defence establishments to consumer production and concluding trade agreements with Hungary, Czechoslovakia and other countries. There was talk of introducing its own currency.

Ukraine's Reaction to the Attempted Coup

Kravchuk did not condemn the coup outright, but did ask for recognition of the supremacy of Ukrainian laws on its territory, which contradicted the coup leaders' statement on the supremacy of Soviet laws throughout the Union. The following day the leadership praesidium condemned the coup by twenty-five votes to fifteen and declared the coup leaders' actions to be 'null and void' in Ukraine. It was also clear that elements in the military and police were against the coup and they made contact with opposition groups to urge the bringing of Ukrainian armed forces under military control with the formation of a Ukrainian National Guard. Rukh condemned the coup from the start and declared its support for Yeltsin. Kravchuk was said to have voted for the praesidium resolution and later telephoned a strong condemnation to Moscow. The initial hesitation by the Ukrainian government increased divisions between the parties. Kravchuk defended himself by pointing out that there were hard-line Communists in the parliamentary praesidium and he was not an elected president who could issue decrees as Yeltsin did. Although communications in the Crimea where Gorbachev was under arrest were under the control of the Ukrainian government, Kravchuk was unable to get through to him.

Communist Party buildings were soon occupied and their assets frozen. There was a fear that Communists, still in a very strong position in the Supreme Soviet, were trying to save themselves by declaring their independence from the CPSU and supporting nationalism. But it was then revealed that the proposed state of emergency had been approved by the UKP, which led Kravchuk to leave the Soviet Communist Party's Politburo and Central Committee. It appears that at some stage he also left the Party itself. The Party was weakened by the resignation of many of its deputies and lost its parliamentary majority. Local authorities in Kiev and western Ukraine acted to occupy Communist

Party offices. The new leader of the UKP, Alexander Moroz, said the Party would separate itself from the CPSU and form an independent party with a new name. There would be a special commission to investigate the Party's complicity in the attempted coup. The feeling among many, however, was that, after regrouping, the Communist Party would remain an important political force. Then, unexpectedly, the UKP was formally dissolved on 4 September after increasing revelations of collusion in the attempted coup.

The Ukrainian parliament also announced the seizure of all-Union property on its territory and the creation of a Ukrainian army and national guard. Ukraine was in a strong position in any negotiations with Moscow or other republics. It provided 70 per cent of the Soviet Union's manganese, 80 per cent of its sulphur and 40 per cent of its titanium. Ukrainian iron and steel production was only slightly lower than in the Russian Federation and, in some consumer goods such as television sets it was actually higher. Its grain output amounted to one quarter of the Soviet Union's production. The vast Donbass coalfield extends into Russia, raising questions about who owned what. The republic needed Russian oil for its chemical industry, but like the Russian Federation, Ukraine was, in principle, able to generate a trade surplus with its neighbours.

The Independence Vote

On 26 August 1991 the Ukrainian Supreme Soviet voted overwhelmingly to declare the republic independent and sovereign, one in which Soviet law no longer applied; all this was to be ratified by a referendum and presidential election on 1 December. The unease felt by Yeltsin's reference to renegotiating boundaries was countered by pointing to the treaty with Russia of November 1990, which stated 'respect for the territorial integrity of each other's existing borders'. Nevertheless a Russian delegation was sent to the republic to calm Ukrainian fears. A Russian–Ukrainian working commission was set up to negotiate economic and defence agreements and a joint declaration issued which, while not mentioning Ukrainian independence, also had no role for the central government. Ukrainian apprehension was not entirely assuaged. A significant development was the decision of Ukraine on 17 October not to sign the economic treaty (see p. 133). Eventually the Supreme Soviet agreed to the initialling of the treaty, but it was clear that they did not think it would have any effect in halting the decline in the state of the economy.

The difference between the attitudes towards independence of western and eastern Ukraine, complicated by the presence of a sizable

Russian minority in the east, had declined dramatically in 1990–1. All the talk after the attempted coup was of independence, even among the Russian community. The situation between East and West Ukraine remained difficult, however, because of the quarrels between the Orthodox Church and the Ukrainian Catholic Church (not to speak of Latin-rite Catholics and Autocephalous Orthodox). A week before the election, Kravchuk, the leading presidential candidate, was saying that Ukraine would not join Gorbachev's proposed Soviet federation. A further blow to Gorbachev came when President Bush let it be known that the United States would give early recognition to Ukraine if it voted for independence; this was a significant change of policy as three weeks before the attempted coup Bush, during a speech in Kiev, had warned Ukrainians against 'suicidal nationalism', as part of his policy of supporting Gorbachev. Everyone realized that a Ukrainian vote for independence would end Gorbachev's efforts to preserve some form of union. Gorbachev did not help his cause by hectoring speeches to the Ukrainians saying that independence would be against common sense and a catastrophe. Yeltsin also expressed opposition to independence, recognizing that it would create difficulties for Russia if Ukraine introduced its own currency and army.

In the event, Ukraine voted overwhelmingly for independence and elected Kravchuk president on the first ballot. More than 90 per cent voted and over 80 per cent of them voted yes. Even strongly Russian areas such as the Crimea and the Donbass coal-mining region returned a yes vote. While Gorbachev responded by saying, unconvincingly, that the independence vote did not mean Ukraine would break with the Union, Yeltsin quickly recognized Ukrainian independence. Western powers indicated that they would give recognition as soon as assurances over meeting the former Soviet Union's agreements and treaty obligations had been received.

Independent Ukraine

On Kravchuk's return from Brest, the Ukrainian parliament ratified the Commonwealth of Independent States agreement with the Russian Federation and Belarus, but voted to amend a section which guaranteed the territorial integrity and inviolability of state borders only within the framework of the CIS. It wanted an unqualified guarantee. It also wanted member states to create their own armies by 'reforming units of the armed forces of the Soviet Union stationed on their territories'. The issue of a separate currency became crucial. It was seen as more than a symbolic break from the perceived colonial-type relationship of the past where every significant decision was taken in

Moscow. It was to be the best way to defend the Ukrainian economy. In the interim, a coupon system was developed for basic goods. As well as the money price, purchasers had to hand over an equivalent number of coupons. People from other republics had no access to these coupons and a separate market in coupons was created. There was a strong feeling that the country should reorientate itself towards the West, including eventual membership of NATO and the European Community. Ukrainians realized that they did not have the skills, the technology and the finance to survive in the immediate future without western help. At independence, only 2.5 per cent of Ukrainian trade was with market economies.

Some of the Soviet Union's nuclear arsenal was situated in Ukraine. But in its declaration of sovereignty the Supreme Soviet declared that Ukraine would 'abide by the three non-nuclear principles: not to participate, not to produce and not to obtain nuclear weapons'. Both opposition and Communists agreed that nuclear weapons would be handed back to Moscow. This view was soon to be modified. It was realized that eliminating nuclear weapons on their territory would enhance the nuclear strength of the Russian Federation of which both sides remained very suspicious. They wanted the Soviet command and control system to be replaced by an inter-republican collective nuclear security body. Meanwhile nuclear weapons would remain on Ukrainian soil for an unspecified time and Ukraine wanted joint control over their use. In October a further significant defence decision was taken to set up the republic's own armed forces. The Ukrainian Defence Minister, General Konstantin Morozov, claimed jurisdiction over 'all military units' on Ukrainian territory, thus raising questions about the command and loyalty of the Soviet army. The control of the nuclear-armed Black Sea Fleet was another crucial issue. The Russians moved quickly to transfer their most modern aircraft carrier, the *Kuznetsov*, from the Black Sea to Murmansk in the Arctic. It was clear that this dispute was going to be difficult to resolve.

In addition to the Russians, Ukraine has a significant number of other ethnic minorities on its territory. More than a quarter of the population is not Ukrainian. There are half a million Jews, as well as Hungarians, Belarusians, Poles, Greeks, Germans, Tatars, and so on. The government tried to carry the minorities with them. In November an All-Ukrainian Inter-Ethnic Congress met in Odessa and voted overwhelmingly to support independence. Nevertheless there were problems. For example, Romania raised the issue of territories in Ukraine lost to the Soviet Union under the Nazi–Soviet Pact of 1939. There were also long-standing disagreements with Poland and Hungary over the treatment of their minorities, while the mainly Russian Crimea seemed likely to try to secede.

Moldova (Moldavia)

Introduction

The majority of the people of Moldova (formerly Moldavia) are Romanians and speak Romanian, but the tsars tried to dilute their domination by encouraging other ethnic groups to settle there. As a result the Romanians are a much smaller proportion of the urban population than they are in the countryside. After alternating between Turkish and Russian rule, the region known as Bessarabia became Russian in 1878. National feelings came to the surface again on the outbreak of the Revolution in 1917. In December of that year a National Council was set up on the model of a similar council in Ukraine, and Bessarabia was proclaimed an autonomous constituent member of the Federation of Russian Republics. The situation was complicated by the breakup and disorder on the military front. The National Council had to send to the Romanian army for help. Romanian troops occupied Bessarabia in January 1918 but it was asserted that the move had no political significance. The council, again following Ukraine which had broken its link with Moscow, then proclaimed Bessarabia an independent Moldavian republic. This could not last, as the republic had no means of financial support. In March the council voted for the incorporation of Bessarabia into Romania with rights of provincial autonomy. The defeat of the Germans and the union of all Romanians in one state led to full incorporation into Romania, recognized by the Treaty of Paris in 1920.

The Soviet Union never accepted this arrangement and the Second World War revived the question. Romania joined the war on the side of Nazi Germany in May 1940 and, in June, the Soviet Union presented it with an ultimatum demanding the cession of Bessarabia and northern Bukovina. Two days later the province was occupied by the Red Army. The German attack on the Soviet Union gave the Romanians another chance, and they had reoccupied the province by the end of 1941. With the defeat of Germany the position changed once more. By the armistice of September 1944 the Romanians agreed to cede Bessarabia to the Soviet Union. The northern Ukrainian tip and the southern Danubian districts were incorporated into Ukraine while the centre was joined to the Moldavian Autonomous Soviet Socialist Republic to create the Moldavian Soviet Socialist Republic.

In June 1989 tens of thousands of people demonstrated in the capital, Kishinev, to 'mourn' the establishment of their republic on 28 June 1940. They demanded the recognition of Romanian as the official language and a return to the use of Latin script rather than the Cyrillic imposed in 1948. Similar demonstrations had taken place earlier in the year with speakers demanding the resignation of senior government and Communist Party officials and calling for the creation of a new republic to include southern Bessarabia (strategically near Odessa) and northern Bukovina, which they believed had been unjustly and illegally incorporated into Ukraine. The use of the Cyrillic alphabet now became the symbol and focus of discontent among a large number of Moldavia's 4 million people. The Movement for the Defence and Support of *Perestroika* was formed to support both *perestroika* and also the cultural identity of Moldavia. The republic's Communist Party took a hostile attitude towards the movement, banning a demonstration to commemorate the mass deportation of Moldavian peasants by Stalin. Violent attacks were made on organizers when the demonstration was finally held. The Party refused to publish the movement's relatively moderate programme in the Party-controlled press. The result was to turn a basically cultural movement into a nationalistic one.

At the same time the movement diversified. A hitherto unobtrusive cultural and music club named after the Moldavian writer, Alexei Mateyvich, became an organizational focus of nationalism. It was now accused of fomenting inter-ethnic tensions by demanding the departure of non-Moldavian 'undesirables'. Next came the Green movement, drawing attention to the degradation of the urban and rural environment, for which they blamed Moscow. A League of Students was also established and a student demonstration protesting at the Party's hostile response to their pro-*perestroika* programme was savagely broken up. This led to the turning of a student Komsomol meeting at Kishinev University into a large demonstration of several thousand people demanding a correction to official accounts of earlier events, restoration of the Latin alphabet, and the return to the university of buildings taken for government use. Some concessions came, the Party accepting that, as an experiment, a newspaper and a magazine should be printed in Latin characters. The local Party also called for the republic's Supreme Soviet to prepare a new law on the status of the Moldavian language. *Izvestia*, the official Soviet government newspaper, commented that the issue was a 'minefield':

> The Party and government leadership avoid public discussion of the language question, while the representatives of the intelligentsia and the students have no access into the rooms where decisions are taken. (Steele, 1989a)

In the autumn of 1989, after a huge rally of three-quarters of a million people coming from all over Moldavia and the Moldavian areas of the Ukraine, Moldavian was proclaimed the official language – causing a hostile reaction from the Russian immigrants.

By the end of 1989, after the fall of Nicolae Ceausescu, the Communist leader in Romania, the atmosphere had changed, and people were talking of independence, or union with Romania. The link with Romania was crucial but, as in the Baltic republics, the Moldavians also rejected the Nazi–Soviet Pact whose secret protocols had enabled the Soviet Union to absorb Moldavia. They also saw a close analogy with the two Germanys, but moderates felt that independence or unity with Romania were for the distant future. More immediate problems had to be faced such as social and economic difficulties, and ethnic questions. As well as the areas now in Ukraine, there was the eastern part of Moldavia around Tiraspol, where Russians were in a majority. The Gagauz (Christian Turks) were also asserting themselves. Economic and trade relations with Moscow were too close to break quickly, and Moscow flatly rejected any suggestion of reunion with Romania. Like those in other republics, Moldavia's moderate radicals envisaged some form of confederation of sovereign states based on a new all-Union treaty and a new constitution.

The Communist Party emphasized its ability to concentrate resources on reviving the economy, but was hampered by its past record. After violent clashes between nationalist demonstrators and the security forces in November 1989 a new Party Secretary, Pyotr Luchinsky, was appointed. A native-born Moldavian, Luchinsky was a conciliator and made a good first impression. But a nationalist group, the Stefan the Great Movement, the leading opposition umbrella opposition organization co-ordinating the campaign for the forthcoming election, was able to make an emotional appeal with the slogans of 'Liberty' and 'Unity' which the Communist Party could not match. In addition, there was the Popular Front, which was not calling for immediate independence or unity with Romania, but did demand autonomy, a new constitution, monetary reform, demilitarized status, a multi-party system, and a renewal of national culture and identity. The republic, its members believed, should have full control over its natural and human resources. The Communist Party would lose its monopoly and privileges.

The Russian Revolt

The question of the ethnic minorities was serious. The Russian political organization, Unity, was for loyalty to the Soviet Union. The Russians made up 13 per cent of the population but had a disproportionate share of economic power. A narrow strip of land on the Dniestr river had been attached to Moldavia to help dilute the Romanian population. It had a 26 per cent Russian population and Romanians there were very assimilated. Supported by other minorities, especially the Ukrainians, they staged pro-Soviet political strikes in the autumn of 1989 and brought trains and some factories to a halt for several weeks. In January 1990 a referendum in Tiraspol, the second city and 87 per cent non-Moldavian, voted overwhelmingly in favour of the status of an autonomous republic within the Soviet Union. Vladimir Rylyakov, chairman of the Tiraspol Council of the Union of Workers' Collectives, said the vote was a weapon in case the nationalists tried to secede from the Soviet Union. He saw Tiraspol joining with the towns of Bendery, Dubossary, Rybnitsa, and Grigoriopol, with their surrounding districts, to form an autonomous republic–'a very strong economic force' - with a population of 750,000 and a major part of Moldavia's industry. Tiraspol's referendum was declared unconstitutional by the Moldavian government, and Rylyakov said that his organization had had its official registration withdrawn. But it continued to hold rallies and demonstrations.

In November a number of people were killed and wounded in clashes between ethnic Russians and the police near the town of Dubossary. The Russians now declared independence and planned their own elections. Gorbachev sent a special envoy, Marshal Akhromeyev, to negotiate with the Russians. His first proposal was that the Russians should call off their elections in return for the Moldavian Supreme Soviet solemnly declaring that it would sign the new Union Treaty and not seek incorporation into Romania. This did not meet with much success. The spokesman for Unity, Vladimir Solonar, saw the Russians' action as a negotiating tactic to try to have Moldavia divided into a federation, with three separate areas, one for the Gagauz, one for the Moldavians, and one for the Russians. He strongly denied that the campaign was backed by the Communist Party in an effort to regain its influence. But it was clear that the Dniestr Russians had close contacts with Soyuz, the group of conservative deputies in the all-Union CPD in Moscow. The Russian area, he argued, was never part of pre-war and Romanian-ruled Bessarabia. It was only Romanian during the wartime occupation. In the same month the Russians completed their unofficial elections and faced confrontation with both the Moldavian and Soviet governments. Soviet soldiers were in the region.

The Gagauz Revolt

Another prominent minority, the Gagauz, 14 per cent of the population, feared that independence would mean domination by Moldavians without the protection of Moscow. They were therefore trying to gain independence for their area. In August 1990 they declared their own republic and followed it by holding elections in October. As election day approached, armed Moldavian volunteers from Kishinev moved on the town of Koran to block the elections. The Moldavian Supreme Soviet proclaimed a state of emergency in the Gagauz districts, and Soviet interior troops were sent to the area to restore order. Violence flared at the end of November, when Moldavian nationalists attacked checkpoints on the Romanian border, demanding the withdrawal of Interior Ministry troops guarding the Gagauz minority. Moldavian and Gagauz representatives had agreed on a withdrawal of all 'volunteers' and the establishment of a conciliation commission. But tension arose when the unofficial Gagauz soviet elected a president. The Moldavians claimed that the Gagauz were being manipulated by Moscow to undermine their own nationalist aspirations. They argued that the Gagauz were Russified, supporting Russian interests, and with most speaking Russian rather than Turkish. On 30 December the Moldavian Supreme Soviet voted to comply with an order from Gorbachev that the Gagauz and the Russians must rescind their declarations of independence, and a law which made Moldavian (Romanian) the official language rather than Russian must be reviewed. The two minorities agreed to obey if the Moldavians did so as well.

Reaction to the Soviet Crisis

While the Soviet Union made limited cultural and political concessions, the new government in Romania, aware of Romania's dependence on Soviet trade, also tried to dampen the Moldavians' aspirations. But both governments were overtaken by events. In February 1990 the Moldavian Popular Front won the elections to the republic's Supreme Soviet. Although cautious, it had steadily increased its demands for closer relations with Romania. Early in May the Soviet authorities agreed to open the frontier for one day. Organized by Moldavian cultural associations (ostensibly non-political) hundreds of thousands crossed the frontier into Moldavia in a demonstration of unity. In June, a similar event enabled thousands of Moldavians to enter Romania.

The Moldavian Communist Party was steadily losing influence and credibility in the Romanian population. Its organization began to disintegrate and it split into three factions. The radicals, mainly intelligentsia, tried to get the Party to support *perestroika* and nationalist aspirations. They wanted to break with the CPSU. But they met with little success and tended to resign to join Democratic Platform. The centre tried to follow the Gorbachev reform policies, but was hampered by lack of support among the Party bureaucracy. The conservatives were well organized with support among Party officials and were based in Russified cities and the all-Union industries. Their strongest organization was the Joint Council of Workers' Collectives (OSTK) established in the factories to the east of the Dniestr river and the main force in the self-proclaimed 'Dniestr Soviet Socialist Republic'. The Gagauz areas also gave support to them. The conservatives had support in Moscow and among the military, upheld traditional authoritarian Soviet rule, were confrontational in their attitude to the Moldavian government, and at loggerheads with the official republic Party's leadership. Their policy was to split Moldavia into three republics. The official leadership of the Party seemed unable to stem the loss of membership or to find a consensus to unite the factions.

In June 1990 Moldavia followed other Soviet republics in passing a declaration of sovereignty, saying that Soviet laws would only take effect when its Supreme Soviet ratified them. The Supreme Soviet adopted the Romanian name of the republic, Moldova, and declared all residents to be Moldovan citizens. One of the manifestations of the weakening legitimacy of the Soviet government was an increasing avoidance of the military draft. The Moldovan government was apprehensive that the Soviet army might intervene for this reason. A tense period followed with Moldova anxiously assuring Moscow that it could handle the situation itself. The government finally gave in to Moscow and revoked its law under which the Moldovans were not obliged to obey the draft and could not be punished for refusing to serve. Events in the Baltic republics continued to have an impact. A 'National Salvation Committee' appeared in Tiraspol. Various threatening noises were made about troop movements and the commander of the garrison in Odessa, General Morozov, said the secession of Moldova would not be permitted since too much blood had been spilt in obtaining the territory in 1940. A government crisis followed, with the President, Mircea Snegur, trying to resign, saying that he was being put under Communist pressure.

The Response to the Attempted Coup

The Moldovan government immediately condemned the coup and banned Soviet newspapers supporting it. Anti-coup demonstrations took place in the capital and called for the banning of the Communist Party. The Communist Party leader, Grigorii Yeremei, resigned from the CPSU Politburo and the Central Committee. Within a few days the government had banned Communist Party organizations from all government departments and arrested leaders of the Russian and Gagauz communities who were said to have supported the coup. The Russians responded by threatening to cut off power and gas to the rest of the republic. A week later Moldova joined other republics in declaring its independence, a decision of Romanian deputies, since Russian and Gagauz deputies boycotted the vote. President Snegur also consolidated his position by being popularly elected (albeit unopposed) in December. Although Snegur still talked of eventual reunion with Romania he made clear that this was a long-term prospect. The Moldovan economy was so integrated with other Soviet republics that any other attitude was unrealistic. It was also a reflection of the relatively unstable situation in Romania itself.

In spite or because of the independence declaration, the disputes with the Russians and Gagauz continued to simmer. Both minority groups held referendums at the beginning of December 1991 (declared illegal by the Moldovan government) and both voted for independence by large majorities. The 'Dniestr Republic' also held a presidential election at about the same time and elected Igor Smirnov. The area had already created its own police force and republican guard as well as appointing a defence minister and taken the army under its control. It was refusing to pay taxes to the Moldovan government. The difficulty for the rebels was that they were not recognized by either Yeltsin or Gorbachev. The Dniestr area has no border with Russia. On the collapse of the Soviet Union Moldova joined the Commonwealth of Independent States. But its economic situation remained serious and inextricably tied to other former Soviet republics. The disruptive ethnic disputes remained unresolved and explosive. The future was therefore uncertain and hazardous.

Notes

1 For an account of the Ukrainian Insurgent Army see the article by Laba Fajfer in *Problems of Communism* 27 (5), September – October 1988, pp. 77–84.
2 In 1986 there was a major nuclear disaster at the Chernobyl power station causing widespread and long-lasting contamination in Ukraine and Belorussia.

14

The Baltic Republics Regain Independence

Introduction

The pre-twentieth century histories of the Baltic states are varied. As feudal possessions of the Teutonic Knights the Latvians and Estonians were Protestant subjects of German landowners. The Lithuanians are Catholics and, in the medieval period, were joint rulers of a Polish–Lithuanian empire extending from the Baltic to the Black Sea. All three came under Russian control when Peter the Great defeated the Swedes and established Russian power in the Baltic, together with the creation of a new port and capital, St Petersburg. The defeat and collapse of the tsarist regime in the First World War and the Revolution gave the Baltic states an opportunity to assert their independence, but Poland took advantage of the civil war to seize southern Lithuania (including Vilnius). Economic depression in the 1930s destroyed the republics' mainly agrarian exports and led to large-scale emigration to the United States. Quasi-fascist regimes were established in all three republics. These could not agree on their international role. Latvia and Estonia wanted to develop co-operation and to include Poland. But Lithuania, with a history of government by Polish princes, was preoccupied by what it perceived as the Polish threat, and preferred to look towards Moscow or Berlin. Poland did try to persuade both Baltic and Scandinavian states to form a defensive military alliance, but with no success.

The Nazi–Soviet Pact of 1939 forced the Baltic states to accept the deployment of Soviet troops for mutual protection and in 1940 they were absorbed into the Soviet Union. After the Nazi invasion of 1941 there were anti-Soviet revolts and numbers of Baltic troops fought for the Nazis, but the Nazis ignored their new declarations of independence. After the re-establishment of Soviet rule, a ten-year guerrilla war was fought, with support from United States and British intelligence. Large numbers of Baltic inhabitants were deported to the Russian Federation, while many Estonians and Latvians fled to Sweden, where they continued to campaign for independence. However, Sweden recognized the annexation and handed over some refugees to the Soviet Union after the war, but other western powers never formally recognized its legality. Although Soviet rule was acknowledged *de facto* it was denied *de jure*. The three republics were much affected by rapid industrialization, including urbanization, the proportionate increase in industrial workers and decline of rural workers, the expansion of education and the rise in the standard of living. The Communist Party in the republics had a low native ethnic membership but a higher level in the leadership cadres.

Immigration

Immigration, especially of Russians, was a serious cause for concern and the presence of these sizable Russian populations remained a difficulty even after independence came, following the coup. Such immigration has not significantly altered the ethnic composition in Lithuania, but has done so in Latvia and Estonia, where there has been a substantial decline in the ethnic native proportion of their populations. These anxieties were confirmed when the results of the 1989 population census were published. It revealed that Latvians, for example, only just made up a majority in their own republic. Whether the influx of Russians *actually* threatened the indigenous culture had not yet been objectively studied, but the belief that it did caused much dissatisfaction.

Was immigration covert Russification, as was alleged by nationalists? Lithuania had the least immigration but the greatest resistance to Soviet rule, especially in the period 1944–50 and in the early 1970s. Immigration was probably closely related to economic development, which was further advanced in Estonia and Latvia. Their other attractive qualities (such as a higher standard of living relative to other Soviet republics) also encouraged immigration. There were mitigating factors. Immigrants were geographically concentrated in the industrial centres, but diffusion was increasing and may have been accelerated by the agro-towns policy (the policy of integrating rural villages into urban agricultural communities). The urban middle class had great significance. It was more culturally conscious than in, say, Belorussia, Moldavia and the Central Asian republics. A large proportion of native dissent had been among students and the intelligentsia, and was linked to the big rise in the number of students in the 1960s.

Economic Factors

The Baltic states have used western standards as their criteria of comparison when considering their prosperity and standard of living, which sustained their discontent. Their position in the 1980s owed much to a high level of investment (a Moscow decision) and immigration. Until the advent of Gorbachev, their future also seemed to depend on these factors. They had shown hostility to Khrushchev's economic regionalization plans and to Brezhnev's emphasis on the 'drawing together' of peoples. It should be noted, however, that not all deviations from central policy were nationalistic. They could be local decisions made in order to enhance the role of the local bureaucracy in decision-making. Among the many complaints that the Baltic states had against the Moscow authorities was the lack of republic-level control over major industries, the size of whose workforce (largely Russian) was unknown to them. This made it virtually impossible for them to organize their own economies properly. Most such industries paid no taxes locally and ignored anti-pollution laws.

Language, Religion and Culture

Language had always been a source of potential tension. Russians did not learn the native language and over the years there had been a decline in the number of native language titles published, although those that were had increased circulations. There had been a rise in mixed marriages in urban areas but apparently little language erosion. In spite of Russian immigration the local cultures remained vigorous but, until independence, they were hampered by the pressure on people to learn Russian while the Russians did not come under similar pressure to learn the indigenous languages. There was also no provision for native language instruction outside the republics. In Lithuania the Catholic Church is closely identified with ethnic, political and cultural institutions. In Latvia and Estonia the population was originally forcibly converted and the majority Church – Lutheran – was a German institution until the twentieth century. Therefore it is not so close to the indigenous nationality in these republics. Nineteenth-century Russification in Lithuania was resisted by religious leaders and organizations. In Latvia and Estonia it impinged more on the Baltic German organizations and paradoxically assisted the emergence of a stronger national identity by weakening the hold of the Baltic Germans.

The Effect of Glasnost and Perestroika

A major effect of *glasnost* was to precipitate a crisis in the Baltic Communist Parties, which led to their loss of political control. Each party was divided into those who were either in favour of, or opposed to, *perestroika* (or, at least, its pace). In addition, tensions emerged between the native and immigrant populations and an open debate developed on secession. In 1989 there was real fear of a collapse of authority, the imposition of martial law and even direct rule from Moscow. Unlike the Caucasus and Central Asia, where there was ethnic unrest and violence, the Baltic republics adopted a calmer, more gradual approach to political reform. They moved step by step, making it very hard for Moscow to stop them. All three republics had Popular Fronts, set up in 1988, originally in support of *perestroika* but soon to develop into political parties. Roughly a third of their memberships were Communists and all three also had radical wings which were the first to demand full independence, a cause which came to be embraced by virtually all the people of the indigenous nationalities and also eventually by many immigrants. They played down socialism in their programmes and advocated a western-style market economy and a multi-party system.

There were also outright pro-independence parties in each republic, as well as organizations which claimed to be non-ethnic but in effect represented the immigrant communities, led by the Russians (Interfront in Latvia, Intermovement in Estonia and Unity in Lithuania). These were particularly worried about efforts to make each republic's native language the official one, and to restrict immigration. Russians were becoming increasingly unhappy and in November 1990 took part in a meeting of 'Soviet internationalists' (that is, believers in preserving the Soviet Union) from all over the Soviet Union who vowed to fight 'fascist' nationalists in the republics. They demanded guaranteed rights as minorities and the continued incorporation of the Baltic republics into the Soviet Union.

Economic Aspirations under Perestroika

On 1 January 1990 the Baltic republics formally went over to a system of economic autonomy. They were all planning to issue their own currencies during 1990, and eventually to make them convertible (far too optimistic a timetable). They wanted to change over to western-style market economies, introduce their own tax system and some form of land ownership and private property, encourage private enterprise and win control over, or remove altogether, industries directed from Moscow, especially defence industries. But establishing a market economy in a small republic closely tied to a major power with severe problems of its own would have been a highly complex task even if Moscow did not obstruct it. It would involve a dismantling of the system of tight, centralized control, of deciding who was to control, for example, the factories then run directly from Moscow, how prices were to be set, and what sort of tax system should be introduced. Complete political independence was even more complicated. Each republic required substantial help from the West, particularly to support new currencies, as well as western investment and development aid. In such a situation it was essential that independence be achieved as peacefully and amicably as possible.

All the Baltic republics produced light industrial goods, of high quality by Soviet standards and not available elsewhere in the Soviet Union. Latvia was the centre of the Soviet computer industry. The republics did have a prosperous agricultural sector (again, by Soviet standards). But these were not competitive in the West unless the whole level of the economy could be raised. Thus they were very dependent on the former Soviet market. They all had to consider what they contributed to the Soviet Union and how they would manage as independent states. In Estonia a reminder of their vulnerability came in August 1989 when the leaders of Russian workers in heavy industry (controlled directly by Moscow), and of local railwaymen, called a political strike over a law limiting the voting rights of recent immigrants. There was serious disruption of vital supplies, especially petrol. Moscow threatened tough new sanctions unless the Baltic states abandoned attempts to set up their own economic institutions. The fear that Moscow would interfere with their relative economic freedom was borne out in the autumn of 1990. The Soviet Prime Minister, Ryzhkov, told the Baltic leaders that their economic independence had, in effect, been suspended as a result of their actions. In addition, at about the same time, it became clear that the talks between Lithuania and the Soviet government had all but broken down.

Independence

The Supreme Soviets of all three Baltic republics unilaterally declared themselves independent (Lithuania, in March 1990, was first and went furthest) and rejected the central government's law on secession on the grounds that they were never legally part of the Soviet Union. All claimed that they were occupied states. They also rejected the idea of a referendum (especially under the restrictive conditions imposed by Moscow). Estonia and Latvia tried to distinguish their moves from those of Lithuania, which had been subjected to an economic blockade after its declaration, by talking of a transitional period before they became effective. They called on Moscow to start talks on a transfer of power and to set up arrangements for the phased withdrawal of the Soviet army from their territories. Difficulties occurred over military service, with the Estonians, for example, passing a law permitting Estonians to do civilian work service in the republic, rather than in the Soviet army. As a result, Gorbachev issued decrees saying that the Latvian and Estonian declarations had no juridical force, but he did not mention economic sanctions or other punitive measures. Although insisting that they obeyed the law, he did appear to offer some form of confederal status within the Soviet Union. At the same time, Estonia and Latvia supported Lithuania, and the three presidents met to ensure a united front. Gorbachev's response was equally complex. In some ways he treated all three republics the same, and in others he was gentler with Estonia and Latvia than with Lithuania.

The three republics revived the Baltic Council, originally created under the Treaty of Concord and Co-operation of 1934, which would enable them to meet regularly to co-ordinate their foreign policies, although the council's recommendations would not be binding on them. It consisted mainly of representatives of the three Popular Fronts. In March 1990 the council issued a declaration in support of the republics' independence and in May the three republics held joint talks. They signed four documents committing them to joint action. These included a request to become members of the United Nations and the Conference on Security and Co-operation in Europe. However, the three republics did not have a very good record of co-operation with each other. One of the difficulties was always disagreement over which language to use, although they were all reluctant to use Russian. Two of the presidents were Communist Party leaders, regarded by the Lithuanians and by radicals in their own republics as too accommodating to Moscow. Economic co-operation between the republics was hampered by their dependence on the Soviet Union and the similarities of their economies; they all lack raw materials. Soviet control meant that the Soviet economic sanctions on Lithuania could not be alleviated by the other two republics.

Gorbachev insisted that all three republics must revoke their independence declarations before he would hold talks with them. In June he became somewhat more conciliatory, agreeing to meet the Lithuanian leaders even if they merely suspended, rather than-revoked, their declarations. All three Baltic presidents attended Council of the Federation meetings, encouraged by Yeltsin's presence as President of the Russian Federation. He supported their independence aspirations and strongly campaigned for a revised union treaty to govern relations between the republics. However, when talks on revision began, the Baltic republics refused to participate on the grounds that they were not part of the Soviet Union. Gorbachev accused them of violating the Soviet constitution and also the Helsinki Accords which 'reject arbitrariness' in resolving European frontier problems. In August the Russian Federation agreed a draft treaty with Latvia in which each recognized the other as 'independent legal entities'; this was the closest Yeltsin, as Russian President, came to formally backing Baltic independence before the abortive coup.

By the autumn the three republics had lost the unity which they had hitherto displayed, and had begun bickering among themselves, while Lithuania and Estonia were going through internal government crises. The three republics were taking an ambivalent line. They said they had formed a united front but each took a different path towards independence, although they were planning to strengthen their economic and political co-operation in mutual self-defence against pressure from Moscow. Negotiations of various sorts were in progress with the three republics separately, although it was not clear what status these talks had (certainly from the point of view of Moscow it was different from that of the republics). Those with Lithuania had most significance but they broke down quite quickly. Meanwhile, attempts by the Baltic states to attend the CSCE in November as observers failed in spite of intense lobbying by Denmark and five other countries. Most countries did not want to embarrass Gorbachev or weaken his position. It was made clear in December, when the all-Union Supreme Soviet gave outline support to the draft Union Treaty, that the three republics would not be allowed to negotiate special status until they had agreed in principle to sign the treaty, although they could make declarations or reservations at the time of signing. If they did not sign they would be bound by the more restrictive 1922 treaty.

Soviet Pressure on the Baltic Republics

The biggest problem for the Baltic states was the presence of the Soviet military, who tended to be regarded as an occupying force. The constant denunciation of the Soviet army by the Baltic governments created considerable tension. For the republics the greatest cause for concern was the military's political activities. Latvia attempted to stop the supply of goods and services to the army until negotiations were initiated on their status. There was a furious response from Gorbachev and the Defence Minister, Marshal Yazov. All three republics wanted to negotiate on the number of troops stationed in their territories, but the central authorities regarded the troops as entitled to be there because they were regarded as being in their own country – that is, the Soviet Union. In the autumn of 1990 the Latvians were prevented by a joint force of naval personnel and OMON (or 'Black Berets', these being a specially trained force of Interior Ministry troops)[1] from executing a court order entitling them to take over a building belonging to the pro-Moscow Communist Party. There was a great outburst of hostility and frustration against the military and fears were expressed that they would combine with Russian factory workers to pressurize the government into signing the new Union Treaty. This was a greater fear in Latvia than in the other two republics because only 52 per cent of the Latvia population was of the indigenous nationality. Nevertheless, similar fears were expressed in Lithuania and Estonia, fears ultimately borne out by the military action of January 1991.

Military Intervention

The events of January 1991, with the associated violence, were preceded by growing tension and the feeling that 'something was about to happen'. Among the many crises of the Soviet Union at this time, that of the Baltic republics seemed to suggest to conservatives in Moscow that the only way to save the Union and stop the move towards independence was to impose authoritarian rule. However, this would have all the usual vicious connotations and probably not succeed. Nevertheless, the decision to send paratroopers to Lithuania to find military draft-dodgers and deserters did, in retrospect, seem to have been part of a plan to create a situation where the elected government could be suspended and superseded by a pro-Moscow substitute waiting in the wings. Demonstrations and strikes by some of the Russian and Polish populations were organized by the pro-Moscow Communist Party. The commander of the Baltic military district supported these moves 'in the name of many thousands of servicemen'. Gorbachev said that he had been inundated with requests to intervene to restore the Soviet constitution and political and social rights, together with presidential rule. He accused the Lithuanian authorities of trying to restore 'the bourgeois system', a phrase uncomfortably associated with the pre-Gorbachev era.

Yeltsin threw in his lot with the Baltic states by flying to Estonia and issuing a joint appeal to the United Nations Secretary-General for an emergency conference on the crisis. Yeltsin also appealed to Russian soldiers in the Baltic not to follow orders to use force against civilians, a more angrily denounced by Gorbachev as 'a gross violation of the Soviet constitution'. The suspension of military operations in the two republics after a short time may have been partly due to international reaction after people were killed in Lithuania but also, and more directly, to differences between politicians and military in Moscow. For radicals, in Yeltsin's words, 'economic reform has been blocked, democracy betrayed, *glasnost* trampled upon'. Belatedly Gorbachev condemned those who sought power other than through constitutional channels, an implicit reference to the 'Committees for National Salvation' which mysteriously sprang up and tried to take power in Lithuania and Latvia. He also called on the army to be disciplined and not to listen to appeals to join the political struggle. Shortly afterwards he set up panels to resume discussions with each of the three republics.

Intermittent incidents continued, especially attacks on border posts set up by the three republics. The republics believed that much of this was designed to provoke a reaction on the part of governments and population, in order to provide an excuse for army intervention and the imposition of presidential rule. In letters to President Vytautas Landsbergis of Lithuania and Anatolii Gorbunov of Latvia, the Soviet Deputy Minister of Defence, General Mikhail Moiseyev, said that illegal armed forces were being set up in Latvia and Lithuania, using local recruits. He threatened that if the governments of the republics did not carry out the resolution of the Council of Ministers on the question of the call-up for military service 'the General Staff of the armed forces of the USSR reserves the right to adopt whatever measures necessary to ensure that this resolution is fully implemented' (Fast, 1991).

The Referendum on the Union and the Attempted Coup

All three Baltic republics refused to take part in the national referendum on the Union declared by Gorbachev for 17 March 1991, and announced that they would hold referendums of their own. The three referendums resulted in overwhelming votes for independence, making it clear that many non-indigenous inhabitants must have voted in favour. The announcement of the coup was accompanied by military and naval activity in the Baltic republics, including a naval blockade and the occupation of television stations. The head of the Baltic military command declared a state of emergency and announced that all government decisions would have to be approved by him. Estonia and Latvia proclaimed their complete independence (as Lithuania had already done) and called on the West to recognize them. The failure of the coup was received cautiously and suspiciously at first, but there soon came a realization that these events could lead to the rapid achievement of full-scale independence. The next step was the banning of the local Communist Parties, the taking over of Communist property, and the freezing of Communist Party assets. The KGB was disbanded.

In effect, Soviet political and military power collapsed after the coup, leaving the republics' governments in charge, much to their surprise. The supporters of the Soviet Union among the Russian minorities found themselves without a reliable political base. Most accepted independence as a fact, but were apprehensive about the future. Food prices were rising rapidly and the huge enterprises in which most working-class Russians had jobs were unlikely to compete effectively in the new economic situation unless converted to other tasks. Russian workers, together with disgruntled members of the Soviet army and security forces (such as OMON) could still have mounted a last-ditch Communist resistance to independence. However, the Russian Federation and the Baltic states were, for the time being, enjoying good relations, owing to their common resistance to the attempted coup and the federation government's support for Baltic independence. A week later pressure was growing for diplomatic recognition of the independence of the three states, led by the Russian Federation and the Scandinavian countries. It came very rapidly, together with membership of the United Nations. The Provisional Government of the Union of Sovereign States (the post-coup governmental arrangement which lasted from August to December 1991) made recognition of Baltic independence one of its first acts. The next step was the negotiation of the withdrawal of former Soviet forces from the Baltic republics. This was likely to be slow and difficult for logistical reasons and the strategic importance of the area. Claims by the central government (and, possibly, after the breakup of the Soviet Union, by the Russian Federation government) for compensation for investment and property built in the Baltic republics were likely to be met by counter-claims for ecological damage caused by Soviet factories and military installations.

Ethnic Minorities in the Republics

A continuing problem was that of the ethnic minorities in the now independent republics. Lithuania, for example, was talking of asking its Polish (8 per cent) and its Russian (9 per cent) minorities to sign loyalty pledges if they wished to have citizenship rights, even if they had been born in the republic. Both Russian and Polish minorities were suspected of supporting the coup. The problem was worse in Latvia and Estonia where much larger Russian communities lived mainly segregated lives and did not speak the national language. Partly for ethnic reasons and partly because of tight Russian control in smaller Russian minority towns, the bulk of the ethnic minority representatives in the Baltics were Communist. The minorities tended to see the nationalistic governments of the republics as hostile to them, and therefore they did not feel inclined to declare support. Meanwhile the Council of Europe deferred membership applications from the new republics until they were satisfied on constitutional provisions for citizenship for minorities. The West was also in a position by means of aid to help resolve the tension among the ethnic minorities, which was likely to grow with unemployment and other economic difficulties.

Economic Prospects

The economic prospects were bad but not as bad as for some other former Soviet republics. By Soviet standards they were relatively advanced, but were heavily reliant on supplies from other republics. There were inevitably serious transition problems. Trade with Russia was of overriding importance. Ports such as Ventspils in Latvia exported Russian oil and gas. Apart from coal shales in Estonia, the three republics were entirely reliant on the Russian Federation and Ukraine for energy. They agreed to send observers to meetings on the economic agreement being negotiated after the coup and also remained very interested in any economic developments and agreements following the formation of the Commonwealth of Independent States. They had a need to belong to some sort of economic community, because if, for example, the Russian Federation insisted on their paying world prices for their energy, their economies would be in serious trouble. Western aid to the three independent republics was vital, but before the sudden acquisition of independence only the Scandinavian countries had thought seriously about it. The three republics were looking to the Scandinavian countries to help them in common projects such as the setting up of a Baltic investment bank. Among other things the bank (together with the World Bank and the Bank for Reconstruction and Development) would help joint projects for energy, transport and communication. It had been assumed by others that Moscow would block any moves that were made and the United States was not very forthcoming about financial aid. It offered relatively little and expected the Baltic republics to rely mainly on the Scandinavian countries and Germany, while the United States provided for their security.

Foreign and Security Policy

The foreign affairs of the three republics were transformed, not only by their own independence, but by the reunification of Germany, a democratic government in Poland, the reviewing of their neutral status by Sweden and Finland and, above all, by the collapse of the Soviet Union. A conference in September 1990 agreed on measures to cut pollution in the Baltic, while thirty-two Baltic cities formed a union in September 1991 to create new links across and around the Baltic Sea. Many other Baltic organizations were springing up. These developments were (at the end of 1991) in the very earliest stages of discussion. The future security of the region was of concern to the West. The presence of former Soviet army and naval forces in Kalliningrad (part of Russia but only accessible through Lithuania) was a particular problem. Arms cuts might have helped to solve these issues but, meanwhile, the countries of the Baltic and Eastern Europe were virtually defenceless, unprotected by NATO and exposed to the unsettled situation among the former Soviet republics.

Conclusion

From the Soviet point of view the problem of the Baltic republics was complex. Economically, the republics were closely integrated into the Soviet Union and continued to be so after independence. Lithuania's borders were not the same as they had been before the Second World War and their President, Vytautas Landsbergis, was seen as unnecessarily provocative. There were important Soviet national security interests and a substantial amount of economic investment was involved. The central government argued that the minorities in the republics had already experienced discrimination and human rights violations. But it was the Baltic states which exposed the inherent contradiction of Gorbachev's policy of greater liberalization while maintaining the empire intact. The memory of independence gave powerful impetus to the independence movements and was reinforced by international law as well as the disavowal of Stalin's crimes by Gorbachev's government. Other republics watched and learned from the Baltic states' tactics. Estonia adopted a cautious approach and developed ties with Yeltsin, as well as improving its economic position. Latvia managed to get support for independence from the bulk of its large Russian population, which undermined Soviet allegations of nationalist discrimination against minorities. Lithuania took a direct approach, declaring independence and surviving an economic blockade. All three began to form their own police and security forces. Attempts by the military to intimidate or even replace the governments of Lithuania and Latvia were largely thwarted by the resistance of the population and international opinion. In the end, the Soviet leadership was forced to agree to far-reaching concessions. Independence finally came with unexpected suddenness after the collapse of the coup.

Notes

1 The Special Purpose Militia Detachments (OMON or 'Black Berets') were formed in Moscow in 1987. They had units in all major cities and were directly under the control of the Interior Ministry rather than the local police force. Specially trained and disciplined, their main tasks were riot control and dealing with serious crimes. At first they were recruited from ex-army personnel but, with the deterioration of relations between the republics and the centre, they were more and more drawn from young nationalistic Russians.

15

The Central Asians: Independence Thrust Upon Them

The five Islamic republics of Central Asia are composed of diverse nationalities. The region contains over 50 million people in an area amounting to a quarter of the Soviet Union. The Soviet frontier divided ethnic groups from their fellow nationals in adjoining countries, simply marking the limits of tsarist expansion which the Soviet Union inherited. Except for the Azeris in Iran, the Soviet component of these nationalities was the larger. The Soviet Union (and Russia before it) was exposed in this region to influences from the Islamic world. To Muslims, the Soviet Union's defeat in Afghanistan represented just the latest chapter in a 700-year clash of cultures. With the exception of Tajikistan, whose language is a form of Persian, the languages of Central Asia are of Turkish origin. (There was resentment at the conversion into the Cyrillic alphabet of their languages because it had the effect of further isolating the Central Asians from related nationalities abroad.) It was Turkish reforms of the nineteenth century that inspired the Jadid reform movements, and many looked to Turkey as a model of what they would like to become. But, paradoxically, this Central Asian region was historically dominated by Iran and is Persian in culture, as is Afghanistan.

Pre-revolutionary Islamic Russia

In the nineteenth century pressure from tsarist Russia caused the Central Asian lands to become Russian protectorates. The resulting social and economic changes created a reformist Jadid ('New') movement which had links with the wider Islamic world. Opposition from the conservative clerical and political establishment drove the reformers to co-operate with the Bolsheviks. Marxist ideas had penetrated the Islamic regions of Russia before 1917, but had their own special features, including an emphasis on the rising of the oppressed, a strong preoccupation with nationalism rather than the class struggle, a revolution emanating from the countryside rather than the city led by the peasants and the bourgeoisie (not the industrial proletariat), and a belief that Marxism and Islam were not incompatible. All this is part of the history of the impact of the modern West on the Islamic world and the desire to use such impact to precipitate reform. Thus before 1917 the Jadidists had been part of a great Islamic reform movement. After 1917 their existence became entirely tied to the Bolsheviks. Really, for the Jadidists, the Revolution came too early. The Jadidist priority was independence, and they could not reconcile this with the more populist demand for social reform of the backward masses, who were Sunni Muslims and not predisposed to conflicts with authority.

Disaffection after the Revolution

With the success of the Bolshevik Revolution the Islamic reform movement was absorbed into the Revolution and at the same time contained by it. The Bolsheviks created a Socialist Republic of Turkestan and two ostensibly independent 'people's' republics of Bukhara and Khvarazm. But there was disaffection with the ethnocentric policies of the Bolsheviks. One of the most notable expressions of opposition was the clandestine Erk Party (later called the Turkestan Socialists, 'Turkestan' referring to the whole Soviet Islamic area), made up of strong Muslim nationalists in the 1920s. The Emir of Bukhara tried to lead a revolt against the Bolsheviks, and this became the start of the Basmachi movement. The Jadidists were divided, on the one hand, into those who joined the Basmachi against Soviet rule – wanting a restoration of the pre-Soviet order – and on the other, into those who preferred the gains of the Revolution and the restructuring of Islamic society within the Soviet system.

The harsh treatment of rebels by the Red Army and the flight of the Emir of Bukhara to Afghanistan gave a new impetus to the Basmachi movement. It now involved all those opposed to the Soviets, but its weakness was the fact that it was not united. Rather, it was a multitude of disconnected and sometimes warring rebel bands. For a time Enver Pasha tried to unite them but he was defeated and died in August 1922. Central Asia now benefited from conciliatory measures (including the New Economic Policy). The population was tired of the disturbances, and a Soviet promise of a return to order was seen as a sufficient incentive to abandon the Basmachi movement. Deprived of popular support, the movement gradually weakened, but remained strong in Bukhara for several years more (rebel groups were still being captured at the end of 1929). As late as 1931 the movement gained strength from the resistance to collectivization.

Until 1923 the Soviet authorities intervened relatively little in the republics. Policy in Central Asia reflected this and was also in line with Lenin's insistence on winning over the Muslims, but *not* in an imperialist way. Thus for a time the Bolsheviks tolerated increasingly hostile states in the region. Then they came to realize that the world revolution would not happen, and so turned to reconstituting the empire. There was a change in Islamic policy and the local Communist Parties were thoroughly purged. The question of integrating the republics was raised. At first an economic union was created, with an Economic Council for Central Asia. But the reality was that integration into the Soviet Union was seen as inevitable. A conference in 1924 voted unanimously for this and in 1925 the whole of Turkestan was reorganized, with the Socialist Republic of Turkestan and the People's Republics of Bukhara and Khvarazm disappearing to make way for the Soviet Republics of Kazakhstan, Kirgizia, Tajikistan, Turkmenistan and Uzbekistan. With the reorganization of Central Asia the Jadid aims of a United Turkestan were ended. The creation of the separate Soviet republics with their own languages, one of which was non-Turkic Tajikistan, ended hopes of a regrouping and unification of all of Central Asia. Needless to say, the Soviet authorities also firmly discouraged any such ideas. Stalin destroyed what was left of the pre-Revolution reform movements.

Western commentators have sometimes argued that Soviet policy in Central Asia was inexorably expansionist, Afghanistan being the most recent example. In fact, the record is one of forays outwards to control adjacent regions where threats existed, followed by retreat. This was true of interventions in Iran in both World Wars, and of the occupation of Sinkiang in the 1930s. It was also proved true of the intervention in Afghanistan. Within Soviet Central Asia, Soviet policy was one of *rapprochement* rather than of assimilation. Russian was promoted as a *second* language and the federal structure retained in the 1977 Constitution. Other Soviet policies inadvertently encouraged nationalism. For example, people such as the Uzbeks were far more integrated under Soviet rule than they had ever been before. Previously they were a collection of clans and groups with ninety-two dialects. Religion and culture became a uniting force in the face of Soviet colonialism. But throughout all this time vestiges of the idea of an all-Muslim nationalism persisted, as continuing official attacks on the idea indicated.

Nationalism was seen as compatible with Communism, and there was a strong belief among Central Asian nationalists that true Communism could only be realized in the East. In historical studies the question whether historical development was revolutionary or continuous had been discussed, with the latter interpretation being preferred by Islamic scholars, and ethnic values being given preference over class values. Even before the outburst of nationalism in the Gorbachev period there had been a stronger assertion of their own brand of Communism as their bargaining position improved with population increase, greater literacy, and increased strategic importance. Attempts had been made to get more local autonomy and greater representation in Moscow (that is, more important jobs for Muslims). The unofficial leaders of these moves were the Uzbeks. The new assertiveness also involved a stress on the federal status of the Soviet Union, the state-hood of the Muslim republics, and an identification with the Third World rather than with East European states.

Contacts with the Islamic World

The Central Asian people, being Islamic, retain many obvious features of Islamic culture. Soviet Islam contained communities of three branches of Islam: the Sunni, who have wide external contacts, and the Shi'a and Ismailis, who have fewer outside links. There was distrust of the non-Islamic West. After the Revolution religion was still practised but became more private and conservative. Both Islam and Orthodox Christianity were mercilessly harried in the 1930s; then came a period of accommodation and desperate appeals to patriotism during the Second World War. In the deportations of 1943–4 all but one of the nationalities involved were Muslim. There was a cynical use of Ortho-dox clerics and Islamic mullahs in the Brezhnev years to promote Soviet foreign policy by means of carefully vetted official delegations sent everywhere, from the Middle East to the World Council of Churches.

Almost all Soviet Islamic communities have significant groups of corresponding nationality abroad, so the question arose: where was the national centre of these groups and what was the relationship of Soviet Islam to the Islamic world in general? Soviet propaganda at first ig-nored, and then played down, ties with the wider Islamic world and emphasized solidarity with the Russian 'elder brothers'. Contact with the Islamic world was gradually re-established after 1953 and Islamic elites sometimes had radical views, for example, that part of Afghani-stan should be annexed because this would strengthen Islam's position in the Soviet Union. Central Asians also wanted to be at the forefront of development and modernization in Asia but the Soviets reserved this role for Russians. Non-Russians were not trusted except as technical advisers and in promotional activities. The reward exacted from Mos-cow for keeping to this limited role was less pressure on religion. The invasion of Afghanistan by the Soviet Union in 1979 was welcomed because it was seen as giving Soviet Muslims a better bargaining position with Moscow. During the campaign there was at first much contact between fellow Muslims in the army and administration, with no Russian control. But after February 1980 there was a reversal of policy, Muslims being replaced by Russians.

As far as contact with the Russians was concerned, although they lived side by side in two unequal parts, there was relatively little contact in rural areas. Mixed collective farms had been abandoned in the 1930s but there were later attempts to revive them. State farms had always been more intermingled, with Russians predominating. In education, real contact had begun in secondary education and in the army. This had had little effect on local culture but was profound among the intelligentsia. Russian was the second language and there had been some introduction of Russian words into the local languages. This had reduced their unique character and potentially tended to cut them off from associated languages outside the Soviet Union. Overall, however, the policy of Russifying the languages had little impact, except in the mass media.

The Economy of Soviet Central Asia

Central Asia certainly became politically and strategically more important after the Second World War, because of a population explosion and, in foreign affairs, the unfriendly relations with China with whom the Soviet Union shared a common border. In some respects the region benefited from Soviet control. The standard of living was higher than in neighbouring Iran, Pakistan and India; there were better roads, education and health services. The Central Asian republics gained from intense industrial development in the 1930s under Stalin and (in the 1950s) from the 'virgin lands scheme' of Khrushchev in North Kazakhstan. Oil and gas were developed, and there was huge investment in cotton. But by the 1980s the period of economic expansion was over. On the whole living standards were lower than in other parts of the Soviet Union although there had been big improvements in later years. The region's economy (based on cotton and extracting industries) still had colonial features. The population remained largely agricultural and there had been a selective adoption of modernization. The main characteristics of the manpower situation included a surplus of labour, low productivity, a high birth-rate and low emigration. All of this was having an increasing impact on the civilian economy and military manpower. One view was that economic pressures would cause Central Asians to emigrate, while another was that Central Asians would not emigrate and Moscow would invest heavily in the region. Migration would most likely cause a problem of ghettos. It was more probable that Europeans would leave Central Asia because of increased competition from trained native workers, the Islamization of urban life, the growth of violent unrest in the region and incentives to go to labour deficit areas (which, however, would not solve labour deficit problems). As with many Third World countries there had been heavy migration from the countryside to the towns, and the Soviet attempt to limit mobility by using the internal passport system to insist that everyone be registered in a particular place appeared to have broken down in many parts. People lived 'illegally' with relatives.

Glasnost, Perestroika *and Nationalism*

The concept of a 'Soviet nation' had not eroded Islamic identity. The Soviets had aimed to emphasize differences among Muslims and to replace the old social order. The second aim was achieved but the differences between Muslims remained and merely reinforced their concept of nationhood. The future of Soviet Central Asia depended on retaining the Islamic republics and suggestions of abolition which surfaced in the 1960s were dropped. The central authorities came to realize that Islamic culture was very resistant to abolition and harsh repression might be counter-productive. Also the Soviet Union needed good relations with the Middle East and South Asia. Commentators such as Allworth (1990) stress the two levels of Soviet Asian life, the official Soviet and the unofficial local. Political power in the five republics has always been held by an elite of traditional clan leaders who were also very influential within the Party. These leaders had significant popular consent and such loyalties were keeping the old Party machines in control. They leant towards more independence combined with authoritarian rule, rather than democracy. Many political leaders who emerged in the late 1980s were closely linked to leaders of the Brezhnev period. This continuity was explained mainly by the fact that the Communist Party coexisted with, rather than replaced, existing systems of authority.

By the time Gorbachev became Party General Secretary, it seemed that a take-off point had been reached. Cultural nationalism had been established and the political movement was gaining momentum. A rapidly modernizing society was still based on a colonial type of economy and a highly centralized political system. The ingredients for an outburst of nationalism were there but there was no effective anticipatory response from the central government. The main features of Gorbachev's initial policy was not the containment of discontent but rather an increasingly far-reaching purge of corrupt elements from local Party and state bureaucracies. The Party Secretary in Uzbekistan,

Sharaf Rashidov, died in mysterious circumstances as investigations got under way. Uzbek officials had falsified the cotton statistics for years, and each group brought in to replace the previous corrupt leadership was itself involved in similar activities. The troubles which started at the end of 1986 transformed the situation. Gorbachev attempted his 'revolution from above' and produced the first major outbreak of unrest in Central Asia since the 1920s, namely, the riots in the Kazakh capital, Alma-Ata, in December 1986. Anti-Russian feeling here (a Russian, rather than a Kazakh, had just been appointed First Secretary of the local Party) went together with the hostility of other Kazakhs for the Ulus-Juz (Great Horde) clan of southern Kazakhstan, who had come to control the local Party patronage system. Further violence followed in many areas, including the Fergana Valley of Uzbekistan and the capital of Tajikistan, Dushanbe. In nearly all cases local hostility between ethnic groups was manifested alongside a growing anti-Party and anti-Russian feeling.

Each of these conflicts had its own distinguishing features, but there was also a common pattern of long-standing resentment of Soviet treatment of ethnic groups, as well as hostility between them. This came into the open after the relaxation of Soviet control, and because of worsening economic conditions, which also generated widespread unrest and frustration. Usually there was a common sequence of events: after violent clashes, there came a government show of force that was either too late or too excessive or both. The Soviet authorities sometimes dismissed the demonstrators as 'thugs' or 'hooligans', and tried to suppress detailed information about what actually happened by closing the region to visitors and the mass media. The question arose in each case whether the outburst was a conflict between warring ethnic groups or a protest against Communism, or both. Another question was whether the action of the Soviet authorities was simply to restore peace, or to punish opponents of the regime and to prop up officials loyal to the Party and to Moscow.

Gorbachev seemed to find it difficult to understand this outburst of violent nationalism. He apparently saw it as a plot by local corrupt, power-hungry men to stir up national passions for their own ends. But even where there was some truth in this, there was also a strong element of protest against economic and social conditions, manifesting itself in resentment against supposedly favoured minorities, and against the Russians. The initial programme of reform from above, imposed by Moscow on a passive but reluctant Central Asia, had given way to violent protest from below. The issues in Central Asia were brought to the fore by the overall changes in the Soviet Union itself and the region had, in this sense, been reactive. But there were certain special factors at work, such as widespread underemployment, lower levels of health and literacy, and a serious housing shortage. The development of agriculture had produced extensive ecological problems. Much of the predominantly female workforce in agriculture had been affected by pesticides. Thus resentment at control from Moscow and at Russian settlers in Central Asia was worsened by the impact of Gorbachev's *perestroika*.

Ironically, it was the relative lightness of Moscow's rule over the region, allowing the indigenous societies and cultures to survive instead of being replaced, which gave rise to the difficulties the Soviet Union faced. Soviet power brought many benefits: improved economic output and standard of living, promotion of health and education, and, with time, integration into the apparatus of power. Failure was to a great extent due to an inability to understand the need for decentralization. The rigidity of the Soviet centralized economic and political system made economic progress, for example, seem a function of decisions taken in Moscow and as being organized for the benefit of the centre. Thus people believed that they were being exploited and that the specific wealth of their republic was being taken away.

The new concern about ecology, with anxiety about pesticides in cotton, and the drying up of the Aral Sea, provided an ideal issue with which to attack the centre. Thus the first concern was, not so much lack of democracy or ethnic rights, as over-centralization of decision – making and lack of economic freedom. The new Kazakh president, Nursultan Nazarbaev, initiated a regional meeting of top leaders of the five Central Asian republics at Alma-Ata in June 1990. It resulted in far-reaching agreement on economic, environmental, cultural and political co-operation, with provision for a permanent staff to be located in Alma-Ata. The leaders criticized Soviet mismanagement of the economy and environmental damage, in particular the destruction of the Aral Sea. However, political independence was likely simply to entrench their economic backwardness and dependence on the Russian Federation. They would also have a huge environmental bill which they could not pay. They believed that the environmental disasters had been caused by the policies of the Soviet Union and that therefore the central Asian republics should not shoulder the bill. They traditionally had not been interested in total independence, but with higher birth-rates among the indigenous peoples and Russians leaving the area this could have altered. The central government in Moscow made much of the need to protect the minorities in the republics. Another factor, the landlocked character of the area, could have militated against breaking ties with the Russians. Certainly it was noticeable how many minority ethnic groups – including the Kurds in Turkey and the Azeris in Iran as well as those groups in Soviet Central Asia – really did not want full independence, but rather the acquisition of greater political and economic influence within a multinational entity.

The Resurgence of Islam

The Islamic revival, and struggles between different tendencies, did not begin until after Soviet power in Central Asia showed signs of disintegrating. There were clear signs of a revival of interest in their Islamic past and a great demand for copies of the Koran and other Islamic literature. However, it was difficult to interpret exactly what this meant. Because of the suppression of official teaching of Islam, the beliefs and practices of most Central Asians were of a popular, often superstitious, character. But there was little evidence of organized religious opposition as such. Despite reports of Iranian and Afghan mujahidin influence, little proof of this came to light. Nevertheless, religion was experiencing a significant revival. Mosques were being built all over Central Asia and some mosques confiscated by Stalin in 1937 were returned to religious use.

There was growing Islamic activism in bordering states, such as radical Sh'ias in Iran, the mujahedin in Afghanistan and the fundamentalist Jamaat-el-Islami in Pakistan. Confusion in Central Asia was something they believed could be taken advantage of and they had already supplied funds, arms and literature. But many observers thought it doubtful that world Islam, although growing in influence, posed a serious political threat. Iranian influence was limited because, with the exception of the Tajiks, most Soviet Central Asians belong to the Sunni rather than the Sh'ia branch of Islam which predominates in Iran. Insofar as the local leaders had a model, it was more likely to be South Korea or Singapore, both authoritarian but capitalist, rather than the Islamic states on their borders. Moderate Muslims supported the admittedly weak democratic movements, largely through a group called the Islamic Renaissance Party. It was technically illegal everywhere except in Tajikistan and, although it had a nominal leader, Ahmed al Qadi, it developed separately in each republic according to local conditions. It believed in social policies, the rights of non-Muslims and the Koran's teaching not to impose Islam on people by force. Some regarded these sentiments as hiding more fundamentalist beliefs which would emerge if the Muslims won power. Others saw it as an acknowledgment that, after many years of Communist rule, only 5 to 10 million Muslims (out of some 50 million) actually practised their faith. Fundamentalist language could cause ethnic tension and put off foreign investors. There was rivalry between this party and the Central Board of Muslims; the latter was an official body of the Soviet regime, which was therefore regarded with suspicion, although its officials said that pro-Soviet elements had been removed. Outside influences could have affected the outcome of conflict between these two bodies, but neither wanted to become embroiled in politics because of the severity of the problems which the region faced. Others argued that, in the absence of strong secular reformist movements, the Islamic fundamentalists could step in to provide the only viable political alternative.

The loosening of the Soviet hold unleashed something less evident in the Baltic and the Caucasus, namely an international competition for political and economic influence among other Asian states. Regional powers such as Iran, Turkey and Saudi Arabia were interested in taking advantage of the situation. They were simultaneously enticed and alarmed by the apparent breakdown in Soviet authority. To counter any Afghan Islamic influence and to prevent Iranian contact from growing, Moscow encouraged two states to become involved: Turkey and Saudi Arabia. Turkey was developing economic links with the Caucasus and Central Asia. Saudi Arabia was encouraged by Moscow to play a greater religious role.

The roots of the Islamic identity of Central Asians are primarily cultural and internal. The decisive political issue, therefore, was national rather than religious. The movements which emerged asserted the Islamic character of their people, but were not Islamic parties. Their main demands were for greater regional autonomy within the Soviet Union, especially for greater control over their economic resources, or for independence. Events elsewhere (such as the example of Lithuania and violence in Azerbaijan) made independence more attractive and after the attempted coup it was realized that relations with the centre and with the Russians would have to be renegotiated from scratch. Independence came to them anyway, with the collapse of attempts to preserve the Union.

After the Failed Coup

The leaders of the Central Asian republics (still basically the old Communist leadership) were split in their reaction to the coup. President Nazarhaev of Kazakhstan unequivocally condemned it, but the President of Uzbekistan declared that the coup was necessary as *perestroika* had failed, an opinion rapidly reversed when the coup collapsed. Other republic presidents were silent or non-committal. The failure of the coup caused the credibility of most of the Central Asian leaders to be undermined. In the immediate aftermath the republics declared independence (more as a negotiating position than as a declaration of fact) and the President of Tajikistan resigned after criticism of him for being indecisive during the coup. Most expressed support for a very loose confederation of equal, independent states. Concern was created, especially in Kazakhstan with its large Russian population, over Yeltsin's suggestion that frontiers might be renegotiated. Indeed, the domination of Russia in the transitional government worried the Central Asians.

After the announcement by the three Slavic republics that the Union was at an end and they intended to form a Commonwealth of Independent States, the Central Asian republics had to take a rapid decision on their policy in this new situation. After a two-day meeting they decided to join the new Commonwealth, provided they were treated as co-founders with equal rights. But they also stated that they wanted the 'social and' economic realities' of Central Asia to be taken into account, meaning that they were looking for regional aid. A later meeting of the eleven republics of the Commonwealth in Alma-Ata agreed on the inviolability of their present borders, and that the Russian Federation should take over the Soviet Union's seat on the United Nations Security Council. The greatest threat to Central Asian leaders was their weak economies, which tied them inextricably to the Russian Federation, to which they supplied primary products such as cotton, grain and gold and received back manufactured goods. Nationalists complained that they were treated as colonial, one-crop economies, but in the past they may not always have got the worst of the deal. In future their links with the Russian Federation meant that they would be the victims of Russian economic problems, such as hyperinflation.

16

The Caucasus Fights

Azerbaijan

Until the twentieth century Azerbaijan was no more than a geographical area. Before its absorption by the tsars it had fallen mainly under Iranian rule, or enjoyed a relative autonomy in periods of imperial decline. In spite of the traditional Iranian connection the Azeri language is akin to Turkish and, in modern times, it is to Turkey that Azeri nationalists have tended to look. Turkey has been a more natural model for the mainly Sunni Muslim, urbanized intelligentsia who pioneered the nationalist movement. A republic was proclaimed under the name of Azerbaijan during the short two-year Ottoman-Turkish army occupation from 1918. The name was retained under the subsequent British occupation. In December 1918 the Azeri government was recognized by the British commander as the only effective authority in the area. After the evacuation of allied troops, the Soviet regime was proclaimed in Baku in April 1920 and Azerbaijan became part of the Transcaucasian Socialist Federated Soviet Republic comprising Azerbaijan, Georgia and parts of Armenia and other territories. In 1936 this federation was abolished and Azerbaijan was established as one of the all-Union republics of the Soviet Union. Publicly at least, nationalist sentiment waxed or waned according to variations in Soviet policy and strategic considerations towards Iran. The high point for nationalist feelings came in 1941 when, for the second time this century, the Soviet army occupied northern Iran and set up a southern Azeri government, only nominally part of Iran, one of whose key policies was the revival of the Azeri language suppressed by the Shah.

Nagorno-Karabakh

Among the effects of *glasnost* was the bringing to the surface of many national issues which had been unexpressed but simmering for many years. One of these was the question of Nagorno-Karabakh (Mountainous Karabakh), an enclave within Azerbaijan with some 75 per cent of its population composed of Armenian Christians. Although the area was designated as an autonomous region, this in effect gave it very little control over its own affairs. Peoples of two different regions and cultural traditions, the Armenians and Azeris became even more distinct under pre-revolutionary Russian rule. The great majority of the Azeris were poor peasants, cut off from the rapid development of industry, but a small but powerful Armenian middle class rose to prominence in the industrial sector of what would become Azerbaijan. In 1905, at a time of grave political crisis in the empire, Azeris and Armenians clashed in the streets of Baku. In March 1918 Communists allied with Armenian nationalists to suppress a Muslim revolt, but in September of that year, when a Turkish army occupied Baku, Azeris massacred thousands of Armenians in revenge for the 'March days'.

When Soviet power was established in Azerbaijan Nagorno-Karabakh was at first declared a part of Armenia in a gesture of fraternal solidarity, but in 1923 it became an autonomous region within Azerbaijan largely to please the Turks. For sixty-five years the Karabakh Armenians lived in an uneasy relationship with the dominant Azeris, occasionally protesting about their separation from the Armenian republic. Only in 1988 did this become organized, with mass rallies to demand their right to merge with Armenia. The issue provoked considerable ethnic unrest in both Azerbaijan and Armenia and caused a serious refugee problem as Armenians throughout Azerbaijan fled to Armenia while Azeris in Nagorno-Karabakh tried to leave. On 15 June the Azeri Supreme Soviet voted to reject the demand for the secession of Nagorno-Karabakh, a decision endorsed three days later by the Supreme Soviet in Moscow.

In January 1989 Moscow announced that, in view of the troubles, it was introducing 'a special form of administration' but with Nagorno-Karabakh remaining an autonomous region incorporated into Azerbaijan. The wording of this statement implied that Moscow was taking some form of direct control over the region (and a Kremlin commission was sent in shortly afterwards). This was disappointing to the Armenians, because it did not satisfy their aspirations, and to the Azeris, when they found they had only nominal control over the region. Moscow had clearly decided on a 'get tough' policy and all eleven of the Armenian Karabakh Committee, which had organized mass rallies on the issue in 1988, were arrested, but the committee apparently continued to operate. The arrest of the Armenian nationalists attracted international attention. Gorbachev made a speech in Ukraine in February in which he said that he favoured raising the status of autonomous regions but would not tolerate separatist movements. This was not merely aimed at Armenia and Azerbaijan but at all areas where such tensions existed.

The Supreme Soviet disbanded the emergency administration from January 1990 and put Nagorno-Karabakh firmly back under the overall control of the Azeris, although its local government was run by the Armenian majority. As a result, serious rioting and attacks on Armenians occurred in Baku from 13 January. There were tell-tale signs that this three-day pogrom was carefully planned. Many Azeris and some Soviet journalists blamed the local Communist Party and security authorities. There was little but circumstantial evidence and rumour, but if elements in the Party leadership were responsible, they were apparently trying to restore their authority among Azeris. Armenians and Azeris had slipped back into their historic relationship of bitter enmity, with the Armenians seeing themselves as a Christian enclave defending western civilization while being surrounded on three sides by Turkey, Iran and Azerbaijan – all Islamic.

With violence reaching virtually the intensity of war, Gorbachev declared a state of emergency and sent in further troops, saying that the situation had 'reached the point of murders, robberies, and attempts at armed overthrow of Soviet power and at changing by force the state and social system enshrined in the constitution of the USSR' (Steele and Rettie, 1990). On the whole, the Soviet authorities were for a time relatively restrained in their response to the considerable violence. Perhaps this was because they were afraid of arousing the whole Islamic world, or perhaps because, especially after the massacre in Tbilisi, the Georgian capital (see pp. 247–8), it was not Gorbachev's policy to come down heavily on inter-ethnic disputes. There was a danger that the Soviet army might become the target of attacks. An additional factor was the failure to effect even a limited improvement in economic circumstances.

The arrival of Soviet troops was welcomed in Armenia although feelings had hitherto been mixed about a Soviet army presence. Armenian activists had previously accused the Soviet army of tacitly siding with the Azeris in the territorial disputes between the republics and of not doing enough to protect Armenians. Unable to extinguish centuries of hatred, the Soviet army settled for the role of intermediary with occasional interventions, making sure that neither side permanently gained the upper hand. Azeri nationalists responded by blocking roads and railway lines in an attempt to stop the troops reaching Baku and other trouble areas. The troops opened fire in Baku on 19 January. It was clear that the Soviet authorities had lost control of the situation in large parts of Azerbaijan. What authority there was came from the Popular Front and, in Baku, the 'Council of National Defence'. The Azeri Supreme Soviet demanded the withdrawal of Soviet troops within forty-eight hours and voted to suspend the state of emergency. They also threatened a referendum on secession. Meanwhile Armenia was being effectively blockaded.

Moscow's reaction was confused. The Defence Minister, Yazov, told reporters in Baku that the army's aim was to 'destroy the organizational structure of the Popular Front leaders' who wanted to seize power. Earlier, the Interior Minister, Bakatin, had hinted at co-operation with 'healthy forces' within the Front. The Popular Front in Baku said that it had offered peace talks to Moscow and would guarantee law and order in the city, if the Soviet troops withdrew. This was rejected and Moscow made clear that it wanted to restore the authority of the Communist Party in the republic. Increasingly, the dispute between the two republics took on an anti-Russian tone. Armenians had traditionally seen the Russians as fellow Christians and protectors against the Islamic Turks and Azeris, but now they were perceived as having betrayed the Armenians by failing to ensure Armenian control over Nagorno-Karabakh. They alleged that the Azeris were conducting an economic blockade against Armenia and Nagorno-Karabakh. By September the Nagorno-Karabakh region and the neighbouring Shaumyan district had declared themselves independent of Azerbaijan. They said that the Soviet constitution and laws were in force in their areas, thus distancing themselves from the Azeri declaration of sovereignty.

Soviet policy dramatically changed as a result of Azerbaijan's support for the coup. Armenians were helped to return to their villages from which they had been forcibly removed earlier in the year. An agreement on a cease-fire and an end to the blockade in the area was to be followed by talks between Azerbaijan and Armenia mediated by Presidents Yeltsin and Nazarbaev. But fighting soon broke out again with Azeris being forced from their villages by Armenian fighters, while the blockade continued. A serious deterioration in the situation occurred in November, when the Azeri parliament voted to abolish the autonomous status of Nagorno-Karabakh and declared that it would be governed by a 'National Unity Council'. The Armenian President announced that he regarded this as tantamount to a declaration of war on his republic. An intervention by Gorbachev had little effect. Early in 1992 a human rights team expressed serious fears of the Armenians in Nagorno-Karabakh being annihilated by the Azeris, who increasingly appeared to be threatening an assault on the territory. In the event, it was the Armenians who slowly gained the upper hand.

Nationalist Movements in Azerbaijan

The problem of Nagorno-Karabakh and the violence connected with it had complicated the nationalist situation in Azerbaijan, but otherwise Azeri nationalism had demands similar to those made by nationalists in other Soviet republics, namely de-Stalinization, a purge of the Party bureaucracy, and political pluralism. The democratic traditions of the area were weak and it had been comparatively easy for the Party leadership to claim that nationalists were an unrepresentative minority. The Popular Front was a loose coalition of nationalist and Islamic groups. It was officially recognized in October 1989, and by then was credited with being the real power in the land, having pushed the Azeri Communist Party into the background. Its long-term demands were full autonomy for the republic within the Soviet Union, the right of unrestricted association with Iranian Azeris, and an end to what it called the 'strongly pro-Armenian bias of the Kremlin'. It eventually split into two factions when a moderate section, disagreeing with the Front's policy calling for unity with the northern provinces of Iran, left to form the Social-Democratic Federation. This group also strongly opposed the Communist Party's monopoly of power in the republic and campaigned for greater pluralism and the removal of Party leaders said to be corrupt. It condemned the violence against Armenians and claimed that they may have been organized by the KGB.

There were clear signs of the Party losing it grip. Azeri Communists were publicly burning their Party cards but in effect the Party had lost control since the summer of 1989 when the Popular Front had taken over in the turmoil of the Nagorno-Karabakh dispute. The Party tried to repair the situation by sacking its leader, Abdul-Rahman Vezirov, and replacing him with the Prime Minister, Ayaz Mutalibov, but the real negotiations for a cease-fire were being carried out by the Armenian National Movement and the Azeri Popular Front. Ever since the arrival of the Soviet army Baku had been under curfew and a form of martial law. As the election approached in October 1990 the army refused to allow anyone but residents entry to Baku, officially to prevent trouble-makers raising tension before the vote. Opposition election groupings such as the Democratic Bloc saw it as a device to keep out observers and other election helpers. In contrast to the situation in many other republics the Communist Party, in spite of the crisis it faced, seemed likely to win the election, as the Democratic Bloc contested only 218 of the 360 constituencies. The Popular Front, which had appeared on the verge of taking power in January, before the arrival of the troops, was part of the Democratic Bloc and had 158 candidates.

The Communist Party leader, Mutalibov, steered a cunning course of publicly opposing some of Gorbachev's measures (to gain national credibility) while supporting him on the main question of keeping Azerbaijan in the Soviet Union. He said that the Popular Front had overplayed its hand with extremist slogans and use of force. He pointed to the formation of a Council of National Defence in January, allegedly aimed at launching a military coup. The Popular Front and the left of the Democratic Bloc argued that the behaviour of Soviet troops intimidated people. By killing at least 143 people (according to the official count) arresting several Popular Front leaders, and sacking many of their supporters from their jobs, the Party authorities managed to frighten people into reverting to support for the status quo. In the event the Communist Party easily won the elections. The Popular Front accused the Communists of electoral fraud by causing obstacles and delays in the electoral commissions, so making it impossible to register many Popular Front candidates. In addition, their leader, Ekhtibar Mamedov, had been in prison since the January troubles.

Relations with Iran and Turkey

The revolution in Iran had had a great impact on all the Islamic areas of the Soviet Union, not because of its fundamentalist principles, but because it demonstrated that revolution was possible and could be successful in overthrowing a seemingly entrenched political regime. In an attempt to break out of its isolation, Iran tried to improve relations with Moscow. This included a pledge not to interfere in the Soviet Union's internal affairs, even though this might be a time of maximum opportunity for doing so. Serious nationalist disturbances broke out along the Azeri–Iranian border early in 1990. It appears that the rioters broke down frontier fences and demanded free access to, and trade with, Iran or even unification. The disturbances seem to have been spontaneous in origin. Nakhichevan, where they began, is an isolated enclave geographically cut off from the rest of Azerbaijan by Armenia. It is prone to a special militancy, and it may have been the backward, rural population, more susceptible to fundamentalism, which was the first to move. Once it had happened, however, the Azeri Popular Front had to identify with it.

In this conflict the Soviet Union advocated talks with Iran to make it easier for families to cross the border. An Iranian delegation visited Moscow. In fact, the Iranian mullahs, having problems with their own multinational state, themselves viewed with alarm the growth of pan-Azerbaijanism. Like the Soviets, they felt that if one of its ethnic minorities established a national state, others would follow and Iran would lose up to half its territory and population. In Turkey the press also showed great enthusiasm for developments in the Caucasus, but it was not official Turkish policy to encourage the kind of ideals which once conceived of the Turkish-speaking regions of the tsarist empire as a natural part of a great pan-Turkish commonwealth. Educated and more modern-minded Azeris look towards Turkey out of ethnic kinship and as an example of an Islamic but secular state which has adjusted to the modern western world. Thus neither Turkey nor Iran had shown any strong inclination to take advantage of the ever-growing nationalism in the Soviet Islamic republics. But if the turmoil grew, both knew they would find it harder and harder not to become involved.

The Attempted Coup

President Ayaz Mutalibov welcomed the coup and called it the natural consequence of policies which had brought chaos over the last few years. Although he tried a rapid turn-around, Azerbaijan's relations with Moscow, hitherto favourable, were badly damaged. By the end of August the republic had declared independence. Its Supreme Soviet also announced the creation of a national defence force and the lifting of the state of emergency which had been in force since the Baku riots. After the coup opposition groups demonstrated, demanding the postponement of the presidential elections, which were due on 8 September. It was not at first clear whether Mutalibov would follow the Moscow decision to suspend the Communist Party but he eventually resigned the Party leadership, dissolved the Party and seized its property. In the space of eighteen months he had switched from being a loyal Soviet Communist to a 'non-Communist' supporter of independence. The most dramatic post-coup development was the announcement on 10 October of the 'nationalization' of Soviet military hardware on Azeri territory, together with a recall of Azeris serving in the Soviet armed forces. This was the first challenge to the integrity of the Soviet armed forces.

At the presidential election Mutalibov was the only candidate as the election was boycotted by the opposition, who declared it undemocratic because of not having been allowed to organize. He announced that a new party, provisionally known as the Republican Democratic Party, would replace the Communist Party. The survival of the Communist old guard in Azerbaijan – albeit under another name – surprised outsiders. Mutalibov was supported by a majority unwilling to risk the unknown, while the opposition would have liked to remove him but did not know how. The more moderate wing of the divided Popular Front was willing to hold round table discussions with Mutalibov. His position had been weakened in Moscow and abroad since his initial support for the coup but the prospects for democracy rather than authoritarian nationalism were not bright.

With the final collapse of the Soviet Union in December and the formation of the Commonwealth of Independent States, Azerbaijan had to come to terms with an unexpected and unwanted degree of independence. The Azeris had great problems in establishing the new republic as a viable independent state and looked to the Commonwealth for the external economic support and security which they had always felt they needed. In spite of the neo-Communist victory, Azerbaijan was more advanced politically than the Central Asian republics, with a large opposition and independently minded intelligentsia. Economically, it lagged behind. There was no privatization programme and, although the republic is rich in oil, there were no laws allowing foreign investment. The Nagorno-Karabakh crisis was worsening and seemed likely to attract increasing international attention and even intervention.

Armenia

Moscow's Policy towards Armenia

The events in the Caucasus following the outbreak of the Russian Revolution were very confused. Attempts to create an independent Armenian state were unsuccessful, because of hostility from Turkey and the changing, uncertain policies of the western powers. A Transcaucasian Federated Republic had been formed which, within a few months divided into three parts. The Armenian portion became a republic which was taken over by the Armenian Bolshevik Party (aided by Soviet troops) in the revolt of February 1921. In the autumn of that year an alliance between the Soviet Union and Soviet Armenia was announced. In 1922 the Transcaucasian Socialist Federated Soviet Republic was formed. It was split up in 1936 and the Armenian Soviet Socialist Republic came into being. A massacre of Armenians in Turkey in 1915 (denied by the Turks) had become a focal point of the Armenians sense of grievance and injustice. Many Turkish and Iranian Armenians emigrated to the republic, and the portions of the former 'Armenia' which lay in Turkey and Iran lost their identity, although Armenians still exist there in some numbers. In 1946–7 the Armenian refugees in Syria and Egypt began moving into Soviet Armenia. The Armenians speak an Aryan language and are Orthodox Christians, but are without natural allies. Azerbaijan is hostile, while Turkey has been a particular enemy since the massacres earlier this century. There is no sympathetic state nearby or particular strategic reason for the West to show concern as they did, for example, over the Baltic republics.

The government faced further difficulties in its economy as unrest grew with, at different times, Azerbaijan imposing a rail blockade and a general strike being called in Georgia. Moscow was insisting that Armenia repeal its decision to nationalize all the assets of the Armenian Communist Party and Komsomol and return land to the peasantry. Most of the period of *glasnost* and *perestroika* was dominated by growing demands for independence and the dispute with Azerbaijan over the

Armenian enclave of Nagorno-Karabakh (see pp. 235–8). In May 1990 the Armenian Supreme Soviet demanded guaranteed links between the republic and Nagorno-Karabakh. They also voted to suspend the spring call-up of conscripts into the Soviet armed forces. These decisions were taken while large demonstrations in Yerevan, the capital, urged the Supreme Soviet to assert its independence from Moscow.

In August a prominent nationalist (and supporter of restoring Nagorno-Karabakh to Armenia), Levon Ter-Petrosyan, had become president of the republic by popular election. Later in the month another leading nationalist, Vazguen Manoukyan, was elected Prime Minister. Both men had previously been arrested and imprisoned by the Soviet authorities as members of the Karabakh Committee. A new government was formed and the Supreme Soviet had placed before it a resolution advocating full independence from the Soviet Union, while a more moderate resolution was supported by the Armenian Communist Party. It was not clear then or after the Soviet Union had disintegrated, how an independent Armenia could survive, economically or defensively.

Nagorno-Karabakh and the Armed Guerrilla Forces

In July Gorbachev had issued a decree threatening military force against all 'illegal armed units' which failed to surrender their arms and disband within fifteen days. This was primarily aimed at the Armenian nationalist guerrillas who had become well organized and even ambushed and captured Soviet troops, seizing their weapons, military vehicles and artillery. Originally formed to defend Armenian settlements against armed groups from Azerbaijan, the guerrillas had more and more directed their operations against Soviet forces. The Armenian authorities may well have been condoning their existence and they were never likely to comply with the decree. Instead, there were demands for the setting up of a separate Armenian army. As the deadline for compliance was reached President Ter-Petrosyan secured an extension and a promise that force would not be used. The biggest paramilitary group, the Armenian National Army (ANA) reluctantly agreed to be controlled by the Armenian Supreme Soviet.

Rivalries between the militias had brought the republic to the brink of civil war. There were vendettas and attacks by armed bandits on villages. The ANA had more men under arms than all the other militias put together, but political support for the Armenian Nationalist Movement (ANM), the first nationalist party to emerge and with a majority in the Supreme Soviet, was being eroded. Many felt that the ANM was too cautious in the moves to independence, and militia leaders resented having to be under the control of the Supreme Soviet. These discontents could have led to a shift in military balance.

The election of a nationalist president had clearly calmed the situation, but the outstanding problem, relations with Azerbaijan and a resolution of the Nagorno-Karabakh issue, remained very delicate. In spite of Ter-Petrosyan's conciliatory efforts, ANA attacks on the Azeri border continued, and matters came to a head at the end of August when a deputy and several other people were shot dead by the ANA at their headquarters. This gave rise to a state of emergency and an ultimatum to the ANA to surrender its arms. If it did not do so, the troops of the Interior Ministry and the KGB would be ordered in. There was a confrontation at ANA headquarters, which was a critical test of the new Armenian government's ability to bring order to Armenia and thus justify less subservience to Moscow. The ANA leaders finally gave in and told their supporters to lay down their arms and obey the republic's authority. But serious clashes occurred between Soviet forces and Armenian militias in the spring of 1991.

Armenia increasingly began to accuse Moscow of supporting the Azeris against itself. Certainly large numbers of refugees had arrived in Armenia over the previous three years, starting with the ethnic riots in Baku in 1988, and later from Nagorno-Karabakh and the Azerbaijan–Armenia border areas. From Moscow's point of view Azerbaijan was a far more important ally than Armenia. Armenians felt that Moscow was determined to support the allegedly shaky regime of Ayaz Mutalibov while Armenia was being punished for demanding independence (a referendum was to be held on 21 September 1991). It appeared that the Soviet army was co-operating in deporting back to Armenia the Armenians living in Azerbaijan near the border with Armenia or in Nagorno-Karabakh. In the face of violence Gorbachev seemed to be aiming at creating a no-go area on the high plains separating the two sides.

The Effect of the Attempted Coup

The immediate response of Ter-Petrosyan to the attempted coup was restrained; the government and most public bodies supported this cautious attitude. His approach was usually one of moderate pragmatism and had wide support. The Armenian Supreme Soviet voted to declare 'independence' on 23 August, going further – in theory – than any other republic except Lithuania, although it did stop short of openly advocating leaving the Soviet Union. The declaration had provocatively proclaimed Armenia's 'inalienable right' to Nagorno-Karabakh. The newly named Republic of Armenia claimed the right to have its own army; unlike other republics it already had the nucleus of an army in the thousands of guerrillas who had stolen many weapons from Soviet troops. The KGB still controlled the border with Turkey, but the guerrillas had far more control of the border with Azerbaijan. The coup had a dramatic effect on relations with Moscow. The Azeri government supported the coup and, as a result, Soviet troops no longer supported it. Instead, they became neutral and were soon helping Armenians to return to the villages, now recaptured, from which they had been forcibly deported. As both Azeris and Armenians had their own armed forces the security of these returning villagers was very uncertain. It soon became clear that Yeltsin of Russia and Nazarbaev of Kazakhstan favoured talks. But the two sides were far apart. It was to be expected that final agreement would be very difficult.

Independence

It was once thought that the Armenians, as a Christian nation and victims of Islamic oppression, would always look to the Soviet Union for protection. But increasingly they favoured independence outside the Soviet Union, although they were prepared to sign an economic treaty with the other former Soviet republics. The support for independence grew rapidly when Soviet soldiers helped to deport Armenians from Nagorno-Karabakh. One development of all this was an attempt to restore relations with Turkey, although memory of the massacre of Armenians by Turks and incorporation of western Armenia into eastern Turkey was still very strong. However, they needed good relations with neighbours if they were to be independent and they had common economic interests with Turkey. The referendum in September 1991 overwhelmingly supported independence, which was promptly declared by the Armenian parliament. Subsequently, Armenia joined the Commonwealth of Independent States. Apart from the difficult task of establishing its independence on firm foundations, it was still preoccupied with the ever-growing crisis over the Armenians in Nagorno-Karabakh.

Georgia

Georgia has had a turbulent history with periods of independence as well as domination by Iranians, Mongols and others. Under Russian control from 1783, the country experienced varied fortunes. In the 1905 revolution the whole of the Caucasus was involved in a civil war and although the disorders, which affected Armenia more than Georgia, died down in the following year, the Russian government ruled strictly through the bureaucracy, army and the police. In 1914, however, the Georgians joined in the war in support of Russia and the allies but repressive measures were maintained; hence the Revolution of 1917 was strongly supported. The independent Transcaucasian Federated Republic, set up in 1917, split into three republics in 1918 but Georgia came to terms with the Soviet government in 1920 and received *de jure* recognition of independence from the League of Nations in January 1921. A month later Soviet troops invaded and took over the country, ostensibly to protect minorities such as the Ossetians. The Transcaucasian Socialist Federated Soviet Republic was formed in 1922 with headquarters at Tiflis. In 1936 this republic was dissolved and the Georgian Soviet Socialist Republic created. Stalin – although in origin a Georgian himself – purged his fellow nationals as much as he did anyone else. However, it is a complicating factor that for many, especially older, Georgians Stalin is still a hero. In a bizarre distortion of nationalism, some even saw de-Stalinization as a form of discrimination directed against Georgia by Moscow.

Corruption had become a problem in the republic. In 1972 the ageing First Secretary of the Georgian Communist Party was deposed while on holiday. The Central Committee elected as his successor the leader of the coup, the Interior Affairs Minister, Eduard Shevardnadze (later Soviet Foreign Minister under Gorbachev). A large-scale purge of dissidents followed, with 25,000 being arrested in the next two years, events denounced by Amnesty International. One dissident, eventually imprisoned in 1976, was Zviad Gamsakhurdia, later the Georgian President. Two years later he recanted and was released, a move seen by some as a selling out to the KGB and by others as a ploy by dissidents to enable him to organize the national liberation movement. These events help to shed light on some aspects of Soviet–Georgian relations in the Gorbachev period.

The nationalist movements aimed at independence ultimately but, in the interim, for economic autonomy and 'telling people the truth'. The movements were sparked in September 1988 by a green issue, opposition to a huge hydro-electric scheme which would have submerged historic sites, and by the failure to transfer the David Guaredja monastery to the Church (during a general reopening of churches) from its use as an army headquarters. A protest in November with a demonstration of 30,000 people was much larger and was about the proposed changes in the Soviet constitution concerning the republic's right of secession and the authorities' power to intervene directly 'in the case of threat'. It ended when Moscow announced concessions. Nevertheless, nationalist feeling was still very strong. Further independence demonstrations took place in February 1989 in spite of warnings from the police that they were illegal.

The Tbilisi Massacre

The situation in Georgia deteriorated dramatically on 9 April when Soviet troops stormed a demonstration outside the main government building in Tbilisi and killed at least twenty people. A hunger strike and sit-in were being staged by the National Democratic Party of Georgia, the National Independence Party and four more moderate groups. The local police tried to restrain the soldiers without success. This was the worst incident in which security forces had been involved since 1962. The Georgian Party authorities had always taken a tough line to try to prevent the emergence of a Popular Front like those in the Baltic republics. Whether or not they acted on orders from Moscow, the impression was created of a recalcitrant, conservative group of security officials who used Stalinist methods to crush a show of nationalism. Shevardnadze, the Foreign Minister, and formerly, as we have seen, Party First Secretary in Georgia, was sent to the republic to try to calm the situation. Shevardnadze admitted at a Party meeting that 'the methods used to disperse the demonstrators are unacceptable in a society which has taken the road of *glasnost* and *perestroika*'.

Five days after the deaths, the Party Secretary in Georgia, the President and the Prime Minister all resigned. The local KGB chief for two months, Givi Gumbaridze, was named Party Secretary. In shaking up the leadership the Party was following the pattern set in 1988 in the neighbouring republics of Azerbaijan and Armenia. In both places the Party chiefs were sacked, apparently for their inability to halt unrest. A Georgian commission and a Moscow criminal investigation were set up to investigate the charges of brutality. The commission reported that soldiers carried out a 'planned mass massacre' and that the action carried signs of being a punitive operation, committed with especial cruelty. It criticized the media for distorted coverage of the clash and blamed local leaders for 'complete isolation from the people'.

The involvement of central authorities appears to be confirmed by statements in the Supreme Soviet at the end of May when General Rodionov, the local commanding officer, revealed that two Politburo members, including Shevardnadze, joined in the decision to impose martial law and use troops 'to seize the city'. The sacked Georgian Party Secretary, Dzumber Patiashvili, then disclosed that the Defence Minister, General Yazov, had telephoned him the previous day to announce the decision to send troops into Tbilisi. A Deputy Defence Minister was in Tbilisi to take charge and General Rodionov was put in executive control. KGB troops were flown in. Patiashvili's account contradicted everything which had been said before, namely, that the local Georgian Communist Party was in control and requested military help without reference to Moscow. Later Yegor Ligachev, conservative opponent of Gorbachev, said the decision to send troops to Georgia was taken by, the whole Politburo. On the first anniversary of the 1989 massacre rallies were held and there were calls for a boycott of military service and for the union of the many competing Georgian nationalist parties.

Opposition groups decided to boycott the elections on 25 March and, at an unspecified date, to hold their own elections to an opposition congress. This congress would 'control the actions of the republic's government until complete independence is achieved'. The Georgian Supreme Soviet called for negotiations with Moscow on independence saying that 'it considers illegal the 1922 USSR agreement on relations with Georgia' and that the Red Army occupation of Georgia in 1921 was an 'international crime'. Elections to the Georgian Supreme Soviet were eventually postponed until the autumn, while some opposition groups urged an electoral boycott on the grounds that Moscow would never concede independence through the ballot box. The republic's constitution was amended to abolish the Communist Party's monopoly of power and to allow all parties 'to participate on equal terms in the management of the state and public affairs'.

Serious disturbances occurred in July with a political protest which disrupted rail traffic through much of the Caucasus. Several hundred people blocked the track at Samtredia, which was on one of only two lines from the Russian Federation into the Caucasus. The protesters wanted an early recall of the republic's Supreme Soviet to pass a new election law and the registration of all opposition groups so that they could fight the elections fixed for 28 October. Before the elections, opposition groups elected an unofficial congress as they had promised. Two groups, the National Democratic Party (led by Georgi Chanturiya) and the National Independence Party (led by Irakli Tsereteli) divided 136 out of 200 seats between them. However, some nationalist groups (such as the Round Table/Free Georgia group led by Zviad Gamsakhurdia) boycotted the elections to the Congress and supported the Georgian Supreme Soviet elections. Other groups stood in elections to both bodies (for example, the Democratic Georgia group, led by Alexander Dzhavakhishvili). Even the Communist Party was divided, a majority boycotting the Congress, but its 'democratic' faction winning eleven Congressional seats. There were divided opinions as to what the Congress should do. The National Independence Party wanted a campaign of civil disobedience, while Democratic Georgia believed in co-operation between the Congress and the Supreme Soviet in preparing for independence.

After the Tbilisi massacre the Communist Party had virtually collapsed, but it staged a comeback in 1990. It was now as nationalist as any other party in the republic. Ten other blocs, embracing nearly forty groups, contested the elections. Half the seats were elected on a constituency basis (some of which went to a second round), and half by proportional representation through party lists. In the event, the Communist Party was defeated after sixty-eight years in power. The Round Table/Free Georgia alliance won 155 out of 250 seats in the Supreme Soviet. It was supported by other nationalist groups. The Communist Party obtained sixty-four seats. The Round Table leader, Gamsakhurdia, was elected President. He was a writer and philologist who had been gaoled several times for dissident activities and had exploited the reputation of his father, an author and nationalist. At first he adopted a cautious approach to independence, assuming a transition period of about five years during which the Soviet army would remain. A bill to establish the supremacy of Georgia's laws over those of the Soviet Union was to be introduced as well as amendments to the constitution removing words such as 'Soviet', 'Communist' and 'revolutionary'.

Despite an ultimatum from the Soviet army headquarters in Moscow, Gamsakhurdia said in January 1991 that the Georgian Supreme Soviet would keep a law, passed the previous month, which abolished Soviet army conscription in Georgia. The army ultimatum warned that if Georgia refused to enforce the draft, the army might do so itself. Georgia planned to conscript its youth into a 12,000 strong Republican National Guard, which was to be formed in February, and to join them with the 20,000 militiamen of the Interior Ministry. The primary aim of the guard would be to counter armed criminal gangs which had adopted a political façade, but it could also defend Georgia against attacks by the Soviet army. The central government could not treat Georgia like the Baltic states because Georgians were willing and able to fight. There was no sizable Russian minority or old-style Communist Party which could be used to suggest popular support for intervention. There were, however, Azeri, Armenian and Jewish minorities whose discontents could be exploited. More important still, were the demands from the Abkhazians and South Ossetians for more autonomy. Although Georgians saw these demands as inspired by Moscow, it is more likely that they were part of the general tendency to national self-assertion throughout the Soviet Union. Hostility to the aspirations of these minorities was likely to lose Georgia international sympathy.

Abkhazia

The Caucasus, which has more than thirty separate languages in an area about the size of Britain, was the most dramatic illustration of the artificiality of many Soviet internal political boundaries. The Abkhazians had been demanding that their republic (an autonomous republic within Georgia with a population of half a million) should be allowed to secede from Georgia and be upgraded to a full republic. Georgians, who formed a majority of Abkhazia's population, fiercely opposed the idea, as did the Georgian Party leadership. The local Party leader in Abkhazia, Boris Adleyba, was sacked after backing secession. Both Abkhazians, represented by a group called Ayglara (Unity), and Georgians organized demonstrations in Abkhazia in the spring of 1989 as well as in Tbilisi. Georgian nationalists claimed that the Abkhazian protest was instigated by Moscow in order to discredit Georgia's own demands for greater autonomy. As elsewhere, the protests show how *glasnost* had revealed many suppressed ethnic resentments of the previous seventy years, in which anger with Moscow was intermingled with tensions between ethnic communities.

South Ossetia

In January 1990 Soviet troops had to be sent to a remote region of the Caucasus mountains where tension rose between the Georgian and South Ossetian communities. The National Front of South Ossetia claimed that their community was besieged by Georgians, who had been setting up sporadic blockades since the previous November. Ossetians had lived in the area for centuries. North Ossetia, with roughly 300,000 people, was an autonomous republic in the Russian Federation. South Ossetia, with some 65,000 people, was an autonomous region within Georgia. Both speak an Iranian language and have always been cautious about the Georgians. In the Revolution they sided with Russia, and the Georgians put down several uprisings between 1917 and 1920. The South Ossetians feared that an independent Georgia would discriminate against them and they repeatedly called for Soviet intervention. Conflict continued between Georgians and South Ossetians especially after the Ossetians, in September 1990, proclaimed themselves a separate republic. The Georgian Supreme Soviet, in reply, declared the new republic illegal and abolished the Soviet-created autonomous region of South Ossetia. In addition Georgia announced a state of emergency and imposed a curfew.

Gorbachev pronounced these Georgian rulings illegal and ordered their rescinding. He proposed that the Georgian militia should withdraw from the area. Soviet troops would then go in to restore order and the autonomous region would be re-established. The Georgian government ignored this. Its Interior Minister claimed that the South Ossetians were getting their weapons from the Soviet army. Moscow then sent in troops anyway. The serious violence started with these decisions, with both sides believing that Moscow was using the conflict to pressure Georgia into signing the proposed Union Treaty. In March

1991 Yeltsin and Gamsakhurdia, on behalf of the Russian Federation and Georgia, agreed to form a joint police unit to attempt to calm the area. President Gamsakhurdia also offered to negotiate with the leaders of South Ossetia, apparently in an attempt to stave off the imposition of a state of emergency. The Georgians started a rail strike, blocking the ports of Batumi and Poti, in protest at Soviet troop activity in South Ossetia. Tension and sporadic fighting continued.

The Independence Referendum

On 31 March Georgians voted on the question: Do you agree that Georgia's state independence should be restored on the basis of the act of independence of 26 May 1921? Ninety-two per cent of the republic's electorate took part, with 99 per cent of those voting 'yes'. However, this vote has to be interpreted in the light of Gamsakhurdia's statement that only those districts which voted for independence would be entitled to Georgian citizenship which, in turn, would be the prerequisite for the ownership of land. In April the Georgian Supreme Soviet elected Gamsakhurdia as its first executive President, and he was given temporary emergency powers to rule by decree until the elections in May. He soon decreed a campaign of 'national and civil disobedience' against Soviet interests in the republic, in support of its demands for full independence. At the elections opponents of Gamsakhurdia accused him of authoritarian tendencies, but a coalition of parties in favour of independence led by him won power with 87 per cent of the vote. The Communist Party came nowhere. Voting did not take place in South Ossetia. Many, particularly in the ethnic minorities, remained uneasy at what they saw as Gamsakhurdia's increasing authoritarianism. However, the government had said that all those who had roots in Georgia from before 1921 would definitely receive citizenship in an independent Georgia. The opposition candidate in the presidential election, Valerian Adadze, thought that Gamsakhurdia's provocative activities would bring Soviet intervention rather than independence. Both government and opposition still agreed that the demands in South Ossetia and Abkhazia to join the Russian Federation was the work of Moscow, aiming to undermine the independence movement.

The Effect of the Attempted Coup

The growing crisis in Georgia over the ethnic minorities and opposition to Gamsakhurdia's authoritarian style of government was coming to a head as the coup occurred. His first public reaction to the coup was to appeal for calm and to say that he was uninterested in it since it was taking place in 'another country'. Subsequently, there were demonstrations against the Communist Party and Gamsakhurdia demanded its banning and the confiscation of its property. The South Ossetians and the Abkhazians supported the coup because they believed it would prevent the breakup of the Soviet Union. There is evidence that Gamsakhurdia tried to turn the coup to his advantage, and at first gave it his support. The day before the coup the Georgian Prime Minister and other ministers resigned or were dismissed by the President. The sacked Prime Minister, Tengiz Sigua, joined the opposition. Gamsakhurdia talked of a plot against the Georgian government instigated by Shevardnadze, the former Soviet Foreign Minister. Coup decrees were published in Georgian newspapers and a major crisis occurred when he agreed to the Soviet army's demand to disband the National Guard and transform it into police units. It was soon recreated but it remained split as a large number (including the leader, Tengiz Kitovani), refused to resume loyalty to Gamsakhurdia.

The republic was far more preoccupied with its own crisis than the coup. Demonstrations continued as the government banned many exports and clamped down on the press. The demonstrators were demanding the resignation of the President and the government, as well as new elections. Gamsakhurdia accused opponents of being traitors and was prone to see conspiracies everywhere. He arrested political opponents and censored the media. The human rights movement was by now among his most vociferous opponents. Many demonstrations occurred throughout September, sometimes with violence. The former national guards allied themselves with the supporters of former Prime Minister, Tengiz Sigua, and former Foreign Minister, Georgii Khoshtaria.

The Overthrow of President Gamsakhurdia

Eventually thirty opposition groups united in a campaign to oust Gamsakhurdia. They wanted the abolition of the presidency, new elections, the return of the 1921 Constitution and a coalition government. Civil war seemed a real possibility. A session of parliament, called early, suggested that, although Gamsakhurdia was backed by the majority, this support might be slipping away. Large crowds in the streets were still in favour of him, however. After the occupation of the television centre by the opposition and the blocking of roads into the capital, Gamsakhurdia had talks with opposition leaders, mediated by the Patriarch of the Georgian Orthodox Church. He was pressed to agree to an emergency televised session of parliament to discuss a new electoral law. But two days later Gamsakhurdia declared a state of emergency and called on Georgians to come to Tbilisi and help 'liquidate this nest of bandits'. He also set up a National Security Council, directed by him, to control the armed forces, settle ethnic conflict, and enforce law and order. Splits appeared among the opposition. A tense stand-off ensued, punctuated by fighting and terrorist attacks.

By the middle of December fighting had broken out in Tbilisi and Gamsakhurdia had taken refuge in the parliament building, which was besieged by his opponents. The opposition consisted of four paramilitary groups, that of the former Prime Minister Tengiz Sigua, the rebel national guard led by Tengiz Kitovani, the Mhedrioni Society, led by Jaba Iosseliani and the militiamen of Meab Kostava. An extended and violent siege followed during which Georgii Chanturia, leader of the National Democratic Party, imprisoned by Gamsakhurdia, was freed. The rebels gradually got the upper hand, in spite of demonstrations in favour of Gamsakhurdia, in one of which firing took place and some demonstrators were killed. They formed a Military Council, which was designed to replace Gamsakhurdia's government. Notably, the supporters of Gamsakhurdia, thought to exist in large numbers elsewhere in Georgia, did not come to the capital to support him. Gamsakhurdia fled Tbilisi on 6 January 1992. He eventually went into hiding in western Georgia, but attempts to organize armed resistance on his behalf failed. The Military Council steadily established its control over western Georgia where Gamsakhurdia's support had hitherto been strong. It was far better equipped militarily than Gamsakhurdia's supporters, but it remained to be seen whether a firmly based civilian government could be established in the near future. Georgia's ability to operate as an independent state depended on being able to solve the ethnic minorities question. Until this happened the economic situation remained in crisis. Like other republics its economy had been closely integrated into the Soviet system. The Commonwealth of Independent States was not willing for Georgia to become a member while uncertainty and tension prevailed. Neither were other states willing to grant diplomatic recognition.

Epilogue:
The Future

The Commonwealth of Independent States

A summit of the new Commonwealth took place in Minsk at the end of 1991. It reached a compromise on the issue of the military command of conventional forces. While there would be unified command, Ukraine, Azerbaijan and Armenia's insistence on forming their own forces was also accepted. There were concessions by Russia and Ukraine over control of the Black Sea Fleet. The armed forces were a major problem, as they had become the only remaining significant Union body still existing. Former Soviet troops remained in place in all the republics. The army, in particular, was at this time very demoralized and discontented. They were witnessing the disappearance of the Union they existed to defend, Soviet troops were being withdrawn from Eastern Europe and it was no longer clear who was in command of them. Military personnel would be able to transfer their loyalties to their own republics, and even Russians might be prepared to serve in a republic where they had lived for some time and had their homes. There was some talk of a possible military coup but it was hard to see how this could be sustained in the face of the new independence of the republics, and the hostility which would be engendered in them.

Other agreements were signed on external borders, former Soviet property abroad and co-operation in disasters. They agreed on setting up institutions to manage the new Commonwealth, but Kravchuk of Ukraine, in particular, made it clear that Ukraine did 'not intend to form any Commonwealth structures to speak on [Ukraine's] behalf on the international stage' (Rettie, 1991c). He added that Ukraine wanted to be an equal partner in Europe. Clearly there were major disagreements, particularly between Russia and Ukraine, over economic and financial policy. Economic questions included the ownership of resources, especially energy supplies. Western Europe depended on the former Soviet Union for almost half its natural gas, and Eastern Europe's dependence was infinitely greater. The validity of bilateral

financial and trade agreements with former Soviet ministries was now
in question. The future of the Soviet Union's $60 billion foreign debt
was of major concern. It was likely that the republics would seek to
establish their own currencies, which would foment trade disputes.
Russians losing their jobs in loss-making industries in other republics
would be a source of unrest. Other problems involved diplomatic
representation, including Soviet representation at the United Nations
and its permanent seat (and right of veto) on the Security Council. In
the event, Russia took over the seat and the United States, NATO and
the European Community states moved swiftly to give diplomatic
recognition to most of the Commonwealth republics.

The Question of Nuclear Weapons

Among other arrangements included in the new Commonwealth, was
a single, united command over nuclear weapons deployed in the three
Slavic republics and Kazakhstan. It was made clear that the means
would be found for the presidents of these republics to have a veto over
the use of nuclear weapons. The United States and other western
powers had continued to hope until the last minute that some centre
would be preserved, and that Gorbachev – whom they knew and
trusted – would have a role, especially in control of nuclear weapons.
The unfeasibility of this led to considerable anxiety which the declarations of the new Commonwealth by no means entirely allayed. After
James Baker, the United States Secretary of State, had visited Moscow
in December, confusion still seemed to reign over the fate of nuclear
weapons. Baker seems to have thought that the Russian Federation
would remain the only nuclear power in the region with the other
nuclear republics renouncing nuclear weapons. But the Presidents of
Ukraine and Kazakhstan made it clear that their republics would retain
nuclear weapons for the time being, at least. Baker remained convinced
that Ukraine, Belarus and Kazakhstan did, in principle, want to become non-nuclear states.

The West expected the successor states to take on the obligations
of the 1989 Nuclear Non-proliferation Treaty, the 1972 Anti-ballistic
Missiles Treaty and the Test Ban treaties. The 1990 Conventional
Forces in Europe Treaty had not yet been ratified. Lithuania had
already refused to ratify it because it believed it would 'legalize the
presence of Soviet forces' in the republic. Other republics, such as
Ukraine, were thought likely to want renegotiation because the treaty
was based on force reductions from Soviet military districts which
did not coincide with the borders of the new republics. The START
treaty on the reduction of strategic nuclear arsenals was also awaiting
ratification.

Political Problems in the Russian Federation

In spite of the positive intentions of the new Commonwealth, the political mechanisms for co-ordinating policy did not yet exist and, even more important, there was no effective decision-making in the Russian Federation which, in the face of the need for drastic economic reforms, needed strong, government. The Russian Minister of Justice said, 'The present central administrative structure cannot, in principle, function. There is a total paralysis of Russia's state structures' (Nove, 1991).

Yeltsin's Deputy President, Alexander Rutskoi, also made a strong attack on the Russian government. He said, 'There is no governing power and no democracy in Russia.' The Russian 'White House' had become a 'hotbed of intrigue. Nobody knows where we are going and what our ultimate goal is meant to be' (Steele, 1991b). There was already concern over the legal validity of Yeltsin's decrees, which added to the problems of entrenching legality. An example was his decision to merge the former regular police force with the KGB intelligence agency into a new Russian Ministry of Security and the Interior. The head of the Russian Supreme Court judged it 'necessary to suspend' the decree. The Russian media said that the new ministry bore an uncomfortable resemblance to Stalin's NKVD, his main vehicle of repression. There were thought to be too many academics in the Russian government and too few with real political experience who were at the same time committed to democracy and the market economy. All this related to the implication, made throughout his career, that Yeltsin was incapable of exercising power responsibly. Certainly his previous popularity would be greatly tested, now that he was in charge and no longer the anti-establishment hero, able to blame Communist enemies for criticisms of him.

Why Did the Soviet Union Collapse?

Signs of decline and decay were evident before Gorbachev came to power. He himself has admitted that he realized the need for change, although not the type and scale. Ordinary people were of course aware of the huge gap between propaganda and reality. *Glasnost* made available for the first time irrefutable data showing the oppressiveness, lying and duplicity of the Soviet regime as well as its failure to be the happy, efficient well-run society it claimed to be. This knowledge finally undermined its already weakening legitimacy. Gorbachev released reforming energy which, in the end, he could not control. His clear intention was drastically to reform, but retain the essential features of, the old regime, especially the central role of the Communist Party. Not only did he meet strong opposition from vested interests, but he unleashed political momentum from a source long acquiescent in the Soviet Union – the grass roots. This included the centrifugal force of nationalism which perhaps could have been contained except that the inability of the centre to effect significant reform encouraged the nationalities to feel that they could hardly do worse by going it alone and that at least they would be responsible for their own mistakes and costs instead of having to pay for the decisions of the centre.

Hosking (1989) drew attention to the theory of Alexander Yanov, that Russian history shows a cycle of reform imposed from above, followed by a reaction and attempts at more rational reforms leading to stagnation and corruption until the cycle began again. But the Soviet Union of the 1980s and 1990s was a very different place from that before the 1960s. The population was urbanized, better educated and more aware of conditions in the West. The government had renounced the use of force to sustain its rule in order to bolster its claim to be a modern, industrialized, sophisticated society. International opinion would not tolerate such use of force, and the Soviet Union was dependent on trade and aid from the West. Hence, if persuasion was insufficient, the Soviet Union could not survive. In reform ambitious politicians came to see opportunities for advancement, opportunities hitherto unavailable to non-Communists, while reform was also now necessary for the political survival of Communist leaders. Perhaps one of the most significant outcomes of the collapse of the Soviet Union was how many of the 'new' leaders were ex-Communists. Some, like Yeltsin, had definitively renounced Communism. Others, like those in Central Asia, had made relatively little adjustment except to change the name of the Party and to climb on the nationalist bandwagon. In many republics, including the Russian Federation and Ukraine, ex-Communists were still numerous in many political and administrative posts, while they were also endeavouring to get a large stake in the potentially very profitable private enterprise system being established.

Gorbachev

Gorbachev had effectively ensured that the August coup would not succeed by refusing to sign the state of emergency decree, as the coup leaders had expected him to do. But his failure to grasp the significance of what had happened – epitomized by his attempt to argue that the Communist Party still had a role – meant that he could not halt the steady draining away of his authority. Although he made many mistakes – such as appointing the wrong people to important posts and apparently vacillating between support for conservatives and radicals –

he stood firm on two vital points. These were that he would not use force or cynically appeal to extreme Russian nationalist feelings to hold the Union together. It eventually became clear that, without (and probably even with) the use of force, the Union could not hold.

His very considerable achievements at home and abroad could not conceal the impression that he was essentially trying to reform the old order – however drastically – when the increasingly perceived need among opinion leaders and leading politicians was to replace that order. It was this leap that he could not take. Unlike the leaders of the republics, he had not been elected by the people, and the referendum supporting the Union in the spring of 1991, by which he set much store, was too loaded to be reliable. In any case, it had been superseded by changes in public opinion since it was held, as the vote for independence in Ukraine showed. Hence he steadily alienated all sections of society: conservatives for his reforms, radicals for refusing to ally himself unequivocally with them and his insistence that the CPSU could be reformed, nationalists for his failure to comprehend the deep yearning for independence from Moscow, and economists for his failure firmly to grasp the necessity for rapidly implementing drastic changes.

The Future of the Commonwealth of Independent States

Ironically it was President Nazarbaev of Kazakhstan, a friend of Gorbachev's and a supporter of a Union confederation, who planted the idea which ultimately led to the Minsk Declaration. In the spring of 1991 he had suggested that all fifteen republics should meet in Alma-Ata without Gorbachev and work out a new form of co-operation. The idea of an agreement without the participation of the centre was received coolly at first, and seen as a politically self-interested move by Nazarbaev; but it soon seemed increasingly attractive. There was a strong desire among Russians to destroy the old Union but the suspicions of the other republics, fuelled by statements from Yeltsin about renegotiating borders, prevented the Russian Federation simply taking over the functions of the old Union. Ukraine, resentful over its perceived inferior position *vis-à-vis* the federation, became increasingly attracted to breaking from the centre. For Kravchuk of Ukraine the European Community was a model to follow, but the new Commonwealth was as yet much less than that. There was no Commonwealth president or parliament. Agreements were apparently to be reached in meetings of the republic presidents. Some felt that co-ordinating bodies must be created. Already Yeltsin's decree abolishing the Soviet Foreign Ministry had provided for a four-week period in which the Commonwealth would create a 'co-ordinating and consultative mechanism to conduct foreign policy'. But the Ukrainian parliament issued a statement which, among other things, said, 'co-ordinating institutions within the framework of the Commonwealth cannot have governing functions. Their decisions are recommendations' (Hearst, Dyczok and Simmons, 1991).

Nevertheless, at the Alma-Ata conference on 21–2 December it was agreed to set up a committee to manage the Commonwealth's external frontiers and to work out an accord sharing former Soviet property and assets. Each member state would make financial contributions to joint projects. Failure to pay would mean non-involvement in, or the freezing of, the project. The Russian Federation made efforts to allay fears of Russian dominance; it held meetings outside Moscow and sought the agreement of all republics to such issues as control of the nuclear button and the transfer of the United Nations Security Council seat from the Soviet Union to the Russian Federation. This may not have been sufficient, but it probably helped in the early stages of the republics' adjustment to the breakup of the Union, and their reassessment of their relationships with other areas and neighbouring states. The suspicion and hostility to the centre was such that the Commonwealth could only survive by tolerating diversity.

In the end the new Commonwealth would be judged on how effectively it contributed to the successful transition to a market economy as well as the extension and preservation of democracy. Clearly all there was in the early days were declarations of intent. Months or years of negotiation lay ahead; one only has to cite the intense negotiations often necessary in the European Community to realize the magnitude of the problem. The Ukrainian and Belarusian parliaments soon expressed fears of Russian domination of the CIS. It might well have been that, after economic and military reforms had been attained, the republics would see no further need for the Commonwealth. On the other hand, by then it might have acquired a purpose and momentum of its own.

For two centuries the question of how to create an effective and permanent democracy had dominated political thought. In the struggle between those who believe in society as a naturally evolving organism whose strength lies in tradition and firm authority, and those who are convinced that a truly democratic society can and must be rationally planned, the Soviet experience stands out as a spectacular manifestation of the latter and an equally spectacular failure. Whether that failure was the result of wrong analysis, intentions and policies or whether it is inherent in such experiments is a question which will continue to be heatedly argued over. Eclipsed for the present by the Soviet Union's collapse, the ideal of a planned human society maximizing human potential may not have entirely lost its appeal and, if it is ever to be resurrected in a new form, that form will surely be much modified by the Soviet experience.

Appendix A

Soviet Party and Government
Before the Gorbachev Reforms

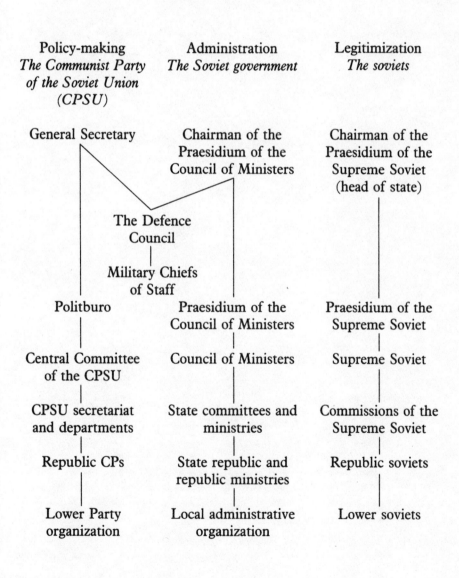

Policy-making *The Communist Party of the Soviet Union (CPSU)*	Administration *The Soviet government*	Legitimization *The soviets*
General Secretary	Chairman of the Praesidium of the Council of Ministers	Chairman of the Praesidium of the Supreme Soviet (head of state)
	The Defence Council	
	Military Chiefs of Staff	
Politburo	Praesidium of the Council of Ministers	Praesidium of the Supreme Soviet
Central Committee of the CPSU	Council of Ministers	Supreme Soviet
CPSU secretariat and departments	State committees and ministries	Commissions of the Supreme Soviet
Republic CPs	State republic and republic ministries	Republic soviets
Lower Party organization	Local administrative organization	Lower soviets

Membership of the three arms of the pre-Gorbachev Soviet government was not exclusive. Gorbachev (like some of his predecessors) was Chairman of the Praesidium of the Supreme Soviet (i.e. head of state) and virtually all ministers and high officials in the government were members of the Party (perhaps holding a Party post) and also deputies in the Supreme Soviet. People such as top civil servants and military officers were not disqualified from being elected to soviets.

Appendix B

The Governmental Structure, Spring to Autumn 1990

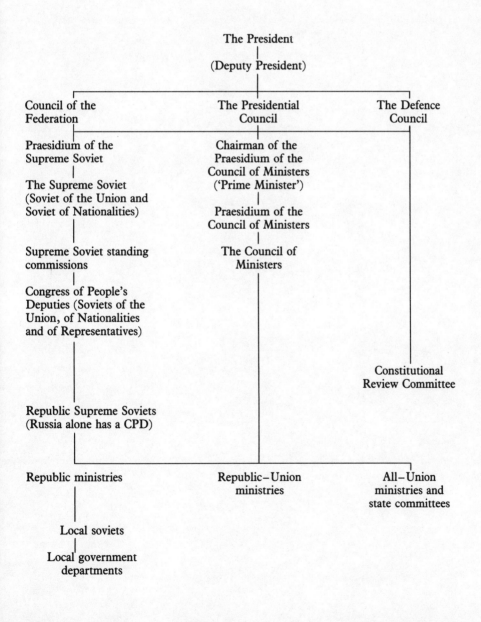

The President

(Deputy President)

Council of the Federation

The Presidential Council

The Defence Council

Praesidium of the Supreme Soviet

The Supreme Soviet (Soviet of the Union and Soviet of Nationalities)

Chairman of the Praesidium of the Council of Ministers ('Prime Minister')

Praesidium of the Council of Ministers

Supreme Soviet standing commissions

The Council of Ministers

Congress of People's Deputies (Soviets of the Union, of Nationalities and of Representatives)

Constitutional Review Committee

Republic Supreme Soviets (Russia alone has a CPD)

Republic ministries

Republic–Union ministries

All–Union ministries and state committees

Local soviets

Local government departments

Appendix C

The Governmental Structure, from early in 1991

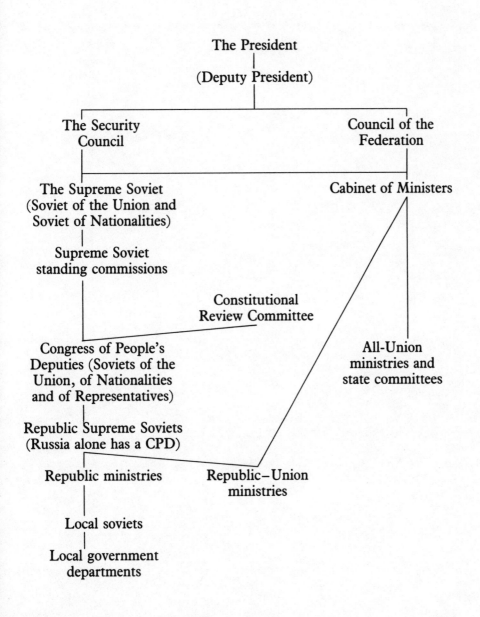

The President

(Deputy President)

The Security Council

Council of the Federation

The Supreme Soviet (Soviet of the Union and Soviet of Nationalities)

Cabinet of Ministers

Supreme Soviet standing commissions

Constitutional Review Committee

Congress of People's Deputies (Soviets of the Union, of Nationalities and of Representatives)

All-Union ministries and state committees

Republic Supreme Soviets (Russia alone has a CPD)

Republic ministries

Republic–Union ministries

Local soviets

Local government departments

Appendix D

The Union of Sovereign States

Provisional Governmental Structure from 5 September 1991 to December 1991

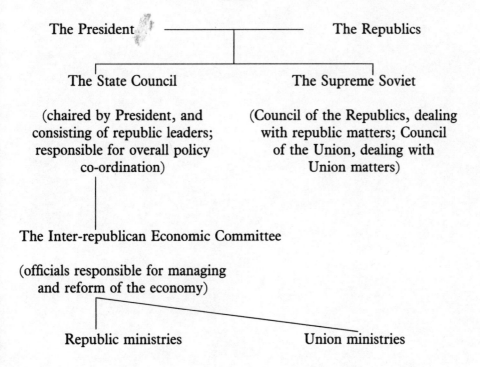

The President ———————————— The Republics

The State Council   The Supreme Soviet

(chaired by President, and consisting of republic leaders; responsible for overall policy co-ordination)

(Council of the Republics, dealing with republic matters; Council of the Union, dealing with Union matters)

The Inter-republican Economic Committee

(officials responsible for managing and reform of the economy)

Republic ministries   Union ministries

Selected Further Reading

Prologue (A Revolution in the Soviet Union)

Brown, A. (2nd edn, 1992) *The Gorbachev Factor in Soviet Politics*, Oxford, Oxford University Press.

Brumberg, A. (1992) 'The road to Minsk', *New York Review of Books*, 30 January, pp. 21–6.

Crawshaw, S. (1992) *Goodbye to the USSR: the Collapse of Soviet Power*, London, Bloomsbury.

Gorbachev, M. (1991) *The August Coup*, London, Harper Collins.

Sheehy, A. (1992) 'Commonwealth emerges out of disintegrating USSR', *RFE/RL Research Report*, 1(1), 3 January, pp. 5–8.

White, S. (3rd edn, 1992) *Gorbachev and After*, Cambridge, Cambridge University Press.

Chapter 1 (The Bolshevik Revolution Triumphs)

Acton, E. (1990) *Rethinking the Russian Revolution*, London, Edward Arnold.

Farber, S. (1990) *Before Stalinism: the Rise and Fall of Soviet Democracy*, Cambridge, Polity.

Frankel E. R., Frankel, J. and Knei-Paz, B. (eds) (1992) *Revolution in Russia: Reassessment of 1917*, Cambridge, Cambridge University Press.

Galili, Z. (1990) *The Menshevik Leaders in the Russian Revolution: Social Realities and Political Strategies*, Princeton, NJ, Princeton University Press.

Koenker, D. P., Rosenberg, W. G. and Grigorsuny, R. (eds) (1990) *Party, State and Society in the Russian Civil War: Explorations in Social History*, Bloomington, Ind., Indiana University Press.

Lih, L. T. (1990) 'Breakdown and reconstitution: thinking about the Russian revolution', *Problems of Communism*, 39(2), March–April, pp. 98–104.

Lincoln, W. B. (1990) *Red Victory: a History of the Russian Civil War*, New York, Simon & Schuster.

Pethybridge, R. (1991) *One Step Backwards, Two Steps Forward: Soviet Society and Politics Under the New Economic Policy*, Oxford, Oxford University Press.

Pipes, R. (1990) *The Russian Revolution, 1899–1919*, London, Collins Harvill.

Chapter 2 (Stalinism: the Regime Bloodily Consolidated)

Blobaum, R. (1990) 'The destruction of east-central Europe, 1939–41, *Problems of Communism*, 39(6), November–December, pp. 106–11.

Bullock, A. (1991) *Hitler and Stalin: Parallel Lives*, London, Harper Collins.

Conquest, R. (reissued 1990) *The Great Terror: a Reassessment*, Oxford, Oxford University Press.

Fitzpatrick, S. (1979) *Education and Social Mobility in the Soviet Union, 1921–34*, Cambridge, Cambridge University Press.

Füredi, F. (1985) *The Soviet Union Demystified: a Materialist Analysis*, London, Junius.

Getty, J. Arch (1985) *Origins of the Great Purges: the Soviet Communist Party Reconsidered, 1933–38*, New York, Cambridge University Press.

Gill, G. (1990) *The Origins of the Stalinist Political System*, Cambridge, Cambridge University Press.

Kemp-Welch, A. (1992) *The Ideas of Nikolai Bukharin*, Oxford, Oxford University Press.

Kuromiya, H. (1988) *Stalin's Industrial Revolution: Politics and Workers, 1928–32*, Cambridge, Cambridge University Press.

Lacqueur, W. (1990) *Stalin: the Glasnost Revelations*, Boston, Mass., Unwin Hyman.

Lewin, M. (1985) *The Makers of the Soviet System: Essays in the Social History of Inter-War Russia*, London, Methuen.

McCauley, M. (1976) *Khrushchev and the Development of Soviet Agriculture*, London, Macmillan.

McCauley, M. (1983) *Stalin and Stalinism*, London, Longman.

MacNeal, R. (1988) *Stalin: Man and Ruler*, London, Macmillan.

Medvedev, R. (rev. edn, 1989) *Let History Judge: the Origins and Consequences of Stalinism*, Oxford, Oxford University Press.

Roberts, G. (1992) 'The Soviet decision for a pact with Nazi Germany', *Soviet Studies*, 44(1), pp. 57–78.

Siegalbaum, L. A. (1988) *Stakanovism and the Politics of Productivity in the USSR, 1934–41*, Cambridge, Cambridge University Press.

Siegalbaum, L. A. (1992) *Soviet State and Society between Revolutions, 1918–1929*, Cambridge, Cambridge University Press.

Tolz, V. (1991) 'New information about the deportation of ethnic groups under Stalin', *Report on the USSR (RFE/RL Research Institute)*, 3(17), 26 April, pp. 16–20.

Tolz, V. and Wishnevsky, J. (1988) 'Materials defending Stalin in the Soviet press', *Radio liberty Research*, 4/88, 21 December, pp. 1–3.

Tucker, R. C. (1991) *Stalin in Power: the Revolution from Above, 1928–1941*, London and New York, Norton.

Volkogonov, D. (1991) *Stalin: Triumph and Tragedy*, London, Weidenfeld & Nicolson.

Chapter 3 (Stalin's Successors: Change and Stagnation)

Amalrik, A. (1976) 'Ideologies in Soviet society', *Survey*, 22(2), Spring, pp. 1–11.

Barghoorn, F. C. (1983) 'Regime–Dissenter relations after Khrushchev: some observations', in S. G. Solomon (ed.) *Pluralism in the Soviet Union*, London, Macmillan, ch. 6.

Bocharov, G. (1990) *Russian Roulette: the Afghanistan War through Russian Eyes*, London, Hamish Hamilton.

Borovik, A. (1990) *The Hidden War: a Russian Journalist's Account of the Soviet War in Afghanistan*, London, Faber.

Breslauer, G. (1982) *Khrushchev and Brezhnev as Leaders: Building Authority in Soviet Politics*, London, Allen & Unwin.

Clemens, W. C., Jr (1989) 'Soviet foreign policy since 1917: achievements and failures', *Survey*, 30(4), June, pp. 87–112.

Cutler, R. M. (1980) 'Soviet dissent under Khrushchev: an analytical study', *Comparative Politics*, 13(1), October, pp. 15–36.

Grigorenko, P. (1983) *Memoirs*, London, Harvill.

Gustafson, T. (1981) *Reform in Soviet Politics: Lessons of Recent Policies on Land and Water*, Cambridge, Cambridge University Press.

Hough, J. and Fainsod, M. (1979) *How the Soviet Union is Governed*, Cambridge, Mass., Harvard University Press.

Kerblay, B. (1983) *Modern Soviet Society*, London, Methuen.

Khrushchev, N. S. (1976) *The Secret Speech*, Nottingham, Spokesman Books.

Lowenhardt, J. (1981) *Decision-making in Soviet Politics*, London, Macmillan.

McCauley, M. (1987) *Khrushchev and Khrushchevism*, Basingstoke, Macmillan.

Parker, J. W. (1991) *The Kremlin in Transition*, vol. 1: *From Brezhnev to Chernenko, 1978–85*, London, Unwin Hyman.

Rutland, P. (1985) *The Myth of the Plan: Lessons of Soviet Planning Experience*, London, Hutchinson.

Sakharov, A. (1990) *Memoirs*, London, Hutchinson.

Scammell, M. (1985) *Solzhenitsyn: a Biography*, London, Hutchinson.

Steele, J. (1985) *The Limits of Soviet Power: the Kremlin's Foreign Policy, Brezhnev to Chernenko*, Harmondsworth, Penguin.

Tökes, R. L. (ed.) (1975) *Dissent in the USSR: Politics, Ideology and People*, Baltimore, Md., Johns Hopkins University.

Troitsky, A. (1987) *Back in the USSR: the True Story of Rock in Russia*, London, Omnibus.

Zaslavsky, V. (1982) *The Neo-Stalinist State: Class, Ethnicity and Consciousness in Soviet Society*, Brighton, Harvester.

Chapter 4 (The Surge of Reform)

Confino, M. (1991) 'Solzhenitsyn, the West and the new Russian nationalism', *Journal of Contemporary History*, 26, September, pp. 611–36.

Cook, L. J. (1992) 'Brezhnev's "social contract" and Gorbachev's reforms', *Soviet Studies*, 44(1), pp. 37–56.

Crouch, M. (1989) *Revolution and Evolution: Gorbachev and Soviet Politics*, Hemel Hempstead, Philip Allan.

Davies, R. W. (1989) *Soviet History in the Gorbachev Era*, Basingstoke, Macmillan.

Dellenbrant, J. A. and Hill, R. J. (1989) *Gorbachev and Perestroika*, Cheltenham, Edward Elgar.

Feher, F. and Arato, A. (eds) (1989) *Gorbachev: the Debate*, Cambridge, Polity.

Gooding, J. (1990) 'Gorbachev and democracy', *Soviet Studies*, 42(2), pp. 195–221.

Gooding, J. (1992) 'Lenin in Soviet politics, 1985–91', *Soviet Studies*, 44(3), pp. 403–22.

Gorbachev, M. (updated edn, 1988) *Perestroika: New Thinking for Our Country and the World*, London, Fontana.

Hasegawa, T. and Pravda, A. (1990) *Perestroika: Soviet Domestic and Foreign Policy*, London, Sage.

Holloway, D. (1989) 'Gorbachev's new thinking', *Foreign Affairs*, 68(1) pp. 66–81.

Hosking, G. (1990) *The Awakening of the Soviet Union*, London, Heinemann.

Jones, A. and Moskoff, W. (1989) 'New cooperatives in the USSR, *Problems of Communism*, 38(6), November–December, pp. 27–39.

Laqueur, W. (1990) *The Long Road to Freedom: Russia and 'Glasnost'*, Boston, Mass., Unwin Hyman.

Legvold, R. (1989) 'The revolution in Soviet foreign policy', *Foreign Affairs*, 68(1), pp. 82–98.

Mote, M. E. (1989) 'Electing the USSR Congress of People's Deputies', *Problems of Communism*, 38(6), November–December, pp. 51–6.

Nove, A. (1989) *Glasnost' in Action: Cultural Renaissance in Russia*, Boston, Mass., Unwin Hyman.

Parker, J. W. (1991) *The Kremlin in Transition*, vol. 2: *Gorbachev, 1985–89*, London, Unwin Hyman.

Paul, E. F. (ed.) (1990) *Totalitarianism at the Crossroads*, London, Transaction.

Richmond, N. I. (1991) 'One step forwards, two steps back: the USSR Supreme Soviet in the age of perestroika', *Journal of Communist Studies*, 7, June, pp. 202–16.

Roberts, C. and Wishnick, E. (1989) 'Ideology is dead! Long live ideology!', *Problems of Communism*, 38(6), November–December, pp. 57–89.

Ryan, M. (1990) *Soviet Society in Figures: the Era of Glasnost*, Cheltenham, Edward Elgar.

Saikal, A. and Maley, W. (1989) *The Soviet Withdrawal from Afghanistan*, Cambridge, Cambridge University Press.

Sakharov, A. (1991) *Moscow and Beyond, 1986–1989*, London, Hutchinson.

Sakwa, R. (1990) *Gorbachev and His Reforms, 1985–1990*, Hemel Hempstead, Philip Allan.

Solzhenitsyn, A. (1991) *Rebuilding Russia: Reflections and Tentative Proposals*, London, Harvill.

Thom, F. (1990) *The Gorbachev Phenomenon: a History of Perestroika*, London, Pinter.

White, S. and Wightman, G. (1989) 'Gorbachev's reforms: the Soviet elections of 1989', *Parliamentary Affairs*, 42, October, pp. 560–81.

White, S. (ed.) (1991) *New Directions in Soviet History*, Cambridge, Cambridge University Press.

Woodby, S. and Evans, A. B. (eds) (1990) *Restructuring Soviet Ideology:*

Gorbachev's New Thinking, Boulder, Colo., Westview.

Yeltsin, B. (1990) *Against the Grain*, London, Cape.

Zaslavskaya, T. (1990) *The Second Socialist Revolution: an Alternative Strategy*, London, Tauris.

Chapter 5 (Soviet Government Transformed)

Afanasyev, Y. (1991) 'The coming dictatorship', *New York Review of Books*, 31 January, pp. 36–9.

Evans, A., Jr (1991) 'Gorbachev's unfinished revolution', *Problems of Communism*, 90(1–2), January–April, pp. 133–43.

Huber, R. T. (ed.) (1992) *Perestroika-Era Politics: the New Soviet Legislature and Gorbachev's Political Reforms*, Armonk, NY, M. E. Sharpe.

Huskey, E. (ed.) (1992) *Executive Power and Soviet Politics: the Rise and Decline of the Soviet State*, Armonk, NY, M. E. Sharpe.

Lentini, P. (1991) 'Reforming the electoral system: the 1989 elections in the USSR Congress of People's Deputies [in Leningrad]', *Journal of Communist Studies*, 7, March, pp. 69–94.

Lloyd, J. (1991) 'What happened to Gorbachev', *London Review of Books*, 7 March, pp. 3, 5–6.

Merridale, C. and Ward, C. (eds) (1991) *Perestroika: the Historical Perspective*, London, Edward Arnold.

Rahr, A. (1991) 'Further restructuring of the Soviet political system', *Report on the USSR (RFE/RL Research Institute)*, 3(14), 5 April, pp. 1–4.

Remnick, D. (1991) 'Dead souls', *New York Review of Books*, 19 December, pp. 70–8.

Reddaway, P. (1991) 'Empire on the brink', *New York Review of Books*, 31 January, pp. 7–9.

Roxburgh, A. (1991) *The Second Russian Revolution*, London, BBC Books.

Sharlet, R. (1992) *Soviet Constitutional Crisis*, Armonk, NY, M. E. Sharpe.

Smith, G. B. (2nd edn, 1991) *Soviet Politics: Struggling with Change*, Basingstoke, Macmillan.

Surovell, J. (1991) 'Ligachev and Soviet politics', *Soviet Studies*, 43(2), pp. 355–74.

Tolz, V. (1991) 'The democratic opposition in crisis', *Report on the USSR (RFE/RL Research Institute)*, 3(18), 3 May, pp. 1–3.

White, S. (3rd edn, 1992) *Gorbachev in Power*, Cambridge, Cambridge University Press.

Willerton, J. P., Jr. (1992) 'Executive power and political leadership', in S. White, A. Pravda and Z. Gitelman (eds) *Developments in Soviet and Post-Soviet Politics*, 2nd edn, Basingstoke, Macmillan, ch. 3.

Chapter 6 (The Decline and Fall of the CPSU)

Chiesa, G. (1990) 'The 28th Congress of the CPSU', *Problems of Communism*, 39(4), July–August, pp. 24–38.

Frank, P. (1990) 'The twenty-eighth Congress of the CPSU: a personal assessment', *Government and Opposition*, 25(4), Autumn, pp. 472–83.

Gooding, J. (1991) 'The XXVIII Congress of the CPSU in perspective', *Soviet*

Studies, 43(2), pp. 237–53.

Hazan, B. (1990) *The Nineteenth All-Union Party Conference*, Boulder, Colo., Westview.

Hill, R. J. (1991) 'The CPSU: from monolith to pluralist?', *Soviet Studies*, 43(2), pp. 217–35.

Hill, R. J. and Frank, P. (3rd edn, 1987) *The Soviet Communist Party*, London, Allen & Unwin.

Millar, J. R. (ed.) (1992) *Cracks in the Monolith: Party Power in the Brezhnev Era*, Armonk, NY, M. E. Sharpe.

Rees, E. A. (ed.) (1992) *The Soviet Communist Party in Disarray: the XXVIII Congress of the Communist Party of the Soviet Union*, Basingstoke, Macmillan.

Robinson, N. (1992) 'Gorbachev and the place of the party in the Soviet reform, 1985–91', *Soviet Studies*, 44(3), pp. 423–44.

Tatu, M. (1988) 'The nineteenth Party Conference', *Problems of Communism*, 38(3–4), May–August, pp. 1–15.

Unger, A. L. (1991) 'The travails of intra-party democracy in the Soviet Union: the elections to the 19th Conference of the CPSU', *Soviet Studies*, 43(2), pp. 329–54.

White, S. (1991) 'Rethinking the CPSU', *Soviet Studies*, 43(3), pp. 405–28.

Chapter 7 (Political Action from the People)

Aage, H. (1991) 'Popular attitudes to perestroika', *Soviet Studies*, 43(1), pp. 3–26.

Brovkin, V. (1990) 'Revolution from below: informal political associations in Russia, 1988–1989', *Soviet Studies*, 42(2), pp. 233–58.

Forest, J. (1991) *Free at Last? The Impact of Perestroika on Religious Life in the Soviet Union*, London, Darton, Longman & Todd.

Fish, S. (1992) 'The emergence of independent associations and the transformation of Russian political society', *Journal of Communist Studies*, 7, September, pp. 299–334.

Friedgut, T. (1979) *Political Participation in the USSR*, Princeton, NJ, Princeton University Press.

Gefter, M. (1991) 'Remembering Sakharov: the misfit', *Russia and the World*, 19, pp. 19–22.

Gustafson, T. (1981) *Reform in Soviet Politics: Lessons of Recent Policies on Land and Water*, Cambridge, Cambridge University Press.

Hosking, G., Ayes, J. and Duncan, P. J. S. (1992) *Independent Political Movements in the Soviet Union, 1985–91*, London, Pinter.

Hough, J. and Fainsod, M. (1979) *How the Soviet Union is Governed*, Cambridge, Mass., Harvard University Press, pp. 524–36.

Lane, D. (rev. edn, 1992) *Soviet Society Under Perestroika*, London, Unwin Hyman, ch. 4.

McNair, B. (1991) *Glasnost, Perestroika and the Soviet Media*, London, Routledge.

Merridale, C. (1991) 'Perestroika and political pluralism: past and prospects', in C. Merridale and C. Ward (eds) *Perestroika: the Historical Perspective*, London, Edward Arnold, ch. 2.

Remington, T. F. (1992) 'Towards a participatory politics?', in S. White,

A. Pravda, and Z. Gitelman (eds) *Developments in Soviet and Post-Soviet Politics*, 2nd edn, Basingstoke, Macmillan, ch. 8.

Sakwa, R. (1990) *Gorbachev and His Reforms, 1985–1990*, Hemel Hempstead, Philip Allan, ch. 5.

Sedaitis, J. and Butterfield, J. (eds) (1991) *Perestroika from Below: Social Movements in the Soviet Union*, Boulder, Colo., Westview.

Skilling, H. G. and Griffiths, F. (eds) (1971) *Interest Groups in Soviet Politics*, Princeton, NJ, Princeton University Press.

Temkina, A. A. (1992) 'The workers' movement in Leningrad, 1985–91', *Soviet Studies*, 44(2), pp. 209–36.

Tolz, V. (1987) ' "Informal" groups in the USSR', *Radio Liberty Research*, 220/87, 11 June, pp. 1–8.

Tolz, V. (1991) 'Proliferation of political parties in the USSR', *Report on the USSR (RFE/RL Research Institute)*, 3(1), 4 January, pp. 12–14.

Tolz, V. (1991) *The USSR's Emerging Party System*, New York, Praeger.

Urban, M. E. (1990) *More Power to the Soviets: the Democratic Revolution in the USSR*, Cheltenham, Edward Elgar.

Zaslavsky, V. and Brym, R. J. (1978) 'The functions of elections in the USSR', *Soviet Studies*, 30(3), pp. 362–71.

Chapter 8 (Economic Disaster)

Åslund, A. (1991) 'Gorbachev, perestroyka and economic crisis', *Problems of Communism*, 90(1–2), January–April, pp. 18–41.

Åslund, A. (2nd edn, 1991) *Gorbachev's Struggle for Economic Reform*, Ithaca, NY, Cornell University Press.

Brooks, K. M. (1990) 'Soviet agriculture's halting reform', *Problems of Communism*, 39(2), March–April, pp. 29–41.

Bush, K. (1992) 'The disastrous last year of the USSR', *RFE/RL Research Report*, 1(12), 20 March, pp. 39–41.

Hanson, P. (1992) *From Stagnation to Catastroika: Commentaries on the Soviet Economy, 1983–1991*, New York, Praeger.

Kontorovitch, V. (1985) 'Discipline and growth in the Soviet economy', *Problems of Communism*, 34(6), November–December, pp. 18–31.

Mars, G. (1992) *The Black Economy in the USSR*, Aldershot, Dartmouth.

Moskoff, W. (ed.) (1990) *Perestroika in the Countryside: Agricultural Reform in the Gorbachev Era*, Armonk, NY, M. E. Sharpe.

Robins, G. S. (1992) 'The Soviet economy and the perestroyka years', *Problems of Communism*, 41(3), May–June, pp. 139–44.

Rutland, P. (1985) *The Myth of the Plan: Lessons of Soviet Planning Experience*, London, Hutchinson.

Tedstrom, J. (1988) 'Soviet cooperatives: a difficult road to legitimacy', *Radio Liberty Research*, 224/88, 31 July, pp. 1–9.

Tedstrom, J. (1990) 'The economics and politics behind Shatalin's plan for an economic union', *Report on the USSR (RFE/RL Research Institute)*, 2(42), 12 October, pp. 1–3.

Tedstrom, J. (1990) 'The Shatalin plan and industrial conversion', *Report on the USSR (RFE/RL Research Institute)*, 2(46), 16 November, pp. 8–11.

Chapter 9 (From Superpower to Supplicant)

Crow, S. (1991) 'The Soviet Japanese summit: expectations unfulfilled', *Report on the USSR (RFE/RL Research Institute)*, 3(17), 26 April, pp. 1–5.

Foye, S. (1992) 'The struggle over Russia's Kuril Islands policy', *RFE/RL Research Report*, 1(36), 11 September, pp. 34–40.

Kanet, R. E., Resler, T. J. and Miner, D. N. (eds) (1992) *The Soviet Union and International Politics*, Cambridge, Cambridge University Press.

Keeble, C. (ed.) (1985) *The Soviet State: the Domestic Roots of Soviet Foreign Policy*, London, Gower.

Laird, R. and Hoffman, E. P. (eds) (1991) *Contemporary Issues in Soviet Foreign Policy*, New York, Aldine.

Pravda, A. (ed.) (1992) *The End of the Outer Empire: Soviet–East European Relations in Transition, 1985–90*, London, Sage/RIIA.

Wallace, W. W. (1992) *Gorbachev and the Revolution in Soviet Foreign Policy*, Aldershot, Dartmouth.

Chapter 10 (Military Confusion)

Allison, R. (ed.) (1992) *Radical Reform in Soviet Defence Policy*, Basingstoke, Macmillan.

Bluth, C. (1990) *New Thinking in Soviet Military Policy*, London, Pinter.

Clarke, D. C. (1992) 'The battle for the Black Sea fleet', *RFE/RL Research Report*, 1(5), 31 January, pp. 53–7.

Davenport, B. A. (1991) 'The Ogarkov ouster: the development of Soviet military doctrine and civil/military relations in the 1980s', *Journal of Strategic Studies*, 14, June, pp. 129–47.

Foye, S. (1992) 'The Soviet armed forces: things fall apart', *RFE/RL Research Report*, 1(1), 3 January, pp. 15–18.

Garthoff, R. L. (1991) *Deterrence and the Revolution in Soviet Military Doctrine*, Washington, DC, Brookings Institution.

Glantz, D. M. (1991) *Soviet Military Operational Art: In Pursuit of Deep Battle*, London, Cass.

Hudson, G. E. (1990) *Soviet National Security Policy Under Perestroika*, Boston, Mass., Unwin Hyman.

Hyde-Price, A. (1991) *European Security Beyond the Cold War*, London, RIIA.

MccGwire, M. (1991) *Perestroika and Soviet National Security*, Washington, DC, Brookings Institution.

Park, A. (1991) 'Global security, *glasnost* and the retreat dividend', *Government and Opposition*, 26, Winter, pp. 75–85.

Pugh, M. C. (ed.) (1991) *European Security Towards 2000*, Manchester, Manchester University Press.

Rusi, A. M. (1991) *After the Cold War: Europe's New Political Architecture*, Basingstoke, Macmillan.

Sherr, J. (2nd edn, 1991) *Soviet Power: the Continuing Challenge*, Basingstoke, Macmillan.

Volten, P. M. E. (1992) 'Security dimensions of imperial collapse', *Problems of Communism*, 41(1–2), January–April, pp. 136–47.

Chapter 11 (The Nationalities Reject the Union)

Armstrong, J. A. (1992) 'Nationalism in the former Soviet empire', *Problems of Communism*, 41(1–2), January–April, pp. 121–35.

Bennigsen, A. and Broxup, M. (1990) *The Islamic Threat to the Soviet State*, London, Routledge.

Denber, R. (ed.) (1991) *The Soviet Nationality Reader: the Crisis in Context*, Boulder, Colo., Westview.

Furtado, C. F. and Chandler, A. M. (1991) *Perestroika in the Soviet Republics: Documents on the National Question*, Boulder, Colo., Westview.

Kirkwood, M. (1991) 'Glasnost, the "national question" and Soviet language policy', *Soviet Studies*, 43(1), pp. 61–81.

Kux, S. (1990) 'Soviet federalism', *Problems of Communism*, 39(2), March–April, pp. 1–20.

Lapidus, G., Zaslavsky, V. and Goldman, P. (eds) (1992) *From Union to Commonwealth*, Cambridge, Cambridge University Press.

Nahaylo, B. and Swoboda, V. (1990) *Soviet Disunion: a History of the Nationalities Problem in the USSR*, London, Hamish Hamilton.

Simon, G. (1991) *Nationalism and Policy Toward the Nationalities in the Soviet Union: from Totalitarian Dictatorship to Post-Stalinist Democracy*, Boulder, Colo., Westview.

Smith, G. (ed.) (1990) *The Nationalities Question in the Soviet Union*, London, Longman.

Solchanyk, R. (1991) 'The Gorbachev–Yeltsin pact and the new Union treaty', *Report on the USSR (RFE/RL Research Institute)*, 3(19), 10 May, pp. 1–3.

Suny, R. G. (1991) 'Incomplete revolution: national movements and the collapse of the Soviet empire', *New Left Review*, 189, September–October, pp. 111–25.

Swoboda, V. (1992) 'Was the Soviet Union really necessary?', *Soviet Studies*, 44(5), pp. 761–84.

Tishkov, V. (1989) '*Glasnost* and nationalities within the Soviet Union', *Third World Quarterly*, 11(4), October, pp. 191–207.

Vakhtin, N. (1992) *Native Peoples of the Russian Far North*, London, Minority Rights Group.

White, S. (ed.) (1992) *The Politics of Nationality in the USSR*, Basingstoke, Macmillan.

Chapter 12 (Russia and Belarus Accept the Inevitable)

Antic, O. (1992) 'Orthodox Church reacts to criticism of KGB links', *RFE/RL Research Report*, 1(23), 5 June, pp. 61–3.

Brovkin, V. (1990) 'Revolution from below: informal political associations in Russia, 1988–1989', *Soviet Studies*, 42(2), pp. 233–58.

Carter, S. (1991) 'Pamyat and conservative communism', *Russia and the World*, 19, pp. 30–1.

Dunlop, J. B. (1992) 'KGB subversion of Russian Orthodox Church', *RFE/RL Research Report*, 1(12), 20 March, pp. 51–3.

Krasnov, V. (1991) *Russia Beyond Communism: a Chronicle of National Rebirth*,

Boulder, Colo., Westview.

Mihalisko, K. (1991) 'The workers' rebellion in Belorussia', *Report on the USSR (RFE/RL Research Institute)*, 3(17), 26 April, pp. 21–5.

Mihalisko, K. (1992) 'Belorussia: setting sail without a compass', *RFE/RL Research Report*, 1(1), 3 January, pp. 39–41.

Orttung, R. W. (1992) 'The Russian right and the dilemma of party organisation', *Soviet Studies*, 44(3), pp. 445–78.

Rahr, A. (1991) 'Yeltsin sets up a new system for governing Russia', *Report on the USSR (RFE/RL Research Institute)*, 3(34), 23 August, pp. 9–12.

Tolz, V. and Teague, E. (1992) 'Political parties in Russia', *RFE/RL Research Report*, 1(1), 3 January, pp. 12–14.

Urban, M. E. (1989) *An Algebra of Soviet Power: Elite Circulation in the Belorussian Republic, 1966–86*, Cambridge, Cambridge University Press.

Urban, M. E. (1992) 'Boris Yeltsin, Democratic Russia and the campaign for the Russian presidency', *Soviet Studies*, 44(2), pp. 187–208.

Wishnevsky, J. (1987) 'The emergence of "Pamyat" and "Otechestvo"', *Radio Liberty Research*, 342/87, 26 August, pp. 1–17.

Chapter 13 (Ukraine and Moldova Break Free)

Bilinsky, Y. (1983) 'Shcherbytskyi, Ukraine and Kremlin Politics', *Problems of Communism*, 32(34), July–August, pp. 1–20.

Bociurkiw, B. R. (1990) 'The Ukrainian Catholic Church in the USSR under Gorbachev', *Problems of Communism*, 39(6), November–December, pp. 1–19.

Gitelman, Z. (1991) *The Politics of Nationality in Contemporary Ukraine*, Basingstoke, Macmillan.

Krawchenko, B. (1985) *Social Change and National Consciousness in Twentieth Century Ukraine*, Basingstoke, Macmillan.

Krawchenko, B. (ed.) (1991) *Ukrainian Past, Ukrainian Present*, Basingstoke, Macmillan.

Nahaylo, B. (1992) *The New Ukraine*, London, RIIA.

Paniotto, V. (1991) 'The Ukrainian movement for *perestroika* – "Rukh": a sociological survey', *Soviet Studies*, 43(1), pp. 177–81.

Socor, V. (1990) 'Moldavian lands between Romania and Ukraine: the history and political geography', *Report on the USSR (RFE/RL Research Institute)*, 2(46), 16 November, pp. 16–18.

Socor, V. (1991) 'Political power [in Moldavia] passes to democratic sources', *Report on the USSR (RFE/RL Research Institute)*, 3(1), 4 January, pp. 24–8.

Socor, V. (1991) 'The Moldavian communists: from ruling to opposition party', *Report on the USSR (RFE/RL Research Institute)*, 3(14), 5 April, pp. 15–21.

Socor, V. (1992) 'Moldavia builds a new state', *RFE/RL Research Report*, 1(1), 3 January, pp. 42–5.

Solchanyk, R. (1991) *Ukraine from Chernobyl to Sovereignty*, Basingstoke, Macmillan.

Tedstrom, J. (1990) 'The economic costs and benefits of independence for the

Ukraine', *Report on the USSR (RFE/RL Research Institute)*, 49(2), 7 December, pp. 11–16.

Chapter 14 (The Baltic Republics Regain Independence)

Arveds Trapans, J. (ed.) (1991) *Toward Independence: the Baltic Independence Movements*, Boulder, Colo., Westview.

Bungs, D. (1991) 'Voting patterns in Latvian independence poll', *Report on the USSR (RFE/RL Research Institute)*, 3(12), 2 March, pp. 21–4.

Bungs, D. (1992) 'Latvia: laying new foundations', *RFE/RL Research Report*, 1(1), 3 January, pp. 61–4.

Clemens, W. C. (1991) *Baltic Independence and Baltic Empire*, Basingstoke, Macmillan.

Girnius, S. (1992) 'Lithuania: a bloody struggle', *RFE/RL Research Report*, 1(1), 3 January, pp. 57–60.

Hiden, J. and Lane, T. (eds) (1992) *The Baltics and the Outbreak of the Second World War*, Cambridge, Cambridge University Press.

Kionka, R. (1992) 'Estonia: a break with the past', *RFE/RL Research Report*, 1(1), 3 January, pp. 65–7.

Laber, J. (1991) 'The Baltic revolt', *New York Review of Books*, 28 March, pp. 58–62.

Parming, T. and Jarvesoo, E. (1978) *A Case Study of a Soviet Republic: the Estonian SSR*, Boulder, Colo., Westview.

Senn, A. E. (1990) 'Toward Lithuanian Independence: Algirdas Brazauskas and the CPL', *Problems of Communism*, 39(2), March–April, pp. 21–8.

Senn, A. E. (1991) *Lithuania Awakening*, Berkeley, Calif., University of California Press.

Taagepera, R. (1989) 'Estonia's road to independence', *Problems of Communism*, 38(6), November–December, pp. 1–26.

Vardys, V. S. (1965) *Lithuania Under the Soviets: Portrait of a Nation, 1940–65*, New York, Praeger.

Chapter 15 (The Central Asians: Independence Thrust Upon Them)

Allworth, E. (ed.) (1990) *Central Asia: 120 Years of Russian Rule*, Durham, NC, Duke University Press.

Atkin, M. (1990) *Islam in Soviet Tajikistan*, Philadephia, Pa., Foreign Policy Research Institute.

Brown, B. (1991) 'The fall of Maseliev: Kyrgyzstan's "silk revolution" advances', *Report on the USSR (RFE/RL Research Institute)*, 1(16), 19 April, pp. 12–15.

Brown, B. (1991) 'The Islamic Renaissance Party in Central Asia', *Report on the USSR (RFE/RL Research Institute)*, 3(19), 10 May, pp. 12–14.

Brown, B. (1992) 'Central Asia emerges on the world stage', *RFE/RL Research Report*, 1(1), 3 January, pp. 51–6.

Broxup, M. (1990) 'USSR: the Islamic threat', *Immigrants and Minorities*, 9, November, pp. 290–302.

Carrère d'Encausse, Hélène (1988) *Islam and the Russian Empire: Reform and Revolution in Central Asia*, London, Tauris.

Critchlow, J. (1991) 'Central Asia: the Russian conquest revisited', *Report on the USSR (RFE/RL Research Institute)*, 3(10), 8 March, pp. 15–19.

Critchlow, J. (1991) *Nationalism in Uzbekistan: a Soviet Republic's Road to Sovereignty*, Boulder, Colo., Westview.

Fierman, W. (ed.) (1991) *Soviet Central Asia: the Failed Transformation*, Boulder, Colo., Weatview.

Gellner, E. (1991) 'Islam and Marxism: some comparisons', *International Affairs*, 67, June, pp. 1–6.

Gleason, G. (1991) 'Fealty and loyalty: informal loyalty structures in Soviet Asia', *Soviet Studies*, 43(4), pp. 613–28.

Lubin, N. (1984) *Labour and Nationality in Soviet Central Asia*, London, Macmillan.

Olcott, M. B. (1981) 'The Basmachi or Freemen's Revolt in Turkestan, 1918–1924', *Soviet Studies*, 33, July, pp. 352–69.

Olcott, M. B. (1990) 'Perestroyka in Kazakhstan', *Problems of Communism*, 4(39), July–August, pp. 65–77.

Ro'i, Y. (1990) 'The Islamic influence on nationalism in Soviet Central Asia', *Problems of Communism*, 4(39), July–August, pp. 49–64.

Chapter 16 (The Caucasus Fights)

Broxup, M. (1992) *The North Caucasus Barrier: the Russian Advance towards the Muslim World*, London, Hurst.

Dragadze, T. (1989) 'The Armenian–Azerbaijani conflict: structure and sentiment', *Third World Quarterly*, 11(1), January, pp. 55–71.

Fuller, E. (1990) 'Round Table coalition wins resounding victory in Georgian Supreme Soviet elections', *Report on the USSR (RFE/RL Research Institute)*, 2(46), 16 November, pp. 13–16.

Fuller, E. (1991) 'The challenge to Armenia's non-communist government', *Report on the USSR (RFE/RL Research Institute)*, 3(18), 3 May, pp. 19–24.

Fuller, E. (1992) 'The Transcaucasus: real independence remains elusive', *RFE/RL Research Report*, 1(1), 3 January, pp. 46–50.

Fuller, E. (1992) 'Georgian president flees after opposition seizes power', *RFE/RL Research Report*, 1(3), 17 January, pp. 4–7.

Fuller, E. (1992) 'Georgia, Abkhazia and Checheno-Ingushetia', *RFE/RL Research Report*, 1(6), 7 February, pp. 3–7.

Lang, D. M. and Walker, C. J. (1987) *The Armenians*, London, Minority Rights Group.

Nelson, L. D. (1992) 'Voting and political attitudes in Soviet Georgia', *Soviet Studies*, 44(4), pp. 687–98.

Parsons, J. W. R. (1982) 'National integration in Soviet Georgia', *Soviet Studies*, 34(4), October, pp. 547–69.

Rost, Y. (1990) *Armenian Tragedy*, London, Weidenfeld & Nicolson.

Suny, R. G. (1990) 'The revenge of the past: socialism and ethnic conflict in Transcaucasia', *New Left Review*, 184, November–December, pp. 5–34.

Suny, R. G. (1991) *The Making of the Georgian Nation*, Bloomington, Ind., Indiana University Press.

Walker, C. J. (1990) *Armenia: The Survival of a Nation*, London, Routledge.

Epilogue (The Future)

Brown, A. (2nd edn, 1992) *The Gorbachev Factor in Soviet Politics*, Oxford, Oxford University Press.

Hosking, G. (1992) 'The roots of dissolution', *New York Review of Books*, 16 January, pp. 34–8.

Lane, D. (ed.) (1992) *Russia in Flux: the Political and Social Consequences of Reform*, Cheltenham, Edward Elgar.

Maiia, M. (1992) 'From under the rubble, what?', *Problems of Communism*, 41(1–2), January–April, pp. 89–120.

Mandel, D. (1992) 'Post-*perestroika*: revolution from above v. revolution from below', in S. White, A. Pravda and Z. Gitelman (eds) *Developments in Soviet and Post-Soviet Politics*, 2nd edn, Basingstoke, Macmillan, pp. 278–99.

Sheehy, A. (1992) 'Commonwealth of Independent States: an uneasy compromise', *RFE/RL Research Report*, 1(2), 10 January, pp. 1–5.

White, S. (3rd edn, 1992) *Gorbachev and After*, Cambridge, Cambridge University Press.

References

Adelman, J. R. and Palmieri, D. A. (1989) *The Dynamics of Soviet Foreign Policy*, New York, Harper & Row.

Allworth, E. (ed.) (1990) *Central Asia: 120 Years of Russian Rule*, Durham, NC, Duke University Press.

Antic, O. (1988a) 'Gorbachev meets with leadership of the Russian Orthodox Church', *Radio Liberty Research*, 218/88, 25 May.

Antic, O. (1988b) 'Celebration of millennium of Christianization of Rus: outcome and prospects', *Radio Liberty Research*, 289/88, 28 June.

Bauman, Z. (1990) 'Totalitarian perceptions', *Times Literary Supplement*, 12–18 October.

BBC (1991) *Newsnight* television programme, 6 September.

Berlin, I. (contributor) (1990) 'The state of Europe: Christmas Eve 1989, *Granta*, 30.

Birch, J. (1991) book review, *Soviet Studies*, 43(5).

Bonner, E. (1990) 'The myth of Gorbachev', *Guardian*, 28 June.

Brown, A. (1991) 'Gorbachev's bitter betrayal', *Guardian*, 20 August.

Bullock, A. (1991) *Hitler and Stalin: Parallel Lives*, London, Harper Collins.

Clarke, D. (1987) 'How could Matthias Rust get to Moscow?', *Radio Free Europe Research*, RAD Background Report, 87, 2 June.

Conquest, R. (reissued 1990) *The Great Terror: a Reassessment*, Oxford, Oxford University Press.

Cornwell, R. (1989) 'Gorbachev fights to save authority of party', *Independent*, 11 December.

Crawshaw, S. (1992) *Goodbye to the USSR: the Collapse of Soviet Power*, London, Bloomsbury.

Davies, N. (1991) 'No Stalinists, simply all the President's men', *Independent*, 20 August.

Ellis, J. (1991) 'Conflict splits the Orthodox Church', *Independent*, 27 April.

Evans, R. (1989) 'Soviet shakeup to fight economic ills', *Guardian*, 12 June.

Fast, T. (1991) 'Baltic games of provocation', *Guardian*, 7 June.

Figes, O. (1989) 'Will the revolution all end in tears?', *Guardian*, 23 December.

Figes, O. (1990a) 'Hail and farewell to the icon', *Guardian*, 30 April.

Figes, O. (1990b) 'Marxists out of step' (review of Z. Galili, *The Menshevik Leaders in the Russian Revolution*, Princeton, NJ, Princeton University

Press), *Times Literary Supplement*, 4–10 May.

Fitzpatrick, S. (1979) *Education and Social Mobility in the Soviet Union, 1921–34*, Cambridge, Cambridge University Press.

Foye, S. (1992) 'The struggle over Russia's Kuril Islands policy', *REF/RL Research Report*, 1(36), 11 September.

Frankland, M. (1989) 'Red retreat', *Observer*, 12 March.

Friedrich, C. and Brzezinski, Z. (1956; 2nd edn, 1965) *Totalitarian Dictatorship and Autocracy*, Cambridge, Mass., Harvard University Press.

Füredi, F. (1986) *The Soviet Union Demystified: a Materialist Analysis*, London, Junius.

Galeotti, M. (1991) 'A critical absence of will', *Russia and the World*, 20.

Getty, J. Arch (1985) *Origins of the Great Purges: the Soviet Communist Party Reconsidered, 1933–38*, New York, Cambridge University Press.

Getty, J. Arch (1990) 'Back in the USSR', *London Review of Books*, 22 February.

Gorbachev, M. (1990) 'Rid party of bureaucratic heritage, says Gorbachev' (Speech to the CPSU Central Committee), *Guardian*, 6 February.

Gustafson, T. (1981) *Reform in Soviet Politics: Lessons of Recent Policies on Land and Water*, Cambridge, Cambridge University Press.

Hanson, P. (1987) 'Converting the inconvertible ruble', *Radio Liberty Research*, 281/87, 16 July.

Hearst, D., Dyczok, M. and Simmons, M. (1991) 'Yeltsin tries to allay fears over Russia', *Guardian*, 21 December.

Hosking, G. (1989) 'Full circle for freedom and openness in the Soviet Union', *Observer*, 13 January.

Hosking, G. (1991) 'The sins of Russophobia', *Times Literary Supplement*, 1 February.

Ingerflom, C. (1990) 'Soviet totalitarianism, myth and reality', *Liber*, 1 February.

Keane, J. (1990) 'The politics of retreat', *Political Quarterly*, July–September.

Keep, J. (1990) 'The missing millions', *Times Literary Supplement*, 5–11 October.

Keesing's Record of World Events (1989) (35(1)) 'Conference on Security and Cooperation in Europe', London, Longman.

Lewin, M. (1985) *The Makers of the Soviet System: Essays in the Social History of Inter-War Russia*, London, Methuen.

Millinship, W. (1989) 'Gorbachov man cometh', *Observer*, 30 April.

Millinship, W. (1990a) 'Gorbachov to bare his claws', *Observer*, 18 March.

Millinship, W. (1990b) 'Gorbachov pulls victory out of a hat', *Observer*, 15 July.

Milne, S. (1990) 'Stalin's missing millions', *Guardian*, 10 March.

Nazarov, A. (1991) 'A front man for the totalitarians', *Guardian*, 20 August.

Nove, A. (contributor) (1991) 'The new face of Russia', *Guardian*, 18 December.

Ostrow, J. (1991) 'Soviet right plays on differing pasts', *Guardian*, 31 January.

Paul, E. F. (ed.) (1990) *Totalitarianism at the Crossroads*, London, Transaction.

Pick, H. (1989) 'Gorbachev outlines common home plan', *Guardian*, 7 July.

Pipes, R. (1990) *The Russian Revolution, 1899–1919,* London, Collins Harvill.

Pringle, P. (1991) 'Map of political power redrawn', *Independent,* 6 September.

Rahr, A. (1987a) 'Why Yazov?', *Radio Liberty Research,* 212/87, 1 June.

Rahr, A. (1987b) 'Restructuring in the KGB', *Radio Liberty Research,* 226/87, 15 June.

Rahr, A. (1991) 'Further restructuring of the Soviet political system', *Report on the USSR (RFE/RL Research Institute),* 3(14), 5 April.

Remnick, D. (1992) 'Dons of the Don', *New York Review of Books,* 16 July.

Rettie, J. (1990a) 'Left and right battle for Soviet party', *Guardian,* 7 February.

Rettie, J. (1990b) 'Ligachev's old socialists never die', *Guardian,* 8 February.

Rettie, J. (1990c) 'Ukraine Soviet republic proclaims sovereignty', *Guardian,* 17 July.

Rettie, J. (1990d) 'Gorbachev turns down Solzhenitsyn proposal', *Guardian,* 26 September.

Rettie, J. (1990e) 'Only market can save Soviet economy', *Guardian,* 17 October.

Rettie, J. (1991a) 'Yeltsin regrets his attack on Gorbachev', *Guardian,* 15 March.

Rettie, J. (1991b) 'Flames of revolt from firestone valley', *Guardian,* 30 April.

Rettie, J. (1991c) 'Key republics split on prices and army', *Guardian,* 30 December.

Roberts, G. (1990) 'Article 6 abolition start of long road', *Guardian,* 6 February.

Roxburgh, A. (1991) 'Final nail in the Party's coffin', *Guardian,* 30 August.

Scammell, M. (1990) 'A great man eclipsed', *Times Literary Supplement,* 16–22 November.

Shatalin, S. (1990) 'As credit runs out', *Guardian,* 9 November.

Shevardnadze, E. (1990) 'Socialism "cannot rely on bloodshed"', *Pravda,* 26 June, quoted in *Guardian,* 27 June.

Smith, G. B. (1988) *Soviet Politics: Continuity and Contradiction,* Basingstoke, Macmillan.

Solzhenitsyn, A. (1991) *Rebuilding Russia: Reflections and Tentative Proposals,* London, HarperCollins.

Steele, J. (1988) 'Gorbachev moves ahead on conference reforms', *Guardian,* 6 July.

Steele, J. (1989a) 'Moldavia minefield troubles Moscow', *Guardian,* 2 February.

Steele, J. (1989b) 'Is the "power struggle" only Western wishful thinking?', *Guardian,* 16 February.

Steele, J. (1989c) 'Yeltsin warns on Gorbachev's influence', *Guardian,* 1 June.

Steele, J. (1989d) 'Deputies turn down Ryzhkov nominees', *Guardian,* 24 June.

Steele, J. (1990a) 'Gorbachev names diverse council', *Guardian,* 26 March.

Steele, J. (1990b) 'Soviet party to split', *Guardian,* 13 April.

Steele, J. (1990c) 'Leading Soviet spycatcher calls for scrapping of the KGB', *Guardian,* 18 June.

Steele, J. (1990d) 'Gorbachev reforms come under heavy attack', *Guardian*, 20 June.

Steele, J. (1990e) 'Ligachev says Gorbachev should go as party leader', *Guardian*, 21 June.

Steele, J. (1990f) 'Soviet radicals break away to form rival party', *Guardian*, 13 July.

Steele, J. (1991a) 'Yeltsin consigns Soviet Union and Gorbachev to history', *Guardian*, 9 December.

Steele, J. (1991b) 'Ally's attack undermines Yeltsin's plan', *Guardian*, 19 December.

Steele, J. and Rettie, J. (1990) 'Gorbachev sends in the troops', *Guardian*, 16 January.

Teague, E. (1986) 'Turnover in the Soviet elite under Gorbachev: implications for Soviet Politics', *Radio Liberty Research*, Supplement, 1/86, 8 July.

Thompson, E. P. (1991) 'Counting the mixed blessings', *Guardian*, 23 August.

Tolstaya, T. (1991) 'In cannibalistic times', *New York Review of Books*, 11 April.

Tolz, V. (1987a) 'Twenty-two-year-old student reveals explosive findings on Stalin purges', *Radio Liberty Research*, 207/87, 3 June.

Tolz, V. (1987b) '"Informal" groups in the USSR', *Radio Liberty Research*, 220/87, 11 June.

Tolz, V. (1991) 'What was the Soviet intelligentsia?', *Russia and the World*, 20.

Tolz, V. (1992) 'Ministry of Security gives new figures for Stalin's victims', *RFE/RL Research Report*, 1(18), 1 May.

Troitsky, A. (1987) *Back in the USSR: the True Story of Rock in Russia*, London, Omnibus.

Tumarkin, N. (1983) *Lenin Lives! The Lenin Cult in Soviet Russia*, Cambridge, Mass., Harvard University Press.

Volkogonov, D. (1991) *Stalin: Triumph and Tragedy*, London, Weidenfeld & Nicolson.

Walker, M. (1988) 'Gromyko's record branded a failure', *Guardian*, 19 May.

Walker, M. (1991) 'Hollow promises revive spectre of Cold War for complacent West', *Guardian*, 20 August.

Weikhardt, G. C. (1985) 'Ustinov versus Ogarkov', *Problems of Communism*, 34(1), January–February.

Yasmann, V. (1987) 'Obstacles in the way of the cooperative movement', *Radio Liberty Research*, 343/87, 16 July.

Index